ROMAN POMPEII

Praise for the first edition:

'He has managed to pack an amazing amount of archaeological and histori-cal material into what is a relatively slim volume … a major contribution to recent trends in Pompeian studies.'
C. V. Walthew, *Classics Ireland*

'Brings into crystal focus such diverse topics as town planning, water supply, prostitution and the ritualised daily routines of the elite.'
JACT Review

In this revised and updated edition of *Roman Pompeii: Space and Society*, Ray Laurence looks at the latest archaeological and historical evidence to present an evaluation of the city of Pompeii that draws on the disciplines of architecture, geography and the social sciences. Pompeii is the focus of many major debates in classical history and archaeology as an essential source of evidence when questioning issues such as city planning, and the working of ancient economies. This study enhances our general understanding of the Roman world.

Pompeii is shown to have undergone considerable urban development, and Dr Laurence emphasises the relationship between the fabric of the city and the society that produced it. Local activities are located in both time and space and Pompeii's cultural identity is defined.

New chapters have been included to reveal how the young learnt the cul-ture of the city, and investigate the role of property development and real estate in Pompeii's growth.

This book is invaluable for students and scholars in the fields of archae-ology and ancient history, as well as rewarding reading for the many people who visit Pompeii.

Ray Laurence is a Special Research Fellow in the Institute of Archaeology and Antiquity at the University of Birmingham. His research interests include Roman urbanisation and the conceptions and representations of ageing in antiquity.

ROMAN POMPEII

Space and Society

Ray Laurence

Second Edition

Routledge
Taylor & Francis Group

LONDON AND NEW YORK

First published 2007
by Routledge
2 Park Square, Milton Park, Abingdon, Oxon OX14 4RN

Simultaneously published in the USA and Canada
by Routledge
711 Third Avenue, New York, NY 10017

Routledge is an imprint of the Taylor & Francis Group

© 2007 Ray Laurence

Typeset in Garamond by Saxon Graphics Ltd

British Library Cataloguing in Publication Data
A catalogue record for this book is available from the British
Library

Library of Congress Cataloging in Publication Data
A catalog record for this book has been requested

ISBN: 0-415-39126-1 (hbk)
ISBN-13: 978-0-415-39126-9 (hbk)
ISBN: 0-415-39125-3 (pbk)
ISBN-13: 978-0-415-39125-2 (pbk)

CONTENTS

FIGURES, MAPS AND PLATES

FIGURES

PLATES

PREFACE TO THE
FIRST EDITION

This book is about Pompeii – a city much studied by others. However, the social meaning of Pompeii has seldom been addressed. Pompeii is an archaeological artefact of immense complexity: after all, it was a city. At times it may appear that I explain aspects of this artefact in historical terms, at others in a more archaeological framework. As a result, this book might be seen by some (e.g. Klejn 1993) as an academic heresy. However, the past should be approached from both perspectives. After all, both subjects seek to explain the same object – the past. The division between these two disciplines is hard to conceptualise. Archaeology confronts history, and history confronts archaeology. By archaeology, I do not mean the narrow perspectives of classical archaeology. The influence of the debates in theoretical archaeology, conducted principally by prehistorians, can be identified in what follows. Too often, ancient historians and classical archaeologists have isolated themselves from the main debates in archaeology and history. Therefore, I have sought to interpret the Pompeian evidence in the light of developments in archaeology and history. I have also drawn upon the methods and preoccupations of architects, geographers and social scientists. The object has been to explain the ancient city of Pompeii in its social and spatial context; and above all to interpret the evidence. The book contains both my own research and a synthesis of the work of others. The latter is included to make Pompeii more accessible to a wider audience. It will be noted that I have concentrated upon public space and social interaction, at the expense of the private or domestic context. There is a reason for this. Domesticity in Pompeii is being approached from a number of new angles, and much of this work has yet to be published. In fact, in the near future, we may look forward to a revolution in the way the Pompeian house is studied. Until this work is published, it will not be possible to account for domestic space in Pompeii adequately. Thus, I leave it to one side and examine primarily public space and the social interaction that took place within it.

The reader should be aware of the Pompeian reference system. The archaeological site was divided into nine regions by Fiorelli in the nineteenth century. These are numbered 1–9. In each region, the *insulae* (blocks) were numbered and each doorway in an *insula* was given a number. Therefore, each location of, say, a house is referred to thus: 9.1.2. In this case, the first number refers to the region, the second number refers to the *insula* block and, finally, the third number refers to the entrance to the building. This allows for easy location of buildings on the site and also on maps of Pompeii.

All references in the text follow the Harvard system, or are standard classical references to ancient texts. References to modern works have been kept under control and tend to refer to the most accessible material available.

Newcastle
August 1993

PREFACE TO THE
SECOND EDITION

Since the publication of the first edition of this book, interest in Pompeii has substantially increased and numerous publications have made an impact on the original work based on a PhD thesis. New work has affected my understanding of the city. Hence, a second edition was seen to be necessary. The format and interest of the book are similar. Readers will find that Chapter 2 has been substantially reworked and that there is additional material on the nature of local identity and traffic flow in Chapter 3. Two new chapters have been added: Chapter 8 on the rental potential of property in Pompeii and Chapter 10 on space and the production of adult citizens. Where possible, a full account of published work has been included where it has affected the original arguments put forward. It has been a pleasure to see interest in the book on the part of others and an engagement with its theses. This has produced agreement and disagreement or identified where readers have found the book confusing. In revising the book, I have tried to include, clarify and discuss the published reactions to the original work. The revised version may produce a clearer vision of the original argument. There are limits to the revisions. For example, the original book was written in the wake of the tail end of the Finley conception of the economy, and strove to move towards a different model that included archaeology. Finley's ancient economy is now an intellectual idea from our past (Horden and Purcell 2000: 101–8; see collection of essays in Scheidel and von Reden 2002 for a retrospective on Finley's legacy). There is not space for a full discussion of the implications of these intellectual changes, or for every comment made on Pompeii since 1993. What I have tried to do is to demonstrate the impact of relevant work on the original text, whilst preserving the original thesis on the interaction of space and society. In re-working the book for a second edition, I have realised the debt I owe to my colleagues whilst at the University of Reading and now at the University of Birmingham, who have found the time to discuss Pompeii and the Roman city. Particular thanks are due to: Joanne Berry, John Creighton, Janet DeLaine, Simon Esmonde-Cleary, Michael Fulford, Gareth Sears and Andrew Wallace-Hadrill. Routledge's anonymous reader made numerous useful points with reference to the original text. In addition, the following have aided and abetted (knowingly or otherwise) the revised text: Colin Adams, Penelope Allison, Julian Bloomfield, Alex Butterworth, Filippo Coarelli, Alison Cooley, Jens-Arne Dickmann, John Dobbins, A. Asa Eiger, Lisa Fentress, Mark Grahame, Lucy Grig, Mary Harlow, Renata Henneberg, Simon Keay, Helen King, Roger Ling, Elio Lo Cascio, David Mattingly, Martin Millett, Henrik Mouritsen, Salvatore Nappo, Felix Pirson, Louise Revell, Andrew Riggsby, Peter Rose and Greg Rowe. Thanks are also due to my undergraduate and postgraduate students, who have raised questions I would not have considered. Likewise, visits to schools drew my attention to the singular curiosity of the young and their fascination with Pompeii. Finally, I would like to thank Richard Stoneman for supporting the original proposal for a book on space and society and, some ten years later, having plenty of enthusiasm for a second edition.

Bondi
March 2006

ACKNOWLEDGEMENTS

Thanks are due to many people who have helped me in my research into Roman urbanism. In Newcastle, Jeremy Paterson (the supervisor of my PhD) has consistently offered help and advice. My PhD examiners, Nicholas Purcell and Tony Spawforth, deserve the warmest thanks for their sound and critical comment. Nicholas Purcell and Andrew Wallace-Hadrill pointed me in the direction of a book about Pompeii, rather than the wider subject of urbanism in Roman Italy: a proposal which received further encouragement from Richard Stoneman. In Pompeii, Baldassare Conticello granted me permission to visit the whole site and Mattia Buondonno made my visit considerably easier. The British School at Rome assisted me financially with two short grants from the Hugh Last fund and a scholarship in 1990–1. None of this would have been possible without their financial support or the library facilities of the school run so humanely by Valerie Scott and her staff. There are many others who deserve thanks. Nearly all the material in the book was presented at numerous seminars and conferences in Leicester, London, Rome, Reading and Newcastle. Rhiannon Evans commented on the final draft of the first edition. Map 3.3 is reprinted by permission of the Peters Fraser and Dunlop Group Ltd. Maps 3.7 and 3.8 appear with the permission of Dr Henrik Mouritsen. Map 5.2 appears with permission from the University of Michigan Press and is taken from T. McGinn, *The Economy of Prostitution in the Roman World: A Study of Social History and the Brothel.* The plan of the House of the Vettii, Figure 7.1, is taken from Wallace-Hadrill (1988), fig. 10, with permission from the British School at Rome. Figures 8.1–8.3 appear with permission from Aristide D. Cartzas. Plans that appear as Figures 8.7 and 8.8 were compiled by Penelope Allison, Jaimie Lovell and Judith Botsai and are reprinted from *Pompeian Households: An Analysis of the Material Culture*, Monograph 42, by Penelope M. Allison (Los Angeles, CA: The Cotsen Institute of Archaeology at UCLA, Monograph 42, 2004). Figure 10.1 appears with permission of Jackie Dunn and is taken from the Pompeiiinpictures website (www.pompeiiinpictures.com). My greatest debt is due to Jeremy Paterson, who found time to discuss, argue, enthuse and offer constructive advice. Any errors that remain are my own.

NOTE ON REFERENCES
TO TRANSLATIONS IN
ENGLISH

Where possible, reference has been given not just to the source material from Pompeii, but also to translations in Alison E. Cooley and M.G.L. Cooley (2004) *Pompeii: A Sourcebook,* Routledge: London. These are simply given after the original reference and an = sign, for example *CIL* 10.787 = E1, where E1 can be located at p. 85 of Cooley and Cooley 2004. This has been done to aid those readers who do not have access to the reference works and/or knowledge of the original languages to utilise them.

INTRODUCTION

Pompeii is one of the most famous archaeological sites in Europe. The thousands of people who visit the remains of this Roman city each day of the year are brought into close proximity to a past which has been preserved by the eruption of Vesuvius in AD 79. As visitors walk down the streets, the scale and nature of the remains make it easy for them to create their own idea of an urban society in the first century AD (see Plates 1 and 2). This experience of the Roman city draws upon the physical reality of the past as it has been preserved: the forum, the houses, the brothels, the theatres, the amphitheatre and, of course, the plaster casts of the dead (Etienne 1992 and Connolly 1979 provide excellent introductions to the site for those who have not visited Pompeii). Frequently, these reconstructions are distinctly idealised. Some of these utopias find their way into art and literature (Leppmann 1968; Wyke 1997: 165–71). Other images and experiences of Pompeii are absorbed into modern architecture and town planning (Unwin 1909), and are indirectly experienced by those living in the modern twenty-first-century cities of Western Europe. Pompeii exists not only in the past but also in the present. The visitors to this ancient city find it is so like their own urban experience in the modern world that they interpret what they see in the light of their knowledge of the modern city. Everything appears to be easily understood and laid out by the heritage industry.

In contrast, Pompeii reveals a very different reality to the 'professional' archaeologist or historian. Although Pompeii has undergone more than two hundred years of excavation and conservation, this has had a relatively small impact upon the disciplines of archaeology and ancient history. The reasons for this have been summed up by Wallace-Hadrill:

> It [Pompeii] is at once the most studied and the least understood of sites. Universally familiar, its excavation and scholarship prove a nightmare of omissions and disasters. Each generation discovers with horror the extent to which information has been ignored, neglected, destroyed and left unreported and unpublished.
>
> (Wallace-Hadrill 1990: 150)

1

Plate 1 The fabric of Pompeii (Vicolo del Balcone Pensile)

Plate 2 Street junction with fountain

The information that is the most accessible for study, at Pompeii, is the physical fabric of the ancient city: the architecture and wall painting. This material is most readily available, whilst it remains conserved. In contrast, the artefacts found alongside the physical fabric of the city have in many cases been lost or dispersed, and can only be rediscovered via the reports of the excavators of the site. This situation has caused much scholarship in the twentieth century to concentrate upon the art and architecture at the expense of a broader cultural investigation of Pompeian society. Even for those scholars interested in art and architecture, Pompeii presents problems. In those areas away from the most-visited parts of the site, vegetation often obscures the object of study (Descœudres and Sear 1987: 13). This can cause areas of the site to be neglected and not examined. The general deterioration of the archaeological remains should not be underestimated (Adam 1980; Ioppolo 1992). The costs of preservation are enormous upon such a large site (see Map 1). In 1993 the excavated area, forty-four hectares of the total sixty-six-hectare site, required funding to the tune of 1,500 billion lire, but the then level of funding only came to some 70 billion lire (letter from B. Conticello in the *Guardian*, 20 January 1993). In the face of the deterioration of the physical fabric a number of initiatives have been taken to record the site. From 1975, an international project, Häuser in Pompeji, has been running to record individual houses with exceptional wall decoration (Strocka 1984, 1991; Michel 1990; Ehrhardt 1988; Seiler 1992; Descœudres and Sear 1987; Eschebach 1982; Peters 1993; Allison and Sear 2002; see also Ling 1997; Ling and Ling 2005 for the British project on the House of the Menander). Also, in the late 1980s, a computer data-base was set up to record the site (Conticello 1990: this supersedes earlier photographic records, e.g. Vlad Borelli *et al.* 1983). This work is still at an early stage. Alongside the work on the computer data-base, an attempt is being made to re-examine and publish some of the lesser-known buildings from Pompeii. In doing so, the authors use the original excavation reports to establish in what state the structure was found, rather than what is preserved today. Also, they have chosen remarkable buildings: the Casa del Marinaio, with a store building on its lower level, and the Sarno bath complex, which may resemble the architecture of the *insulae* at Ostia (Franklin 1990; Ostrow 1990). Such work can only partially compensate for the loss of evidence in the past. Recent reassessments of housing have had a greater focus on theories of social space and the subject of domesticity at Pompeii (see papers in Laurence and Wallace-Hadrill 1997; Grahame 2000; Berry 1997a, 1997b).

There has also been a re-evaluation of our ways of interpreting Pompeian evidence. The method of dating the fabric of Pompeii, which is based upon a typology of masonry fabric and wall painting (the four styles), has been seriously questioned (Dwyer 1991; Allison 1992a, 1992b; Wallace-Hadrill 1990; Laidlaw 1985. Contra: Strocka 1991). The critics of this traditional schema have made a strong argument for a more contextual approach to the *atrium* house. Such an approach would examine the finds, the decoration and the

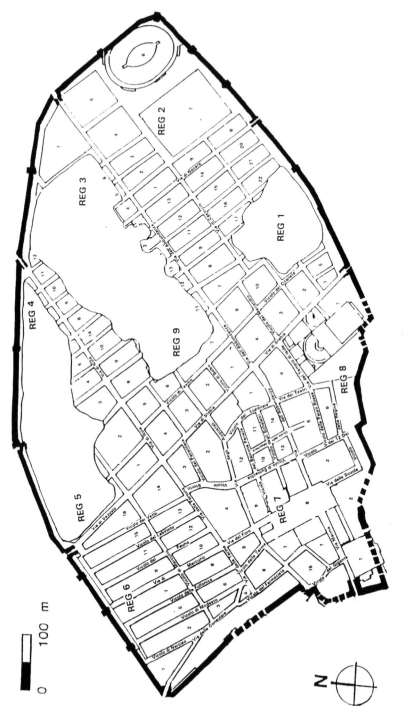

Map 1 Base map of Pompeii

architecture together. Only then could a dating sequence be constructed. However, without further excavation below the AD 79 destruction level, such an ambition will continue to remain unfulfilled (see now Arthur 1986; Nappo 1988; Bonghi Jovino 1984; Berry 1998; Fulford and Wallace-Hadrill 1999; Jones and Robinson 2004 on recent excavations below the destruction level. See also recent excavation reports in *Rivista di Studi Pompeiane*). One dating point that continues to have a role is the earthquake of AD 62. This earthquake, according to Seneca (*N.Q.*6), caused considerable damage to the physical fabric of the city (Andreau 1973; Guidoboni 1989: 139–67 lists epigraphic evidence; see now AAVV 1995). The extent of the damage to the city is difficult to evaluate, not least because the eruption of Vesuvius in AD 79 was also accompanied by a series of seismic events (Plin., *Ep.* 6.16, 6.20). The supposition of 'extensive' earthquake damage in AD 62 has been used to account for a variety of social change in Pompeii (e.g. Nappo 1988; Castiglione *et al.* 1989; Carocci *et al.* 1990). At its most extreme, this form of explanation has been used to attribute a rise of an urban bourgeoisie, which replaced the traditional elite whose fortunes were based upon landed wealth. Mouritsen has exposed the simplistic nature of this argument. He argues that rather than seeing a municipal elite that was closed off to other groups, we should view Pompeian society as fluid with new members entering the *ordo* of decurions frequently throughout Pompeii's history (Mouritsen 1996, 1988). The economic basis for the rise of the bourgeoisie had already been questioned by Andreau (1973). The earthquake of AD 62 would have had a dramatic effect upon urban life, as we shall see in Chapter 2, but there is always a danger that a dated event in a literary source can dominate and eradicate other forms of explanation of social change.

The re-examination of the epigraphic evidence in Pompeii has led to a total rejection of the methods of Della Corte (1965). Mouritsen (1988: 13–27) argues forcefully that the electoral *dipinti* on the façades of houses were not, in most cases, related to the owners or occupiers of those houses; so we can no longer attribute ownership of a house upon the basis of the graffiti on the façade. Equally, the social status of the occupiers of the houses cannot be established solely upon stylistic grounds. Wallace-Hadrill (1990) has proposed through a sample of *insulae* in *Regiones* 1 and 6 that there was a unified material culture that does not highlight discrepancies between wealth and poverty. Wallace-Hadrill's re-evaluation (1991, 1994) of the population of sampled houses and the city as a whole results in similar feelings of frustration. We cannot securely attribute exact numbers of inhabitants to many of the houses in the city (contra Strocka 1991; Wallace-Hadrill 1990: 157). Many of our problems of interpretation are aggravated by the incomplete recording and publication of the finds from Pompeii (Wallace-Hadrill 1990: 187–9; Carandini 1977). A further problem is encountered when the finds are examined. In many ways, the deposition of this material is more complicated than previously thought. Allison has found evidence of hoarding, looting and clearance of valuables from houses prior to and shortly after the eruption of AD 79 (Allison 1992a, 1992b; for final publication of this research project see Allison 2004). Until we fully understand this depositional phase, little can be extrapolated from the evidence of the finds from individual houses in isolation (Allison 2004 does much to resolve these issues, but many of her conclusions are in the form of critique and deconstruction of the work of others). For example, what are the implications of the finds from *Insula* 1.8? A large number of coins, totalling six hundred *sesterces*, were found at a bar 1.8.8–9 (Castiglione *et al.* 1989; compare Crawford 1970: 42 and 1969 no. 245); in contrast relatively few coins were found elsewhere in the *insula* (see Figure 1). Does the sum found at the bar represent a day's takings, or the total capital of the owner of the bar? Did the occupiers of the rest of the *insula* need such sums of monetary wealth, or had these inhabitants left with their money? The latter seems likely, because if we compare the distribution of coin finds to finds of *amphorae* in the *insula,* we find that there is a more even distribution of stored or consumed wealth (*amphorae*) than of movable wealth (coinage) (see Figure 1). The question of how this may reflect social gradations within the *insula* remains uncertain. However, it should be recognised that the coin find at 1.8.8–9 included a significant number of coins from a much earlier period (see Figure 2). Still, we are not sure if these are in circulation or not. What is clear is that Pompeian material culture is cumulative. Dated artefacts such as coins reveal a longevity that should not be dismissed. A similar situation is revealed by dated *amphorae* in *CIL* 4 (2551–9, 5511–28, 9313–17, 10261) (see Figure 3). Twenty-one per cent of all dated *amphorae* were more than thirty years old when Vesuvius erupted. Thus, any artefact assemblage found in a house at Pompeii reflects the accumulated wealth of the inhabitants over more than a single generation. Any interpretation of the finds remains limited until more material is published and evaluated. Such evaluation should be conscious of the wider issues of archaeological deposition. For the 'professional' archaeologist, unlike the guided visitor, Pompeii presents a complex problem that requires solution, but such problem solving is bedevilled by an unsatisfactory body of data, at least for the immediate future. However, such reasoning should not excuse us from an evaluation of the evidence that is available. It is a fallacy that incomplete data cannot be used in the explanation of archaeological phenomena. In the case of Pompeii, this has resulted in an almost complete neglect of the site by archaeologists working upon methodological and theoretical issues (but note Raper 1977). The scope for such work is immense (Dyson 1993). In fact, academic archaeology's relative neglect of Pompeii, the largest urban site in Europe, cannot be excused. In the future, we can look forward to a more rigorous discussion of our methods of interpretation, and theoretical approaches to this unique body of evidence.

The 'professional' historians have also, in the past, neglected Pompeii as a source of evidence and as an object of study. Pompeii was seen as a place for

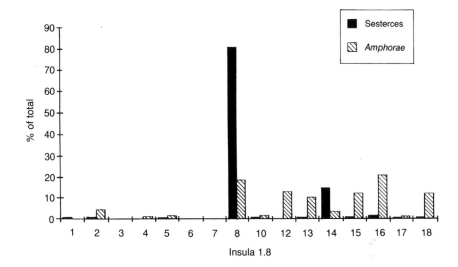

Figure 1 Proportion of coins compared with finds of *amphorae* at each address in
Insula 1.8

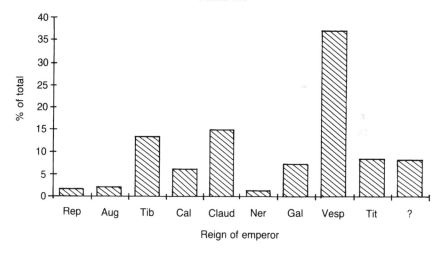

Figure 2 Coins found at 1.8.8–9

the study of art and architectural history and also of the mechanics of elections under the empire (Wallace-Hadrill 1988: 48). However, more recently,
there has been a reassessment of what Pompeii represents and how we
should use such evidence. There was seen to be a real need to relate literary texts, giving details about social life, to the archaeological evidence. The
aim was not to explain the evidence in literary texts but, rather, to examine
the underlying social use and meaning of the archaeological data (Wallace-
Hadrill 1988: 46). This reassessment of the evidence has concentrated upon

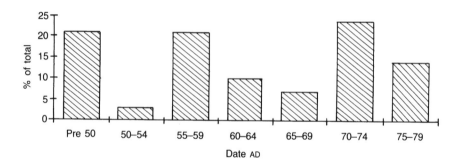

Figure 3 Amphorae with dated *tituli* in *CIL* 4

the *atrium* house, which is seen to be closely related to the social standing of its inhabitant (Wallace-Hadrill 1990). In conducting his study of Pompeian housing, Wallace-Hadrill (1990: 190–2) has examined a sample of 122 houses and differentiates them according to size, function, architecture and decoration. Rather than being a conclusive study of social status and housing, his quantified results present a picture of a diffusion of luxury products from the elite throughout the city of Pompeii. The real value of such work comes out in the application of literary evidence to the explanation of the functions and activities of Roman social life (Dwyer 1991 and, in particular, Wallace-Hadrill 1988; final publication of the project can be found in Wallace-Hadrill 1994). The *atrium* house was well adapted to the rituals of visiting at the *salutatio* and at dinner. The house was equally well arranged for household rituals of a religious nature (summarised by Clarke 1991: 1–29). In this context, the decoration and architecture of the *atrium* house embodied the occupier's social power (Wallace-Hadrill 1991: 226). Moreover, the implications of the Pompeian evidence for the study of a variety of topics in Roman history, for example the Roman family, cannot be underestimated. Pompeii provides a context that can place a control upon the interpretation of our disparate literary sources. For example, housing in Pompeii provides a variety of contexts in which the Roman family existed (Wallace-Hadrill 1991: 225). This underlies the complex relationship between the archaeological evidence from Pompeii and the literary source material. The relationship is reflexive. Literary sources can inform us about the 'social rhythms' that underlie the material culture (Wallace-Hadrill 1988: 48).

Equally, archaeological data from Pompeii can also reveal that missing context that is assumed by our literary sources. In effect, one informs the other. The relationship is not a simple one and needs to be handled with care. Simplistic applications of literary evidence to archaeological data, so common in the past, must be avoided (Allison 1992a, 1992b, 2004). The temptation to reject the literary source material, because it may be unrepresentative, biased, incomplete and from a different context, in favour of a 'purer' archaeological explanation should also be resisted. If we reject the literary sources, we are discarding a body of evidence that is as much a cultural product of Roman society as the archaeological evidence itself (see Laurence 1997, 2004 for more on this matter). Not to use such evidence to inform our own interpretation of the evidence from Pompeii is the equivalent of ignoring the implications of archaeological evidence for the study of Roman socio-economic history (Jongman 1988 expects too much of the archaeological evidence). Both archaeological and literary sources have their relevance for the study of Pompeii, but these sources need to be deployed with care in our interpretation and writing about Pompeii's past existence. Ideally, the historical/archaeological interpretation should satisfy both disciplines. In what follows, both archaeological and literary sources are used to elucidate the nature of the urban experience of the inhabitants of Pompeii.

In the wider context of the study of Roman history, Pompeii has played its part in the definition of the nature of the Roman economy. Not surprisingly, Pompeian evidence was used to reinforce Rostovtzeff's conception of the Roman economy, as closely similar to that of Western Europe and North America in the early twentieth century (Rostovtzeff 1957: 61–73). Rostovtzeff's analysis was by simple analogy between the ancient and modern objects, such as towns or coins (Greene 1986: 14). Stress was placed upon traded goods and the rise of a bourgeoisie. The city was seen to have been a producer of goods similar to the modern cities of the early twentieth century (Rostovtzeff 1957: xii–xiv). It was argued, by Moeller, that one of the major products of Pompeii was textiles, manufacture of which was organised by a guild structure, similar to those associated with medieval Europe (Moeller 1976). Such a simplistic analysis has been effectively destroyed by Jongman's (1988) work on the Pompeian economy. He exposes the paucity of methodology that was associated with the 'modernising' assumptions of Moeller and others (Jongman 1988: 155–86). His work attempted to substantiate the Finley model of the 'consumer city'. This model had been eloquently set out by Finley (1973) in *The Ancient Economy* and was based upon Weber's ideal types of the city (Weber 1958). Finley (1973) had suggested that the ancient economy was embedded in the social structure and the value system of Roman society. He pointed to a passage of Cicero (*Off.* 1.150–1) that suggested that production and trade were unwisely indulged in. Finley concluded that given these social values trade was socially taboo. This outlook derived from literary evidence was combined with Weber's model of the 'consumer city'. The 'consumer city', in contrast to the 'producer city', did not produce manufactured goods for export to external markets. Instead, in the 'consumer city', the agricultural surplus of the city's rural hinterland was consumed by the urban elite. Where manufacturing was undertaken, it was to service the elite with luxury products for conspicuous consumption in the city (Finley 1973: 123–49; Weber 1958: 65–90). This model of the city does not deny that the ancients used coins, traded, manufactured goods, or lived in towns, but what they did not do was to manufacture goods explicitly for an economic trade with external markets (for excellent discussion of Finley's work see Jongman 1988: 28–54 and Greene 1986: 14–16). Although the 'consumer-city' model is very neat and concise, and has become the new orthodox view of how we should view the city and the economy of the Roman Empire, it was not without its critics, who continued to adhere to the modernising concepts derived from Rostovtzeff and others (e.g. D'Arms 1981). To settle this debate once and for all, Jongman applied the model of the 'consumer city' to the extant remains of Pompeii. The model seems to fit the Pompeian evidence, but some evidence is explained away by Jongman (1988: 97–110). Furthermore, Jongman only analyses the archaeological evidence to discredit the theories of others, most notably Moeller, and does not use this source of information to reinforce or falsify his own arguments (e.g. when dealing with *amphorae*, Jongman 1988: 124–30). In many ways, his analysis of Pompeii could have referred to almost any theoretical ancient city. Primarily, he refined the work of Finley and applied it to a geographical location, rather than to an archaeological situation. Such work could have been conducted upon any city in Campania which has a known geographical location. However, given these criticisms of Jongman's application of the model, we have to recognise that the 'consumer city' is by far the best available model that actually defines an ancient city in economic terms (for alternatives see Carandini 1988: 327–38; Engels 1990, to be read with the review by Saller 1991).

In the following chapters, the Pompeian evidence is examined to highlight the role of the city. This analysis is not confined to proving or disproving the validity of the 'consumer-city' model. Certainly, the analysis may highlight the appropriateness or otherwise of the model, but this is not the primary purpose of the book. Underlying the analysis given in the following chapters is the reflexive relationship between urban space and the activities that were conducted by the inhabitants in that space. It has frequently been observed that all behaviour has a spatial aspect to it. For example, the tombs of the dead were located outside the city walls. Should we see individual Pompeians choosing to locate the dead outside the city or did the individual Pompeian have no choice but to place the tomb of a relative there because the dead were spatially located outside the city? In effect, people are born into a spatial world, in which the individual has only a limited choice about the location of activities. However, individuals can fundamentally alter the fabric of urban space. This view of the individual and urban space at times seems to approach a tautology, but this only further underlines the reflexive relationship between space and society. The two entities, space and society, cannot be neatly separated. One is constantly acting upon the other and, simultaneously, the opposite is occurring. Throughout the book, urban activities are analysed within their spatial context. Chapter 1 seriously questions the assertion, within Pompeian studies, that the city was planned. It will be argued that the layout of streets was produced by factors that should not be associated, primarily, with town planning. Chapter 2 examines how the identity of the city was altered from the colonial foundation to the city's destruction in AD 79. The focus is upon the development of civic architecture that reflected the changing identity of Pompeii in this period. In Chapter 3, the level of analysis moves on to a study of local identity and territory within the city. The concepts of neighbours and neighbourhood are fundamental to this study, which utilises the evidence for the distribution of local shrines and the public water supply at a local level. Chapter 4 addresses the location of productive workshops and the nature of production in the city. In particular, the question of whether workshops were concentrated in defined areas is considered. In Chapter 5, deviant behaviour that might have outraged some inhabitants is examined to highlight, for example, whether certain areas of the city were more tolerant of the presence of prostitutes. In Chapter 6, the emphasis shifts to the physical fabric of the city. Through analysis of the use of street frontages, levels of activity are attributed to streets within the city. This highlights streets with high and low levels of human activity in them. In Chapter 7, the spatial arrangement of the buildings adjoining the streets is analysed to establish how the spatial pattern of activity, discussed in Chapter 6, was produced. Chapter 8 undertakes to integrate the implications of work from 1993 through to 2004 on the houses of Pompeii and seeks to suggest that the form of the *insula* blocks was determined, in part at least, by a desire to realise a return in rental income. Chapter 9 examines the variation in the use of space through the day. This establishes a temporal framework, a social product, which placed constraints upon the use of urban space. Following on from this, Chapter 10 seeks to evaluate the role of the fabric of the city in the production of citizens and the social reproduction of *urbanitas* over time. Finally, in Chapter 11, the themes of the book are drawn together to unify the competing views of Pompeii set out in the individual chapters. This final chapter also places Pompeii in the wider context of the study of the Roman city in the first century AD. The book concentrates on the implications of the reflexive relationship of urban space and urban society, so apparent in Pompeii, and uses this relationship to establish a more coherent and all-embracing view of the Roman city than has been presented to us by those using the literary texts, for the most part, whether Moses Finley in *The Ancient Economy* or, now, Peregrine Horden and Nicholas Purcell in *The Corrupting Sea*. Pompeii is a particular city destroyed at a particular time, hence, the evidence, as we shall see, reflects the existence of a city in the first century AD. It is not like any city of Italy of an earlier or later period, since the institutional context of the Roman Empire was not the same as that of Pompeii destroyed in AD 79; a context in which its network of connectivity was very different from that of the earlier periods of its existence (a point clarified by the ceramic evidence analysed by De Sena and Ikäheimo 2003).

1

ANCIENT AND MODERN
TOWN PLANNING

Pompeii was a planned city, like many other Roman cities – or so it is generally asserted by scholars. However, what is meant by 'planned' in this context? Roman colonies founded on green-field sites display Roman planning at its most elaborate. The streets and public space were laid out along geometric lines, which suggests an ordered arrangement. But this has little in common with the modern conception of town planning, which is a complex process for the organisation of modern cities. This modern town planning, unlike Roman 'planning', not only lays out a street pattern, but also organises the use of space and takes account of topography, local transport needs, social concerns, economic parameters, conservation and environmental issues, to name but a few. In contrast, what is known as 'ancient town planning' only addressed the problem of how the city should be laid out. It was Haverfield, the Oxford historian, who originally asserted the notion of the planned Roman city in 1913. His interpretation of ancient towns as planned has never been questioned and has been reproduced recently by Owens (1991). However, in our assessment of urban space in Pompeii, we need to examine how useful the term 'town planning' is for the study of the ancient city. Therefore, in this chapter, the nature of modern and ancient town planning will be evaluated.

Haverfield's book *Ancient Town Planning*, published in 1913, was based on two lectures given in 1910: the Creighton lecture to the University of London and a paper given at the London Conference on Town Planning. The book was not only a study of ancient town planning but also had a strong political message for the twentieth-century reader. As Haverfield stated in the preface:

> The original lecture was written as a scholar's contribution to a modern movement. It looked on town planning as one of the new methods of social reform, which stand in somewhat sharp contrast with the usual aims of political parties and parliaments.
>
> (Haverfield 1913: 2)

In many ways, Haverfield's interpretation was fundamentally influenced by the modern town-planning movement. Therefore to understand his interpretation of town planning, it is necessary to assess the influences upon his original interpretation of Roman city plans.

In the nineteenth century, Britain's cities had undergone a period of rapid growth in both population and area. This growth had been unregulated and, in consequence, the environmental impact had been catastrophic. It was in the period 1900–14 that there was a general realisation of the effects of rapid urbanisation. The statistical surveys of Charles Booth and others had demonstrated that the problem was more widespread than previously thought. This new perception of the urban problem gave rise to a series of intellectual and political ideas that crossed party lines and permeated all levels of society. Britain's failure in the Boer War was blamed upon the poor health of potential recruits. In 1902, for example, 50 per cent of all recruits from Manchester were rejected because of their poor physique. The report of the Interdepartmental Committee on Physical Deterioration, in 1904, associated the poor health of army recruits with overcrowding, atmospheric pollution and other effects of urban living (Ashworth 1965: 167–90; Cherry 1988: 49–73). Therefore, the problems of the cities of Britain were seen, for the first time, to concern the nation. This feeling was summed up by Horsfall in 1908:

> Unless we at once begin at least to protect the health of our people by making the towns in which most of them now live, more wholesome for body and mind, we may as well hand over our trade, our colonies, our whole influence in the world, to Germany without undergoing all the trouble of a struggle in which we condemn ourselves beforehand to certain failure.
>
> (From T.C. Horsfall, *The Relation of Town Planning to the National Life* (1908), quoted by Ashworth 1965: 169)

The health of the nation was a *cause célèbre* of the eugenics movement. Its main concern was the racial degeneration of the British people, in particular, in relation to the rising number of insane (e.g. 1872, 2.2 per 1,000 insane, 1909, 3.2 per 1,000 insane) and also to the decline of the birth rate in the cities (Searle 1976). At the same time, there was a strong campaign for national efficiency, which stressed, amongst other things, the need for industry to be located close to railway yards, and that residential areas should be located away from these areas (Searle 1971). Thus, in effect, this campaign was an early assertion of the need for zoning in the city.

An alternative to these authoritarian campaigns was put forward by the Garden City Association. From 1899, Ebenezer Howard had been asserting that the solution to Britain's urban problems was to create an attractive alternative to urban life, which could be economically sustained. His solution was the Garden City, an ideal form, which he presented in the terminology acceptable to the establishment and, above all, in practical terms. The foundation of Letchworth (1903) firmly demonstrated this. Moreover, the Garden City Association was an important pressure group, which organised conferences on town planning in 1907 and 1908 and also held lectures throughout the country. The appeal of Garden Cities was not to any one group, but crossed political, religious, social and class lines (Hardy 1991).

The outpouring of articles and books in this period advocating town planning is immense. Articles appeared in the *Builder*, the *Sociological Review*, the *Architectural Review* and others, such as the *Race-Builder*. Books on town planning began to appear from 1906 with Patrick Geddes' *City Development,* to be followed in 1909 by Raymond Unwin's *Town Planning in Practice*, which sold widely. It was with such pressure that in 1909 the first Town Planning Act was passed, which acknowledged that city development could no longer be subject to market forces alone.

It should be noted that the advocates of town planning looked to the past for examples to justify their position. In particular, it was the Roman Empire that attracted them. The Roman Empire was an urban culture. It was perceived as a strong empire geared up for conquest. The level of urban amenity and architecture impressed itself upon the early twentieth-century mind. The organised street grid and aesthetic appearance of the ancient city were also important in justifying the civilised nature of a planned urban environment (see, e.g., Unwin 1909: 27–52). Therefore, it should come as no surprise that at the RIBA's 1910 Town Planning Conference there was a morning devoted to 'Cities of the past', and that three of the four papers were upon the ancient world (published in AAVV 1911).

The 1910 Town Planning Conference marked a high point for town planning in Britain. Never before or since has town planning been granted such high esteem. There were 52 papers, 1,200 delegates, and an exhibition at the Royal Academy. In the session 'Cities of the past', Gardner gave an informative account of the Greek city, Haverfield highlighted town planning in the Roman world, Ashby delivered a paper on Rome and Brinckmann accounted for the ideal of town planning from the Renaissance to the present. Haverfield's paper linked modern and ancient planning, with a strong case for a system of planning in the modern world based upon a grid of streets. One of the problems for those, such as Haverfield, who see planning throughout the Roman world is the city of Rome itself. The capital of the Roman Empire displays none of the qualities of planning that had been highlighted by Gardner and Haverfield. This had been recognised by Livy (5.55), who provided an inadequate explanation for the lack of planning in the capital. This lack of planning in Rome was highlighted by Ashby, the Director of the British School at Rome, in his paper. He explained the form of ancient Rome with reference to the physical topography of the site and structural features, in particular the Servian wall. Moreover, he railed against the current tendency of planning in Rome based upon the grid without any respect to extant topography. Significantly, the full force of the town-planning lobby, present at the conference, brushed aside Ashby's discussion of ancient Rome and his objections to modern planning founded upon geometric ideals. In the discussion after the papers, Lanciani highlighted the replanning of Ostia in a fashion similar to an American city. The link between the Roman past and the present was well received by the delegates. The conference itself and, in particular, the session on 'City development and extension' seem to have made an impression on Haverfield and caused him to examine the work of Stübben and Unwin in greater detail (Haverfield 1913: 4 note 1).

Following the 1910 conference, Haverfield revised his paper for publication in book form. The conference paper and *Ancient Town Planning* reveal his feelings about town planning. He insisted that modern and ancient life were not different (Haverfield 1910: 123). He suggested that there should be a system of town planning similar to the Roman grid formation: 'The square and the straight line are indeed the simplest marks which divide civilised man from the barbarian' (Haverfield 1910: 124). He had little time for the recent German planning based upon the curve: 'It has remained for the Teutonic spirit in these last days to connect civilisation with the curve' (Haverfield 1910: 124). For Haverfield, town planning, whether modern or ancient, was: 'the art of laying out towns with due care for the health and comfort of the inhabitants, for industrial and commercial efficiency, and for reasonable beauty' (Haverfield 1913: 11). Here we see the influence of the campaign for national efficiency, alongside Geddes' sociological approach to city planning (on Geddes see Boardman 1978 and Meller 1990). Also, under the influence of Geddes, he asserted that the ancient city under the empire served a region, with its amenities of the amphitheatre and theatre. To back this up, he cited the example of Nucerians attending the amphitheatre at Pompeii in AD 59 (Tac., *Ann.* 14.17 = D34). It is specifically with reference to Pompeii that we see the permeation of modern ideas about twentieth-century planning into Haverfield's analysis of the ancient city (Haverfield 1913: 63–8; see Figure 1.1). He explicitly rejected Mau's (1899) conclusion that the excavated street pattern of Pompeii was laid out in a single phase. Instead, he concluded, from an examination of the plan of the site, that the town had expanded in a number of stages from a smaller nucleated settlement, which was located to the west of the city. This he termed the *Altstädt*, which he associated with the irregular streets close to the forum (a view followed by many today, e.g. Ling 1991: 253, 2005, Carocci *et al.* 1990: 207; see Zevi 1982: 361 for influence of Haverfield in Italian scholarship; compare Richardson 1982). From its original foundation, the city had expanded in a number of phases; these corresponded to the regular streets, for example in *Regio* 6. Because he could not identify a symmetrical grid or, even, a semblance of a grid at the site, he rejected the idea that Pompeii was laid out in a single phase. In other words, Pompeii did not entirely conform to Haverfield's expectation that Roman cities should have a symmetrical grid. Therefore, he had to explain this phenomenon and chose a chronological explanation, in which each block of symmetrical streets represented a different phase in the city's expansion. He ignored an alternative explanation, given by Unwin, that the inexactitude of the layout of streets in Pompeii could be accounted for by the way the planner had utilised natural features, such as contours (Unwin 1909: 49; see also Miller 1992). In fact, the layout of Pompeian *insulae* has a close relationship to the natural topography of the site. *Regiones* 1 and 6, the most regular, are upon land that slopes in a southerly direction. The roughly square *insulae*, to the east of Via di Stabia, are built on an area of ground sloping to the south. *Regio* 8 is dominated by its topography, with streets following the contours of the site. *Regio* 7 displays an irregular pattern, but this may be caused by the pressure on space in this central area. This may have altered the original street pattern. Such a view would not have harmonised with Haverfield's notion of the ancients' strict adhesion to a geometric system of planning. As a result, Haverfield was forced to suggest that the area around the forum was an earlier (uncivilised) pre-historic settlement and that, from this area, the city expanded in a systematic (civilised) fashion. In doing so, he had in mind the modern schemes for the expansion of cities such as Barcelona. There is little real evidence for Haverfield's chronology of town extension in Pompeii (De Caro 1985; Chiaramonte Treré 1986: 16–19; Sakai 1991: 38). Therefore, in the absence of an archaeological chronology for the development of the site, Haverfield adapted the modern notion of town planning to the AD 79 evidence.

This interpretation of the evidence provided a historical justification for twentieth-century planning. Also, in many ways, his work gave the ancient city builder the rationality of the twentieth-century planner, with little account of other factors such as topography. This view of town planning as a geometric grid was outdated by 1913. Geddes' methods of a thorough city survey, displayed at the Cities and Town Planning Exhibition, 1911, giving an account of geography, history, sociology, biology, engineering, aesthetics and architecture, revealed the complexity of town planning in reality, as compared with the drawing-office version based upon geometry (Meller 1990: 157). The complex reality of town planning did not concern Haverfield, who ardently stated that geometry was the key to a civilised urban society similar to that of the Roman Empire.

In the same year as the Town Planning Conference, 1910, Adshead, the first Professor of Town Planning, explained the implications of the Town Planning Act of 1909 in the new journal *Town Planning Review*. He saw planning not only as a means of defining traffic routes, providing parks, buildings, factories and commercial zones, but also as a means to stifle socio-economic problems (Dowdall and Adshead 1910: 39–45). Adshead summarises the planner's dilemma:

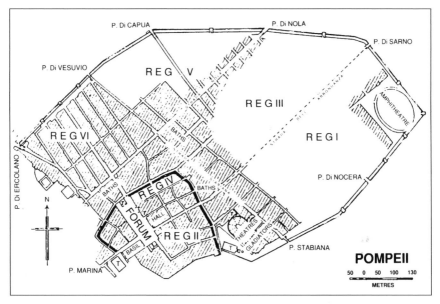

(T = Temple. The area of the supposed original settlement is outlined in black.)

Figure 1.1 Haverfield's Pompeii

The problem of arranging the juxtaposition of the classes or for their separation will constantly present itself, and whilst absolute separation is a policy to be avoided, as being contrary to the natural dependence of the classes upon each other, at the same time to throw them indiscriminately together would be too radical a policy and would most certainly fail.

(Dowdall and Adshead 1910: 50)

What is clear from Adshead's analysis is that, from 1909, the local authorities became interested in planning socio-economic zones in their cities. These zones separated the working class from the middle class, residential areas from industrial areas, etc. In many ways, this is the origin of the urban formations we experience today. These formations had not existed prior to the twentieth century's concern for planning.

The analysis of the city in twentieth-century geography has concentrated upon the definition of economic zoning from empirical evidence (see Figure 1.2). The studies which have resulted have produced a number of models of the city. The most influential of these models are the concentric zone and Hoyt's sectorial model. The concentric-zone model views the city as arranged around a central core containing the government and administrative buildings, and the main business area. This area is termed the central business district (CBD). Around the CBD, there are a series of concentric zones. The first two zones

17

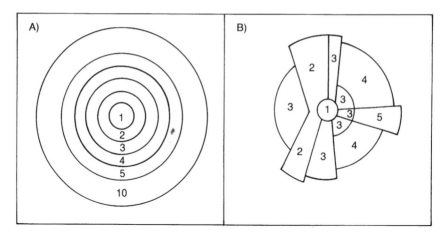

1 Central business district
2 Wholesale light manufacturing
3 Low-class residential
4 Middle-class residential
5 High-class residential
6 Heavy manufacturing
7 Outlying business district
8 Residential suburb
9 Industrial suburb
10 Commuters' zone

Figure 1.2 Models of zoning in the modern city A) Concentric zone model
B) Sectorial model

from the CBD are areas of light manufacturing and wholesaling, the third low-class housing, the fourth middle-class housing, the fifth high-class housing and the sixth out of town manufacturing (Ayeni 1979: 12). In this model, the socio-economic status of residents increases as the distance from the centre increases. The second model, Hoyt's sectorial model, assumes there is a CBD, but suggests that the city is zoned in sectors, according to urban land rents. The zones tend to be associated with transport corridors radiating from the CBD (Ayeni 1979: 12–13). The usefulness of these economic models of the city is limited for the study of Pompeii. Pompeii does not exhibit any traits of socio-economic zoning (Raper 1977). As is argued below, no single social group was confined to, or desired to live, in a separate area of the city segregated from the rest of society. However, the observation that the city clusters around a central CBD may be of some use. In Pompeii, we might be able to identify the forum as the central core around which the city was arranged. The forum was the area in which the administrative, religious, political, symbolic, economic and social functions of the city were concentrated. Also, there was a series of streets that radiated from the forum to the city gates, which formed transport corridors to Pompeii's rural hinterland. However, Pompeii does not appear to have been arranged according to economic zoning, in which the elite were separated from the rest of society. Such economic zoning only appears in cities that have experienced the Euro-American Industrial Revolution in the nineteenth century and Euro-American planning law in the twentieth century (Ayeni 1979: 11–33). Pompeii, then, does not easily fit modern concepts of land use, spatial division or zoning in the British, or European, or North American, or Australasian senses of that word (there is quite a different meaning associated with the term according to the urban culture a person has inhabited).

To begin to understand the nature of urban space in Pompeii, we need to recognise what we are dealing with. The relationship between urban space and society in Pompeii was complex and cannot neatly fit any one single theory (Lefebvre 1991; Harvey 1988; Castells 1977 address this problem in the modern city). The built environment of Pompeii was a product of Pompeian society (Harvey 1988: 196). By studying urban space in Pompeii, we are examining the social relationships and social choices of Pompeian society in space (Soja 1989: 76–93). Therefore, through the analysis of urban space in Pompeii, we come to understand the underlying social structure of Pompeian society.

The relationship between space and society is complex. Urban space in Pompeii reflects the nature of Pompeian society. However, we need to recognise that space is not entirely a neutral commodity (see Hillier and Hanson 1984 for a theory of urban space and Grahame 2000 for full application to *Regio* 6). Not only were individuals born in an urban environment that had already been constructed. Their social choices were made in the context of this urban environment. Moreover, urban space has its own structure and rules: it cannot be arranged in a totally random way. Buildings have to be entered from the street and require an independent entrance for the inhabitants' sole use. Also, the arrangement of the streets is a factor in the non-random structure of space. This would have been a factor at Pompeii. The emphasis upon private property had an effect upon the arrangement of space. This feature of Pompeian society placed a constraint upon the arrangement of space. Equally, the preferences of individuals, the concentration or aggregation of activities, the throughput of people and the ideology of Pompeian society all place their own constraints upon the randomness of space. In effect, it is the urban society that alters the random nature of space and moulds space to its needs. In effect, Pompeii and the urban space it contains were social products rather than planned entities (see Laurence 1997 for pursuit of this theme).

2

RESHAPING PUBLIC SPACE

From Oscan city to Roman colony

The establishment of a Roman colony at Pompeii in about 81 BC was undertaken with the view to the punishment of the town's citizens who had resisted Rome's general, Lucius Cornelius Sulla, in the Social War eight years earlier (App., *BC* 1.39; Vell.Pat. 2.16.2; Orosius 5.18.22 = B1, B2, B4). Land and property would have been taken from the Pompeians and granted to the incoming Roman citizens (Lo Cascio 1996; Zevi 1996 on the process). The situation was reported some nineteen years later as a conflict between the colonists and the Pompeians, with their identities still represented as separate entities (Cic., *Sull.* 60–62 = B15). There was also conflict between them over voting rights and an *ambulatio*, perhaps a portico (see Berry 1996: 254–6 for interpretations of this ambiguous text). The public spaces of the city were reshaped to incorporate the colonists and to create a series of spaces that could have been seen as new or different to what had existed previously. This restructuring of the city's facilities was underwritten by new money coming into the city.

Many of the iconic examples of Roman architecture in Pompeii had already been built at least a generation prior to the arrival of the colonists in 81 BC. The walled enclosure of sixty-six hectares with its street grid can be traced back to the late third century BC and even beyond. Map 2.1 provides a reference point for buildings referred to throughout this chapter. The forum had been laid out in its rectangular format adjacent to the much older temple complex of Apollo (see Plate 2.1). A basilica was in place to the immediate south of this temple and adjoining the forum itself. The Stabian Baths had been in existence for a considerable period of time at the junction of Via dell'Abbondanza, leading from the forum, and Via di Stabia. To the south lay a large theatre adjacent to the Triangular Forum with its temple, forming an integral part of the skyline of the city. Close by were a set of baths, the so-called Republican Baths. The magistrates of the city were involved in the embellishment of the city, whether with a portico, a sundial in the baths or in the laying out of roads (Vetter 1953 nos 8–12 = A8, A9, A10). There was also a sanctuary of Dionysius outside the city's walls (Poccetti 1979). The town

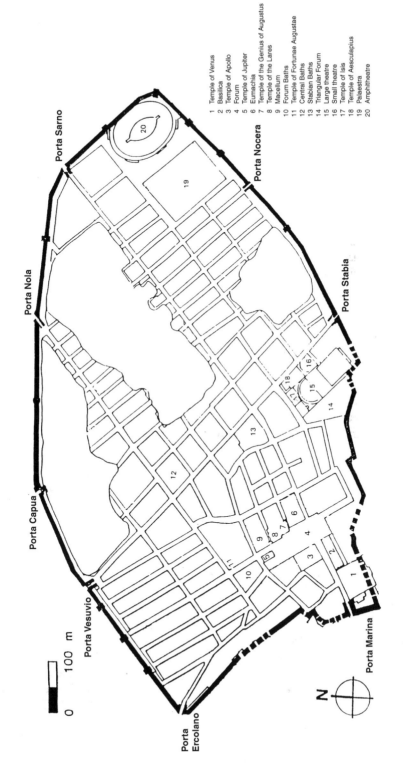

1	Temple of Venus
2	Basilica
3	Temple of Apollo
4	Forum
5	Temple of Jupiter
6	Eumachia
7	Temple of the Genius of Augustus
8	Temple of the Lares
9	Macellum
10	Forum Baths
11	Temple of Fortunae Augustae
12	Central Baths
13	Stabian Baths
14	Triangular Forum
15	Large theatre
16	Small theatre
17	Temple of Isis
18	Temple of Aesculapius
19	Palaestra
20	Amphitheatre

Porta Sarno

Porta Nocera

Porta Stabia

Porta Nola

Porta Capua

Porta Vesuvio

Porta Ercolano

Porta Marina

N

0   100 m

Map 2.1 Public buildings

was also built up with many of the more famous houses stretching back into the third or early second centuries BC.

The outline of the city destroyed in AD 79 was in place when the colonists arrived. However, their arrival marked a new beginning for the city. It was renamed *Colonia Veneria Cornelia Pompeianorum*, a name that reflected the action of foundation by the family of Cornelius Sulla and Lucius Sulla's association with the deity Venus. The re-assignment of property to the colonists remains obscure. What is clearer, however, from inscriptions and archaeology is a reshaping of public space to create an image of a Roman town. The public building projects would have needed human labour for their construction. The influx of colonists and the re-distribution of property or loss of property on the part of Pompeians created the labour resources for the construction of new monuments within the city. It remains unclear as to how long it took for the completion of the work, but there is categorical evidence of it being begun after the colonists' arrival. In 80 BC a new altar was set up in the existing temple of Apollo. The addition of a temple of Venus overlooking the Marine Gate altered the appearance of the skyline of the city. The re-location of the Capitolium at the northern end of the forum re-focused the religious identity of the space on Jupiter, Juno and Minerva (see Plate 2.2

Plate 2.1 The temple of Apollo

Plate 2.2 The temple of Jupiter

and Figure 2.1). To the north of the forum, a new set of baths was constructed (*CIL* 10.819). The need for such a monument, which in many ways dupli-cated the segregated bathing of men and women found in the Stabian Baths, can only be explained in terms of an increase in the number of persons bath-ing in the city (Ling 2005: 56–7). Although it would appear that bathing was becoming more popular with people taking more frequent baths, it would seem more likely that additional features for segregated bathing reflect an increase in population. Part of the Stabian Baths was embellished by the addi-tion of a *laconicum* and a *destrictarium*, alongside considerable restoration of the palaestra and its portico. The money was derived from the sums paid by the *duoviri* (two senior magistrates) on entry into office, and the contract was let out to another party to do the work (*CIL* 10.829 = B11). Such fund-ing was also behind the construction of the smaller covered theatre adjacent to the existing larger theatre (*CIL* 10.937 = B8). The need for a new theatre requires explanation: it may have been constructed to serve the needs of the new colonists or the need to put on two theatre shows at the same time, or perhaps there was simply a desire to have an indoor venue. Whatever the rea-soning, a prime site next to the large theatre was utilised. In the same year as the contract was let for the building of the covered theatre, Gaius Quinctius Valgus, a benefactor also at Aeclanum, Cassino and Frigento, and the

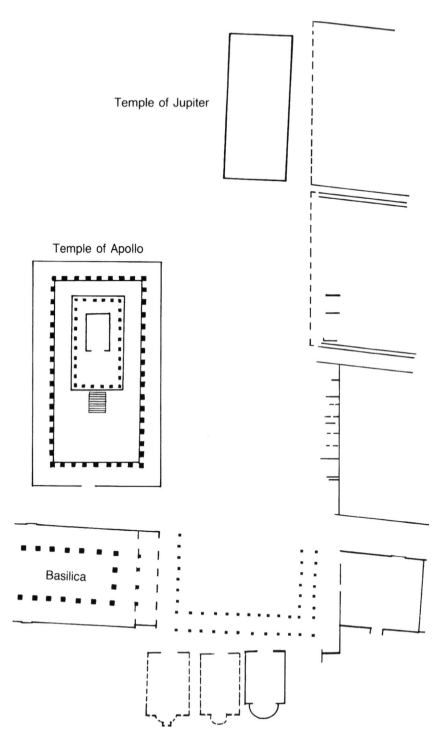

Temple of Jupiter

Temple of Apollo

Basilica

Figure 2.1 Forum in the republic

colonist Marcus Porcius paid for the construction of the amphitheatre on land that they owned and had given to the city (*CIL* 10.852 = B10; Harvey 1973 for the Italian rather than Roman origins of Valgus' wealthy benefactor). An amphitheatre (see Plate 2.3) would seem to have been a feature of colonies like Pompeii, as Welch (1994) has argued. For her, there is a connection back to the military training that the colonists had experienced and a desire to view the fighting of professionals. However, an alternative or additional explanation might be that it was in the colonies that there was an influx of money gained from the booty associated with warfare that created the financial possibility for the embellishment of towns with amphitheatres. In the case of Pompeii, the choice of an amphitheatre was made with a view to the creation of something new and exceptional that could attract people from outside the city, at the same time fulfilling the desire for the spectacle of gladiators on the part of the colonists. After all, on their arrival Pompeii was a city with a forum, temples, baths and a theatre. What structure other than an amphitheatre – a relatively rare building at this date and one that is mostly found in colonies – would have marked the new colony as a place of note? It would have amplified the facilities available and signified the city's identity as a colony of Rome.

Plate 2.3 The amphitheatre

The new colonists' efforts to reshape the city had an impact on almost all existing buildings and the new features of the city inserted within the grid of streets created a new urban form. There would seem to have been a shift away from the Triangular Forum marked by the decline of the nearby Republican Baths. Most of the change was focused on the area around the forum, but the addition of the amphitheatre in the south-east corner of the city created a new pattern of integration between the centre of the city and this outlying area. The city had been re-organised in another way: we have from 47 and 46 BC a list of magistrates of a *vicus* and its associated crossroads (*CIL* 4.60 = E62, see also *CIL* 4.7855 = E64). It would appear from this evidence of a later generation that the city had been divided up into neighbourhoods or *vici* with annually elected magistrates. These neighbourhoods were marked by a series of altars, mostly located at crossroads, at which festivals were celebrated (see Chapter 3). It is the city's magistrates and its structure of government that had changed the city, with inscriptions of these magistrates' actions marking its reconstruction and development. What was created by the Pompeians and by the colonists was a city that displayed many of the features of urbanism found in the later text of *De Architectura* by the Italian architect Vitruvius. Unlike that text, in which buildings are presented in isolation, we have at Pompeii the full ensemble or architectural effect of the spatial relationships between these monuments. The colonists did not obliterate the earlier public buildings. Instead, what changed was the shape of space. The monumental route between the forum, the Stabian Baths, the Triangular Forum and the theatre was extended to include the new amphitheatre in the south-east of the city. The skyline of the city was reshaped to be dominated by the new temple of Venus overlooking the river port to the south-west of the city. On arrival, those travelling to the city would have experienced the new Forum Baths or the newly restored Stabian Baths, and have seen the new Capitolium dominating the space of the forum. However, the impact of these building projects was only realised on their completion and the most notable feature of the Sullan colony prior to, say, 60 BC was the presence of human labour employed in building these structures. This feature may have been a means to employ both the dispossessed Pompeians and the new colonists, who may not have derived all their income from farming and perhaps supplemented the produce of their new land with employment on the city's new public buildings. These construction projects may have been a means to ease the disruption caused by the settlement of Sulla's veterans in the city and its territory.

The imperial city

Our understanding of the public buildings, following the reshaping of the city associated with the arrival of the Sullan colonists, is often integrated into the historical narrative of Rome and the establishment of the Augustan dynasty (or deities). The public buildings at Pompeii are frequently read in the light of Paul Zanker's (1988a, 1988b) interpretation of the monuments of Rome to create a horizon of change associated with the Augustan period (see also D'Arms 1988). There is clear evidence that change occurred in the city's public structures, but it is often difficult to date these changes or to associate deities with the new public buildings in the forum (Gradel 1992, 2003: 103–8). The extensive and detailed survey in the forum led by John Dobbins (1994: 688) has categorically dated at least the building of the temple of Vespasian (perhaps better known as the temple of the Genius of Augustus) and the Eumachia building to the Augustan period (see Figure 2.2). However, it needs to be remembered that what we see today, when we visit the site, is the final rebuild of the city after the earthquake(s) of AD 62 and after.

The forum at Pompeii is a unique architectural space, when compared with the fora in other cities in Italy. In common with other fora (e.g. Paestum), it has a rectangular piazza area (142m by 38m) and, in common with the fora of a number of other Italian cities (e.g. Brescia), it was dominated by a capitolium. However, what are unique are the buildings added to the eastern side of the piazza in a series of piecemeal developments that created a very different public space from what had gone before or what can be found in the other cities of Roman Italy. The shops on the eastern side of the forum were demolished to make way for a series of public buildings. A building complex comprising a *chalcidicium*, a crypt and a *porticus* dedicated to *Concordia Augusta* and *Pietas* was built by Eumachia, a public priestess (see Plate 2.4; *CIL* 10.810–12 = E42. Dobbins 1994: 647; Richardson 1978 for comparison with Rome; see also Richardson 1988: 194–8; Moeller 1975). The niches at the front of the *porticus* contained statues of famous men from Roman history: Aeneas leaving Troy (*CIL* 10.808 = E44) and Romulus, the founder of Rome (*CIL* 10.809 = E45). (See Figure 2.3 for the position and the text of inscriptions.) Significantly, the inscription for the statue of Romulus is an exact copy of that in the Forum of Augustus in Rome (Richardson 1988: 194). Many scholars have sought parallels between this building and the *porticus* of Livia at Rome, which was dedicated to *Concordia Augusta,* built in 7 BC (amongst others Richardson 1978; Zanker 1988b: 320–3, 1998: 93–102). John Dobbins (1994: 648–9, 689) goes as far as to see Eumachia's role in Pompeii as very similar to that of Livia in Rome. However, the *porticus* of Livia as it appears on the *Forma Urbis* has little in common with the *porticus* built by Eumachia in terms of architectural plan, apart from the fact that both buildings have an apse (Rodriguez-Almeida 1980). The buildings were both dedicated to *Concordia Augusta*, and the additional feature of the statues of famous men in the *porticus* of Eumachia in Pompeii has parallels with the ideology of the Forum of Augustus. Decorative elements can also be found that are similar to those on the Ara Pacis. Stylistically, the complex coincides with developments at Rome. However, perhaps we should not rush in and assume that it follows developments there, but instead consider whether the buildings in Pompeii and Rome reflect a cultural shift in

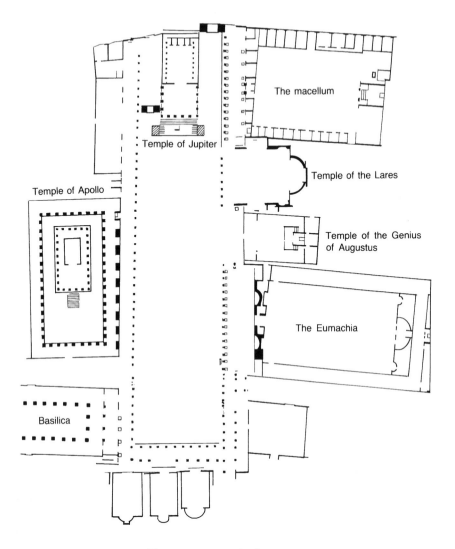

Figure 2.2 Forum in the empire

style towards the celebration of the longevity of the Roman people with reference to *Concordia* and *Pietas*.

The function of this large *porticus* has been hotly debated (most recently by Moeller 1976: 57–71; Jongman 1988: 179–84). However, perhaps we should not be too eager to identify such buildings with utilitarian purposes, especially not with a single function that excludes all others. A *porticus* could have been utilised for a number of purposes. It provided a colonnaded area adjacent to the forum where people could meet, transact business, etc. Therefore, this

Plate 2.4 The Eumachia

porticus may have been used in a similar way to that of a basilica. According to Vitruvius, a basilica should be sited at a warm spot adjacent to the forum so that the *negotiatores* could meet in the winter (Vitr. 5.1.4). One of the groups of *negotiatores* that met in the *porticus* of Eumachia may have been the fullers, who set up a statue to her at the rear of the *porticus* (*CIL* 10.813 = E43). Fentress (2005) argues for an association with the slave trade and sees the building as ideal for the bringing in of goods for auction, but also suggests this was not its exclusive function. Undoubtedly, the *porticus* of Eumachia was used by other groups and for other purposes as well. However, few of these have made an impression upon the archaeological record.

To the north of this *porticus,* a temple was constructed by Mamia, a public priestess (*CIL* 10.816 = E39; see Figure 2.2). The reconstruction of the fragmentary inscription can result in two plausible readings of the deity involved: the Genius of Augustus or more recently Gradel (1992, 2003: 103–8; with Dobbins 1994: 662–3, 1996: 99–103, compare Zanker 1998: 90–3) has made the suggestion of the Genius of the Colony (accepted by Fishwick 1995). The temple is dated by consensus to the Augustan period with considerable repairs after the earthquake of AD 62 (Dobbins, 1992, 1994: 661–8; Richardson 1988: 191–4; Mau 1899: 102–5), but if it is dedicated to the Genius of the Colony, it does not reflect a development in the imperial cult, but

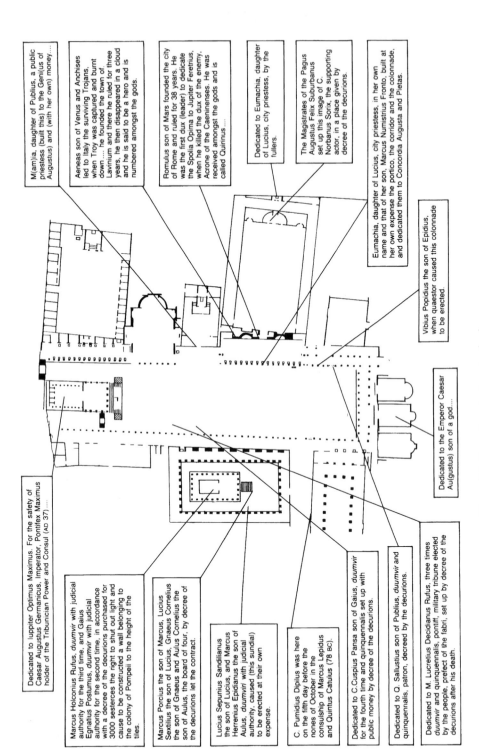

M(am)ia, daughter of Publius, a public priestess (built this) to the Geni(us of Augustus) and (with her own) money....

Aeneas son of Venus and Anchises led to Italy the surviving Trojans when Troy was captured and burnt down.... he founded the town of Lavinium and there he ruled for three years, he then disappeared in a cloud and he is said to be a hero and is numbered amongst the gods.

Romulus son of Mars founded the city of Rome and ruled for 38 years. He was the first dux (leader) to dedicate the Spolia Opima to Jupiter Feretrius, when he killed the dux of the enemy, Acrone of the Caeninenses. He was received amongst the gods and is called Quirinus....

Dedicated to Eumachia, daughter of Lucius, city priestess, by the fullers.

The Magistrates of the Pagus Augustus Felix Suburbanus set up this image of C. Norbanus Sorix, the supporting actor, in a place given by decree of the decurions.

Eumachia, daughter of Lucius, city priestess, in her own name and that of her son, Marcus Numistrius Fronto, built at her own expense the portico, the corridor and the colonnade, and dedicated them to Concordia Augusta and Pietas.

Vibius Popidius the son of Epidius, when quaestor caused this colonnade to be erected.

Dedicated to the Emperor Caesar Augustus) son of a god....

Dedicated to luppiter Optimus Maximus. For the safety of Caesar Augustus Germanicus, Imperator, Pontifex Maximus holder of the Tribunician Power and Consul (AD 37)....

Marcus Holconius Rufus, duumvir with judicial authority for the third time, and Gaius Egnatius Postumus, duumvir with judicial authority for the second time, in accordance with a decree of the decurions purchased for 3000 sesterces the right to shut out light and cause to be constructed a wall belonging to the colony of Pompeii to the height of the tiles.

Marcus Porcius the son of Marcus, Lucius Sextilius the son of Lucius, Gnaeus Cornelius the son of Gnaeus and Aulus Cornelius the son of Aulus, the board of four, by decree of the decurions let the contract.

Lucius Sepunius Sandilianus the son of Lucius, and Marcus Herrenius Epidianus the son of Aulus, duumviri with judicial authority, caused (this sundial) to be erected at their own expense.

C. Pumidius Dipilus was here on the fifth day before the nones of October in the consulship of Marcus Lepidus and Quintus Catulus (78 BC).

Dedicated to C.Cuspius Pansa son of Gaius, duumvir for the fourth time and quinquennalis set up with public money by decree of the decurions.

Dedicated to Q. Sallustius son of Publius, duumvir and quinquennalis, patron, decreed by the decurions.

Dedicated to M. Lucretius Decidianus Rufus, three times duumvir and quinquennalis, pontift, military tribune elected by the people, prefect of the fabri, set up by decree of the decurions after his death.

Figure 2.3 Some inscriptions in the forum

instead a renewal of public religion at Pompeii, independent of developments at Rome. It is a piece of evidence that contradicts the model put forward by Zanker (1988a, 1998) that the forum came to be quickly dominated by the worship of the imperial family. The building to the north of the temple of the Genius, the temple of the Lares, dates from after the earthquake (Dobbins 1994: 685–7). To the north of this building was the *macellum,* which in the imperial period has been seen to have served as a market for the sale of fish and other perishables (De Ruyt 1983: 141–9; Richardson 1988: 200–1; Mau 1899: 94–101). However, recently Alastair Small (1996) has questioned this function since the structure would appear to have had greater use as a cult building. At the eastern end of the *macellum,* there was a new shrine, which contained statues of the imperial family (Zanker 1988a: 28; Richardson 1988: 201; contra Gradel 1992, 2003: 103–8). These have been identified by Small (1996: 120–30) as Agrippina and Britannicus and he suggests the shrine was constructed in the mid-50s AD rather than viewing this shrine as part of a building programme of the Augustan period. In addition, Small (1996: 136) argues that much of the rest of the complex could have been devoted to religion, because the evidence for the use of the building for markets is minimal. Therefore, on the eastern side of the forum by the 50s AD the buildings had expanded to include the Eumachia complex dedicated to *Concordia Augusta* and *Pietas,* a temple to the Genius of Augustus or of the colony, and the *macellum* with its new shrine dedicated to the dynasty of Claudius. There had been an active interest in the worship of Augustus or at least his Genius in Pompeii. This included a *flamen* or *sacerdos divi Augusti* and *magistri* and *ministri Augusti* (Castrén 1975: 68–9; Franklin 2001: 37–40), but the insertion of the imperial cult into the calendar of festivals at Pompeii would not seem to have caused the fundamental alteration of space in the forum in the early imperial period. More important, perhaps, was the development of the cult in the reigns of Claudius and Nero that included both a *flamen* of Claudius (*CIL* 4.1180 = D23) and a perpetual priest of Nero (*CIL* 4.1185, 3884 = D13, D11) during the lifetimes of these two emperors (Small 1996: 130; see also Mouritsen and Gradel 1991).

Alongside the development on the eastern side of the forum, the northern end was also being developed. A series of monumental arches were built in this period. An arch was constructed on either side of the temple of Jupiter (see Plate 2.5 and Figure 2.2). This caused the northern end of the forum to replicate the appearance of the Forum of Augustus or the *Forum Romanum* at Rome, where the temple of *Divus Julius* was flanked by monumental arches (Coarelli 1980: 75–6). It is impossible to be sure about the identification and the dating of these arches or to be certain to whom they were dedicated, but it is probable that they commemorated actions of the imperial family (Richardson 1988: 206–9). The effect would have been to enhance the appearance of the Capitolium with arches on either side of the imperial family. This was complemented by the paving of the forum in Caserta

Plate 2.5 Monumental arch north of the forum

limestone (Richardson 1988: 209–10). In addition, a number of statue bases were erected at the southern end of the forum. Zanker has attempted to identify these with the imperial family (Zanker 1988a: 32–3), but there is very little evidence for following such an assertion.

It was not only in the forum that building activity took place: to the north, an arch commemorating the imperial family was built. The temple of *Fortuna Augusta* was built opposite the Forum Baths (Richardson 1988: 202–6; Mau 1899: 130–2). This temple was built in AD 3 by M. Tullius, a *duumvir quinquennalis*, on his own land (*CIL* 10.824 = E34 dates the temple; see *CIL* 10.820, 821 = E32, E33 on M. Tullius; also Franklin 2001: 27–9). The temple was constructed so that the worshipper had to stand at an angle of 90 degrees to the street (Vitr. 5.1) at a prominent street intersection (Ling 2005: 67–8). This temple seems to have been at the centre of the imperial cult. At the time of its foundation, the first *ministri Fortunae Augustae* were established (*CIL* 10.824; on these *ministri* see Castrén 1975: 76–7 and Mouritsen 1988: 92–9; Franklin 2001: 37–40). These minor officials were drawn from the slaves and freedmen of the city. Their activities were concentrated at this temple, where the majority of inscriptions referring to them are found (Castrén 1975: 76).

To the west of the forum, the temple of Apollo was remodelled by M. Holconius Rufus and C. Egnatius Postumus, and a sundial was added (see Figure 2.2; *CIL* 10.787, 802 = E1, E2; Zanker 1988a: 26). The importance of Apollo in Pompeii's religious calendar is well attested. A. Clodius Flaccus, in his first duumvirate, organised the procession and games of Apollo. The procession held in the forum included bulls, bullfighters, various different types of fighters for the amphitheatre and three troops of boxers. For the games, he funded a pantomime and put up the money to pay the famous pantomime actor Pylades (*CIL* 10.1074 = D41; Beacham 1991: 140–53. On actors in Pompeii, see Franklin 1987). The inclusion of Pylades, one of the most famous actors of the Augustan age, demonstrates the cultural prominence of Pompeii (on culture see Gigante 1979). As *duumvir*, A. Clodius Flaccus provided only part of the entertainment for the festival; others would have supplied complementary elements. In his second duumvirate, A. Clodius Flaccus provided, for the same festival, the procession in the forum, as above, and on the next day a spectacle in the amphitheatre that included thirty pairs of athletes, five pairs of gladiators, another thirty-five pairs of gladiators, and an animal hunt featuring bulls, bullfighters, wild boars, bears and other animals (*CIL* 10.1074 = D41). The festival was clearly a way for the elite to enhance their status and standing in the community (Veyne 1990: 208–34), and the accumulation of ever more elaborate features was the direct result of this competition between them. Finally, the celebration of a festival upon such a grand scale would have brought renown to Pompeii as a centre of culture.

To enhance the performance of these festivals, the large theatre and amphitheatre were refurbished. The theatre was extensively reconstructed and dedicated to Augustus in 2/1 BC (*CIL* 10.833–42 = D51, D52, D54, D55; Zanker 1988a: 33–6, 1998: 107–14; Richardson 1988: 216–18; Mau 1899: 149–50). This prestigious project was financed by M. Holconius Rufus and M. Holconius Celer. It would appear that the rebuilding of the theatre converted it from one suitable for Greek-style games to the recognisably Roman theatre we see today (Zanker 1988b: 325–6, 1998: 108–9). It was in this theatre that the community was seated in a way which reflected the position of each individual in Pompeian society. At the front were the decurions, behind them were the free adult males and at the back were the free adult females and slaves (Rawson 1987). The stage performance commemorated the actions of the gods and ancestors of those watching. The dedication of the theatre to Augustus emphasised to the Pompeians his position in the state. The seating in the amphitheatre was substantially rebuilt in stone in the Augustan period. Wedges of seats were constructed at the expense of individual *duumviri* and, in two cases, by the *magistri* of the *Pagus Augustus Felix Suburbanus* (*CIL* 10.853–7 = D1–5).

The greatest change to the culture and spatial organisation of the city was created when the new palaestra was built adjacent to the amphitheatre (Zanker 1998: 114–15). This new space with its swimming pool, colonnades and planted trees was dedicated to the culture of the gymnasium associated with the training of youths/*iuvenes* for the responsibilities of adulthood (including the martial skills associated with the Roman army) and it eclipsed the earlier centre for such activities: the Triangular Forum close to the now closed Republican Baths, the temples of Isis, Aesculapius, the Samnite

Palaestra, the theatres and the palaestra associated with the gladiator barracks to the south of the large theatre (see Chapter 10). This was also a place to which soldiers visiting the city were attracted (Le Roux 1983). It was in the amphitheatre, in AD 59, that the youths of the city ambushed visitors to the shows from neighbouring Nuceria (Tac., *Ann.* 14.17 = D34). Other bathing facilities, the Suburban Baths, were constructed outside the Marine Gate, and elaboration of the Forum Baths may have been established in response to the new availability of running water from the new aqueduct (Ling 2005: 72; on use see de Haan 2001; Jansen 2001).

Reshaping public space: AD 62–79

The major earthquake of AD 62 (Sen., *Ep.* 6; Tac., *Ann.* 15.22 = C1, C2) can only be understood as exceptional and to be of a different magnitude from the frequent earthquakes experienced in Campania (Plin., *Ep.* 6.20.3 = C12). Seneca's description tends to cause volcanologists to see this event as measurable to above seven on the Richter scale (see Adam 1986). The effect seen in Pompeii was dramatic. John Dobbins' (1994, compare conclusions of Wallat 1997) survey of the eastern side of the forum identifies repair and rebuilding in all the major monuments. However, any assessment of the progress of reconstruction of the public monuments is profoundly limited by the extent of salvage work, particularly in the forum, after the eruption of AD 79. For example, in the *macellum* not only was architectural material salvaged, but also the lead bonding that attached this material to the masonry walls (Dobbins 1994: 685; see other examples in Dobbins 1994 and discussion of evidence by Descœudres 1993 and Zevi 1994). Additionally, there is the problem of how many earthquakes occurred between AD 62 and 79. We know of one from texts, but there may have been others (see papers in AAVV 1995 for discussion). The current consensus is that the forum was in use, rather than under construction and out of use (see Cooley 2003: 31–5 on the historiography of this question). The earthquake may have destroyed much of the city, but it also provided an opportunity for a major overhaul of public space. Nowhere is this more clearly seen than in the forum. Here, the restoration of the existing Eumachia complex, the temple of the Genius of the Colony and the *macellum* was on a lavish scale that included marble imported from Luni to replace architectural and sculptural elements in tufa (e.g. Dobbins 1992, 1994: 659 on the Eumachia complex). The greatest addition to the forum was the Imperial Cult building (Dobbins 1996) that was set at a right angle to the Capitolium. The building itself echoes the developments in architectural form found in Nero's Golden House and might even anticipate the developed sacred architecture of Hadrian's Pantheon in Rome (most recently Dobbins 1994: 685–8). Repairs were also made to the Capitolium, the temple of Apollo and the basilica, but may not have been completed by AD 79 (Wallat 1995; Carroll and Godden 2000). The end result, if achieved by AD 79, was for the buildings associated with the imperial cult in the forum to take on a new format in which marble replaced tufa and new wall decoration created a further impression of grandeur. Such an extensive project of reconstruction took time and considerable manpower (Andreau 1973), but it was one of many that were undertaken by the city. The temple of Venus was being rebuilt on a larger scale than before (Richardson 1988: 280; Mau 1899: 124–9) and the temple of Apollo was undergoing reconstruction (De Caro 1986; Döhl and Zanker 1984: 182). The plan for reconstruction was an ambitious one and may have been supervised by the imperial authorities in the Flavian period (Andreau 1984: 41), or may have been the subject of donations by Nero and the imperial family (*AE* 1985: 283 and 284 = E19 and E20). After all, it was in this period that T. Suedius Clemens, a Roman tribune, examined and recovered public lands (*cippi*, stone markers, at the gates of the city record this: *CIL* 10.10.1018; Conticello 1990: 225; Fiorelli 1875: 404; D'Ambrosio and De Caro 1983: 25; Della Corte 1913; *NS* 1910: 399–401). Little of the restoration work had been completed by AD 79. The temple of Isis had been completely rebuilt, by N. Popidius Celsinus, who was adlected into the *ordo* of decurions for this service at the unusually early age of 6 (*CIL* 10.846 = C5; Richardson 1988: 281–5; Döhl and Zanker 1984: 182–5; Zevi 1994). Repairs were made to the amphitheatre and theatres (Adam 1986: 74).

It remains uncertain whether the aqueduct was reconnected to the water system before AD 79 (Maiuri 1942: 90–4; Andreau 1984: 42; Jones and Robinson 2004; Nappo 1996), so that the city may have once again become reliant upon deep wells for its water supply. However, there were grand plans for reconstruction with work carried out on the existing bathing facilities (Adam 1986: 74). More importantly, a third major bathing complex, the Central Baths, with a large palaestra was constructed after the earthquake of AD 62. The scale, size and design of these baths were of a new type. The bathing block makes no provision for segregated bathing and could have been used for mixed bathing or for men or women only at separate times (see Chapter 10 for discussion). The complex was far from complete by AD 79, but exemplified the new technology of the baths with brick-faced concrete and large expanses of window glass facing the south and west. The presence of windows facing in this direction suggests that its main time of usage was in the afternoon, which might imply that the structure was not of such utility in the morning. The structure was fitted into a single *insula* block with some expansion into a side street (Vicolo di Tesmo) and located in a central position in the city at the intersection of two through-routes (Via di Stabia and Via di Nola); the Stabian Baths were also positioned on an intersection. It was also close to the existing bath complexes. The bathing experience, on completion, would have been different from that found in the other baths of the city. During the day, particularly in the afternoon, there would not have been a need for the lamps found in such abundance in the Forum Baths. The large windows would have lit the spaces for bathers, in a manner found in literature of the time in praise of the lavish baths of Claudius Etruscus in Rome (Mart., *Ep.* 6.42; Stat., *Silv.* 1.5). Whether there would have been the same level of decoration in the Central Baths is unclear, but there were certainly numerous niches already built for holding statuary in the future. When compared with the ill-lit and lower roofed spaces of the Stabian and Forum Baths, this new bath complex would have outshone the existing facilities of the city. There were of course smaller bathing facilities in Pompeii: the Sarno Baths, the Suburban Baths, the Baths of Julia Felix, as well as Crassus' salt water baths.

The earthquake did not change the street grid or the location of the major buildings of the city as such, but the insertion of a new bath building, the Central Baths, at the intersection of two of the major through-routes would have ultimately affected the spatial arrangement of the city and the inhabitants' lives. What we see in the Central Baths and in the forum is the enhancement of the existing arrangements for public life. On completion, the forum and the Central Baths offered a different outlook or perception of urban life in architectural forms that at first sight seemed similar to what had gone before. The new forum presented both the city's inhabitants and its visitors with a space dominated architecturally by the worship of the gods, including the living emperor. Whereas the Central Baths, if completed, would have presented the bathers with a bathing experience that featured light and airy spaces compared with the bathing experience found in the gloom of the aged Stabian and Forum Baths.

The finance behind this redevelopment of the city is difficult, if not impossible, to establish. However, we need to suggest some estimate to place the projects into perspective. To begin with the annual income of the city: Richard Duncan-Jones (1990: 177–8) calculates that the city budget derived from money paid by magistrates and priests entering office would have constituted 35,000 *sesterces* per annum for a North African city in the second century AD. However, it is clear that at Pompeii magistrates paid rather more on entry into office, 10,000 *sesterces* (*CIL* 10.1074 = D8), and we should see as realistic an annual income of 45,000 *sesterces*, from which some 18,000 was paid to the staff of each magistrate (*Lex Coloniae Genetivae* 62, see Crawford 1996: 400 and 422), leaving a surplus of 27,000 *sesterces* per annum. This would yield 459,000 *sesterces* over seventeen years, but it is clear that this money may well have been allocated for games and other celebrations in the city. To it should be added income to the city from rental of lands and income from taxation. The actual landed wealth of the *ordo* of decurions may have amounted to rather more than this: each member had a minimum property qualification of 100,000 *sesterces*, from which we could assume a 10 per cent return per annum, which might mean that the entire *ordo* had a collective income of between 200,000 and 1 million *sesterces* per annum. Over a period of seventeen years, we might suggest that the overall income would have been in the region of 5 to 17 million *sesterces* (see Jongman 1988 for discussion of elite income). Not all this finance would have been available for public projects, since the elite needed to repair their own private property as well.

The question remains to posit a numerical cost on how much the restoration might have cost. Richard Duncan-Jones (1982: 156–62) lists comparable costs from inscriptions in Italy. The repair or rebuilding of nine temples, four sets of baths, the two theatres, the amphitheatre, the aqueduct and the colonnades in the forum can be estimated to have cost between 1.3 million and 3.25 million *sesterces*. Compared with elite income, the cost of rebuilding (either 1.3 or 3.25 million) across the seventeen-year period, taking the higher figure for elite income of 17 million *sesterces*, is affordable or, taking the lower figure for elite income of 5 million, would have been financially ruinous. Importantly, the cultural practice of *euergetism* (including the provision of money for public building projects) tended to be a matter for the individual acting alone or with another member of the elite, rather than a question of the elite pooling their resources. Hence, the cost of rebuilding Pompeii would have fallen on the shoulders of a few members of the elite, rather than the *ordo* as a whole. Few would have been able to finance the building of major projects, similar to those for which we know the prices from inscriptions elsewhere in Italy. Maybe, like the buildings of the early colony, the money came from outside. Given that there is some evidence for imperial intervention at Pompeii, during both Nero's reign and that of the Flavian dynasty, it is not impossible that finance came from the person of the emperor and his family (*AE* 1985: 283 and 284 = E19 and E20). The city was certainly being rebuilt in a new style to reshape the public spaces of social interaction for the future.

The use of these architectural spaces in the forum may have been rather more messy than is suggested by the two-dimensional plans reproduced here. The frescoes from the Praedia Julia Felix show us a forum that features individuals selling goods, reading notices in front of statues, or being publicly beaten (Nappo 1991). However, the location of the individual vignettes of life is defined in the frescoes by the garland-laden colonnades that provide the background to the action of 'everyday life'. The appearance of architecture in these ordinary settings suggests that the rebuilding or reconfiguration of public space had an impact on many inhabitants of the city, as well as on the lives of the elite. Through the 160 or so years from the foundation of the colony, we can see a fundamental continuity of the use of space: the forum, theatres and amphitheatre continued to be the main foci of the city. However, there was considerable readjustment of these spaces to the new demands on the city or interests of the elite in the elaboration of public space: the new Augustan palaestra next to the amphitheatre relocated the cult or institution of *Iuventus* away from its traditional home adjacent to the large theatre and Triangular Forum; the expansion of the forum as a location of sacred architecture at the expense of purpose-built and permanent *tabernae* or shops created a new conception of the forum as a place of religion and worship not just of the Capitoline triad but also of the emperor, even during his lifetime; and the construction of the new bath buildings across the city in a new format utilising window glass created a new form of bathing, in which the body was increasingly visible to the scrutiny of others. Hence, by AD 79, the city had been transformed via the reshaping of the public monuments for a different form of urban culture. What we see at Pompeii is a response to the cultural changes, so apparent in the capital Rome, but also present in other cities on the Bay of Naples. The catalyst for change, however, was often adversity: the settlement of veterans, the turmoil that led to the Augustan principate and its Julio-Claudian successors, the major earthquake of AD 62, and the civil wars that produced the Flavian dynasty. It would be easy to see the *longue durée* of urban history of Pompeii as a process whereby adversity ultimately leads to or produces new urban forms or new investors in the city's fabric, but it needs to be remembered that the process may have continued between these moments of adversity, as is indicated by the setting up of statues of Agrippina and Britannicus in the *macellum* shortly before their demise under Nero (Small 1996). The process of the elaboration of monumental space was continual and should not be seen as a product of any single moment, especially as the initial impetus for the construction of a public building was not realised for several years, if not decades, in antiquity.

3

LOCAL IDENTITY: NEIGHBOURS AND NEIGHBOURHOODS

The terms 'neighbours' and 'neighbourhood' are used frequently in any discussion of the modern city. The city is often viewed as composed of a series of local communities, each with its own identity, which are centred upon a particular neighbourhood. In this conception of the city, each neighbourhood is spatially defined and perceived as a separate entity. However, the term 'neighbourhood', like 'community', is notorious for the variety of meanings attached to it (Bulmer 1986: 17). Some definition of the terminology used in this chapter is necessary. Neighbours are simply defined as those people who live in close proximity to one another. In contrast, a neighbourhood is 'an effectively defined terrain or locality inhabited by neighbours' (Bulmer 1986: 21). This suggests that 'the word neighbourhood has two general connotations: physical proximity to a given object of attention, and intimacy of association among people living in close proximity to one another' (Hawley 1968: 73 quoted in Bulmer 1986: 19). Bert Lott (2004: 18–24) has examined the possibility of the *vici* in Rome corresponding to the North American concept of 'defended neighbourhoods', which he in the end rejects in favour of a meaning of neighbourhood being construed as a 'contrived community' with limited actual cohesion (Lott 2004: 23). The problem of definition defeats the usefulness of either of these terms. The very difficulty of competing notions of neighbourhood, defined not just institutionally via the local government and worship at crossroad shrines in the *vici*, needs to include the division of space and access to key services. These ideas of neighbourhoods and neighbours are examined in this chapter to investigate the possibilities of identifying spatial divisions across the city.

'Neighbourhood' is a term that usually refers to a subset of the city and is identified by a name of a district, such as Kilburn in London within the larger institutional division of Brent. Yet such institutional divisions of the city might compete with others: local identity based on the proximity to a topographical feature, such as Queen's Park, or even basic amenities such as stations in the public transport system. In contrast, the word 'neighbour' is associated with those acquaintances and friends known to a person, as well as those unknown, who live in close proximity to that person's home (Porteous

1977: 68–89). Such concepts were not unfamiliar to those living in the Roman world. The word *vicus* (ward) referred to the institutional nature of a neighbourhood of the city, and those living in that *vicus* were termed *vicani*. This is not to be confused with the term *vicini*, which refers to neighbours (Mouritsen 1990: 146–7). Some names of groups which appear in the electoral notices of Pompeii (Forenses, Campanienses, Salinienses, *Urbulanenses*) have been associated, by modern scholars, with the *vici* of the city (*CIL* 4.783, Forenses, *CIL* 4.470, 480, Campanienses, *CIL* 4.128, Salinienses, *CIL* 4.7667, 7676, 7706, 7747, Urbulanenses = F21–24, F61). Three of these names were also names for three of the gates of the city: the Porta Campana, now Porta di Nola, the Porta Saliniensis, now Porta di Ercolano, and the Porta Urbulanenses, now Porta di Sarno (Castrén 1975: 80; Mouritsen 1988: 67–8). This might suggest that the *vici* were named after the gates of the city. However, it is unlikely that we have a full sample of all the names of the *vici* from our surviving evidence. The correspondence between the names of the gates and the *vici* should not be overstated. The terms cannot be pinned down to any cohesive geographical or social unit, because our evidence is composed of only six electoral notices in four streets (Castrén 1975: 80–2 associates the *vici* with electoral districts and attempts to delimit them on rather spurious grounds). It is rather the historical context of the division of Pompeii into *vici* that provides us with the evidence, which begins to address the question of neighbourhood and local identity (see Lott 2004: 12–18). When the colony had been set up under Sulla, all the trappings of Roman culture had been grafted on to the existing city. These included the local cult of the *Lares Compitales*, and a division of the city into *vici*, local neighbourhoods, with two magistrates being selected for each *vicus* (*CIL* 4.60 = E62 gives a list of *magistri vici et compiti* for 47/46 BC). It is a reasonable assumption that this division of the city into *vici* responded to or, at least, bore some relationship to the system in Rome. Other cities in Italy, for example Rimini (*CIL* 11.377, 379, 404, 418, 419, 421, 6378), were divided into *vici*, and some, such as Puteoli, were also configured into *vici* and *regiones* (Camodeca 1977). What is fundamentally different between the situation in Rome and that of Pompeii, however, is the sheer scale of the division of space and population into their constituent *vici*. Rome with a population verging on 1 million was subdivided into 265 *vici*, whereas the other cities of Italy would appear to have been divided into between five and seven *vici* (Camodeca 1977: 90). Puteoli would seem to have followed the lead of Rome rather more closely than Pompeii (Camodeca 1977: 92). By analysing the relatively abundant literary and epigraphic evidence from the city of Rome, we can begin to gain a broader understanding of the local divisions of the city, which offers us a model from which to measure the degree of conformity or diversity found at Pompeii.

The city of Rome was divided into a number of local units known as *vici*, each with its own pair of magistrates and cult of the *Lares Compitales* located at key crossroads (on *vici* in Rome see Flambard 1977 and 1981; Laurence 1991 and now Lott 2004 for discussion and listing of evidence for late republic and early empire). It was at the shrines of the *Lares Compitales* that the *magistri vici* celebrated festivals such as the *Compitalia*. Thus each inhabitant of the city was a member of a *vicus*, which had magistrates and its own local cult of the *Lares Compitales*. This organisation would have provided each individual inhabitant with a sense of identity and place in the city. The *vici* played an important part in politics, and were utilised by Publius Clodius for the organisation of violent demonstrations in the 50s BC (Vanderbroeck 1987; Lott 2004: 51–60). The administrative division of Rome underwent a fundamental review under Augustus: in 7 BC, the city was divided into fourteen *regiones*, which replaced the four existing *regiones* (Suet., *Aug.* 30). These *regiones* were utilised for organising the administration of the city (Robinson 1991: 9–13). Further, according to Suetonius, Augustus divided the city into *vici* and magistrates were selected annually by lot in each *vicus* (Suet., *Aug.* 30; Dio 55.8 notes that officials had two lictors: Liv. 31.4.5). This is strange: *vici* had existed in Rome prior to this date (e.g. Cic., *Dom.* 54). It would appear that Augustus was altering the spatial configuration of the *vici* to form a new structure that would replace the existing *vici* (contra Lott 2004: 84–98). Later in the same year, Augustus gave the *magistri vici* the images of the *Lares Augusti*. This is known from the excavation of a structure associated with the *magistri vici* close to the Porticus Aemilia (Mancini 1935; Degrassi 1935, 1947; Lott 2004: 91–6, Fig.7a–c). The excavation uncovered a double-sided slab giving details of the annual calendar, a list of consuls from 43 BC, and a list of *magistri vici* from 7 BC, specifically stating that those of 7 BC were the first *magistri vici*. It was to these magistrates that Augustus had given the images of the *Lares Augusti*. The *Lares Augusti* were not a new cult: an inscription refers to their existence in 59 BC (*ILLRP* 200). Not surprisingly, under Augustus they took on a larger role. These *Lares Augusti* were to be placed in the new shrines of the *vici*. Thus, in effect, the new Augustan *vici* associated with the *Lares Augusti* overlie the older *vici* associated with the *Lares Compitales*. It should be stressed that the *Lares Compitales* continued to exist in the city (Suet., *Aug.* 31 refers to the Augustan revival of *Ludi Compitales*). The census for AD 73 recorded 265 of them (Plin., *N.H.* 3.66). The revived cult of the *Lares Augusti* eventually overtook the cult of the *Lares Compitales*. Also, the original division of Rome into *vici* was forgotten in favour of the Augustan division of the city into *regiones* and *vici* (Suet., *Aug.* 30). This was a new division of the city into *vici* and *regiones* and, in consequence, the new shrines did not always coincide with the extant shrines of the *Lares Compitales* (contra Lott 2004: 101). In Augustan Rome, local identity was centred upon the new division of the city into *vici* and the new cult of the *Lares Augusti*.

If we can identify any evidence that such social processes occurred in Pompeii, we can begin to understand the spatial division of the city that formed the basis for an inhabitant's local identity. Epigraphic evidence for the *vici* of Pompeii is not abundant. A single inscription refers to a list of *magistri vici et compiti* for the year 47 or 46 BC (*CIL* 4.60 = E62). This would suggest that Pompeii, like Rome, was divided into *vici*, with magistrates who oversaw the shrines of the *compita* (crossroads) in the republic. Evidence for a reorganisation of this structure, in 7 BC, is derived from a small number of inscriptions referring to the *Pagus Augustus Felix Suburbanus* (*CIL* 10.924, 814, 853, 1042, 1074 = F97, D70, D1, F98, D8; Mouritsen 1988: 94; Castrén 1975: 275–6). We know that the first *ministri* of this *pagus* were established in 7 BC, the same year that the *magistri vici* were set up in Rome (*CIL* 10.924 = F97). Epigraphic evidence also establishes that this *pagus* had *magistri Augusti*, as well as *ministri Augusti* (*CIL* 10.814, 853, 1042, 1074 = F97, D70, D1, F98, D8). I think we may assume that these were established in 7 BC. An epitaph found on a tomb outside the Porta Herculensis (*CIL* 10.1042 = F98) was set up to M. Arrius Diomedes, a *magister* in the *Pagus Augustus Felix Suburbanus.* Underneath the inscription were two carved *fasces* representing the emblems of office. Significantly, in Rome, the *magistri vici* were permitted to have two lictors carrying *fasces* (Dio 55.8; Liv. 31.4.5). It would seem that in Pompeii these *magistri Augusti* also had the *fasces* carried before them as emblems of their office. Therefore, we have evidence for the reorganisation or establishment of the *Pagus Augustus Felix Suburbanus* in 7 BC. This would have been a division of the city's territory close to Pompeii. The *pagus* is well represented epigraphically, unlike other *pagi* and *vici* of Pompeii (but see De Franciscis 1976). However, given the nature of the evidence for the *Pagus Augustus Felix Suburbanus* and how it mirrors the reorganisation of the *vici* at Rome, I think we can infer that a similar reorganisation of the *vici* and the other *pagi* of Pompeii did occur in 7 BC.

This reorganisation of the *vici* should be reflected in the archaeological remains of Pompeii. There are a number of altars found at the crossroads of streets in Pompeii (see Map 3.1 and Plate 3.1). The majority of these altars include paintings of the *Lares* above them (van Andringa 2000 provides a full catalogue of remains; see also Spinazzola 1953: 163–85; Fröhlich 1991). They may also include scenes of sacrifice and images of other gods and serpents (many of the paintings have now faded, and we rely upon earlier accounts for their description: Mau 1899: 233–6; Fiorelli 1875: 81, 82, 108, 175, 214, 249, 273, 303, 324, 343; *NS* 1911: 417–24). The distribution pattern of these altars in the city raises the question of whether the altar was at the centre of a *vicus*. If so, some of these *vici* would be extremely small units of only a few households. More likely, since most of the altars were sited on the major through-routes of the city, they may have been the markers of a boundary between two *vici*. For example, those along Via dell'Abbondanza would have been visible to anyone entering the city at Porta di Sarno as they moved towards the forum. These altars may have defined the linear perimeter between one *vicus* to the south and another *vicus* to the north of Via dell'Abbondanza. The electoral notices mentioning the *Urbulanenses* all appear on the north side of Via

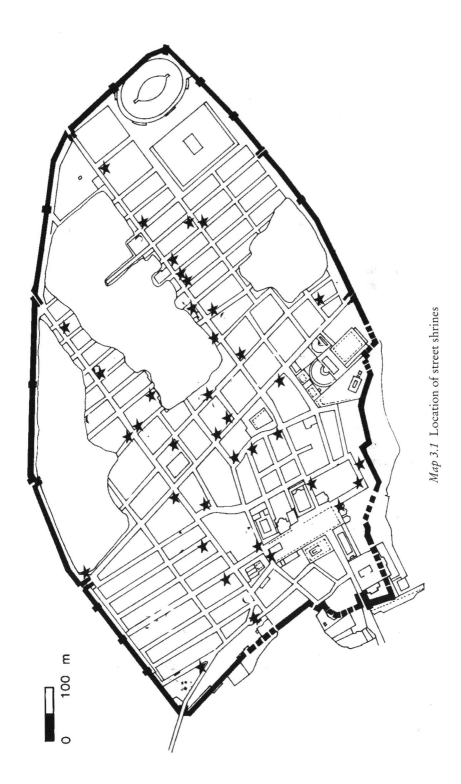

Map 3.1 Location of street shrines

0   100 m

Plate 3.1 Street shrine at the north-west corner of *Insula* 9.8

dell'Abbondanza (*CIL* 4.7676 at 3.4.1; *CIL* 4.7706 at 3.4.3; *CIL* 4.7747 = F61 at 3.6.1). There is also a very fragmentary list of magistrates from the *vicus Urbulanenses* at 9.7.1 (*CIL* 4.7807; see Jongman 1988: 304–6, which should be read with the critique by Mouritsen 1990). None of the altars of the *Lares* from Pompeii included an image of the Genius of Augustus (Mau 1899: 233; Fishwick 1995: 18–19). Therefore, it is possible that these altars were dedicated to the *Lares Compitales* in the late republic. It should be noted that some of the altars had fallen into disuse. For example, the altar at the southeast corner of *Insula* 9.4 was incorporated into the rear wall of the Central Baths. Other altars may have been removed, which might explain the uneven distribution of altars in the city. In the Augustan period, in Rome, the *magistri vici* had been presented with two images of the *Lares Augusti*. These images would appear to have been kept in a central shrine, like that excavated close to the Porticus Aemilia (Mancini 1935). In effect, at Rome, the altars of the *Lares Compitales* were overshadowed by the centralised cult of the *Lares Augusti*. In Pompeii, the structure at 6.1.13 is of a similar nature to that found in Rome near the Porticus Aemilia (Fiorelli 1875: 81; Degrassi 1935; Mancini 1935). There are two other structures that can also be associated with this cult (6.8.14 and 8.4.24, Fiorelli 1875: 122, 343; Mau 1899: 235). The *Lares Augusti* did not replace the *Lares Compitales*. However, in the first century AD, there was a tendency for people to associate more strongly with the *Lares Augusti* rather than the *Lares Compitales*, which may have caused some altars of the *Lares Compitales* to have been neglected or even removed. Therefore, in Pompeii, we are seeing this process of transition, in which the identity of the inhabitants of each *vicus* became concentrated upon the centralised shrine of the *Lares Augusti* rather than the altars of the *Lares Compitales* that marked the boundaries of the pre-Augustan *vici* of their ancestors. This would suggest that in Augustan Pompeii, the shape of urban space was fundamentally altered with respect to the *vici* and the inhabitants' local identity.

Neighbourhoods can also be defined through an examination of the provision of public fountains (Plate 3.2; Jansen 1991; Nishida 1991: 91–8; Eschebach 1979; Eschebach and Schäfer 1983; Mygind 1917 and 1921 provide detailed evidence). These fountains would have been used by people in close proximity to them and provided a point of contact between neighbours (Map 3.2). The fountains are considered to be Augustan in date (Richardson 1988: 51–63; Zanker 1988a: 38–40), and were associated with the building of Pompeii's aqueduct. Unlike aqueducts elsewhere, Pompeii's supply was built to supply high-quality drinking water and water for display in houses, including private bathing facilities, rather than to supply water to new sets of public

Plate 3.2 A fountain in Via della Fortuna

baths (Coulton 1987: 82; Jansen 2001; de Haan 2001). Also, the aqueduct would have provided for the existing demands for water: for the baths, private houses and public supplies. This replaced an earlier system utilising wells and cisterns in the city (see Richardson 1988: 51–3 for wells), as can be seen graphically at a crossroads in Via delle Consolare (Plate 3.3). The deep well behind the fountain was filled up with a deposit that included pottery, lamps and other items. This evidence provided an Augustan date for the fill. As the well had been replaced by the fountain, we can assume that the fountain and, by inference, the aqueduct are Augustan (Richardson 1988: 56; *NS* 1910: 563–7). This suggests either that something was fundamentally wrong with the water supply from wells or that there was a new demand for good-quality water that led the city of Pompeii to undertake the vast expense of building an aqueduct. There was a cultural demand for good clean aqueduct-borne water in Augustan Italy. Vitruvius (*De Architectura* 8) has a long discussion about the supply of water to cities and, in particular, drinking water. Vitruvius is quite specific that water from the plains and low-lying regions was of poor quality. However, sources in the mountains and, especially, in forests away from the sun were more suitable (Vitr. 1.7). Later, another author, Frontinus,

Plate 3.3 An Augustan fountain at the junction of Via delle Consolare and Vicolo di Narciso

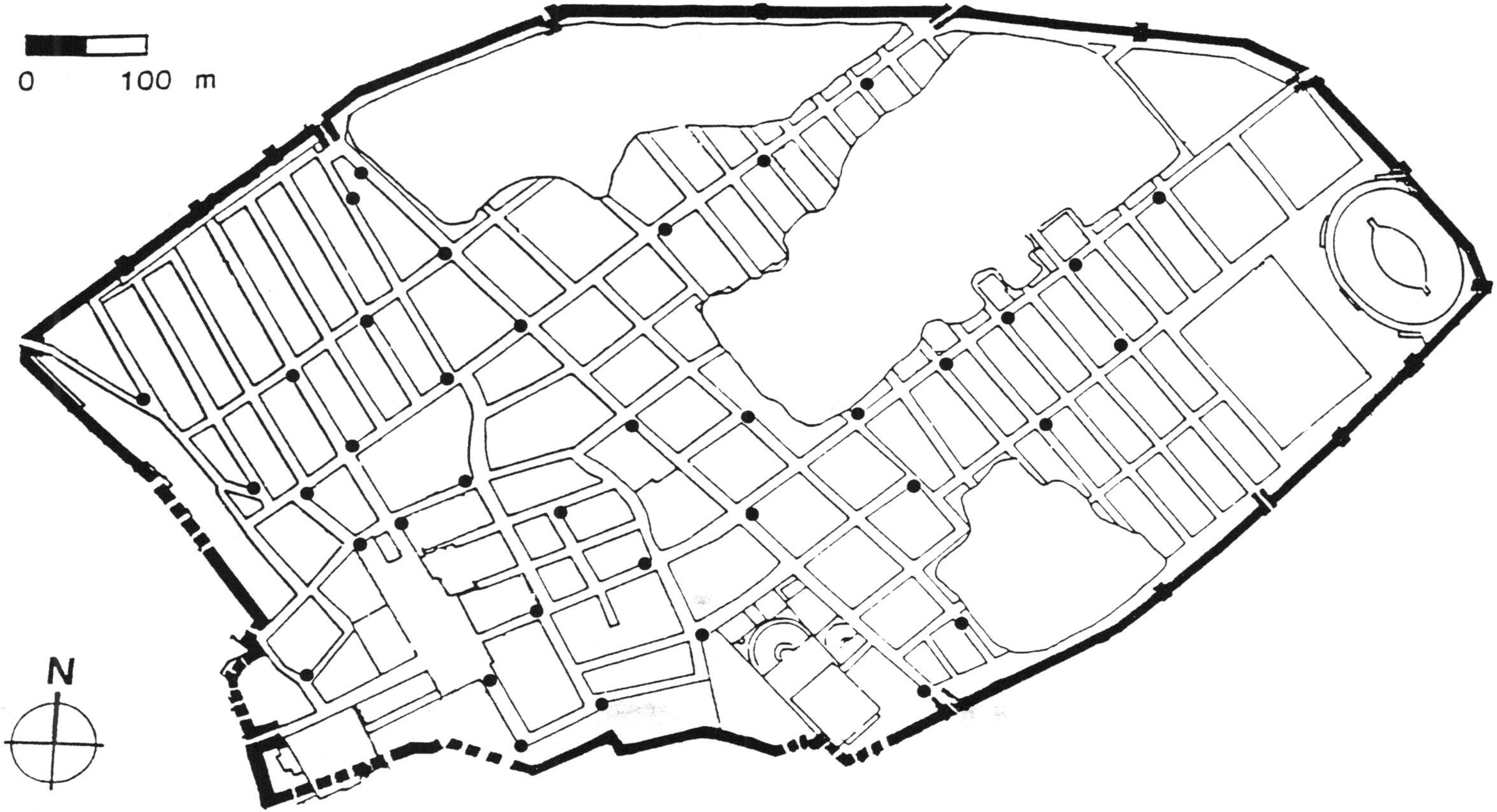

Map 3.2 Distribution of fountains

was preoccupied with the provision of clear drinking water to the people of Rome. He is emphatic that good-quality water should be reserved for drinking, whereas poor-quality water was more suitable for the baths, fulling and other uses (Front., *Aqu.* 2.92). In Augustus' reign the supply of water to the city of Rome had increased by 78 per cent according to Frontinus' figures (Front., *Aqu.* 2.65–71). The Augustan date of Pompeii's aqueduct may suggest that, as with many other public-building projects in Pompeii at this time, we are seeing a desire to imitate developments in Rome and provide good-quality drinking water (compare Front., *Aqu.* 1.24).

The supply of water to Pompeii is strikingly similar to Vitruvius' description of how it should be done (8.6). The water arrived in the city at a *castellum* (reservoir) at the highest point in the city (Plate 3.4). In the *castellum* the water was divided into three, with one of these divisions receiving significantly more water; water left the *castellum* in three large pipes. Vitruvius suggests (8.6.2) that the central pipe, which received more water, should be for the pools and fountains of the city; a second pipe was for the baths, which provided the city with revenue; and a third pipe provided water to private users who would pay for its use. Clearly, Vitruvius considered that the supply of water to fountains and pools should be at least one-third or even

Plate 3.4 The *castellum* at Porta Vesuvio

half of the total amount of water delivered to the city by the aqueduct. This suggests that many people in the Roman cities of the first century AD utilised a public supply of water (in Petr., *Sat.* 70 slaves carried water in *amphorae* in Trimalchio's house. It is unclear whether they drew the water from a public or private fountain. Trevor Hodge 2002: 304–5 sees the supply as adequate for the population level). In Pompeii, many of the houses had their own internal water supply (Jansen 2001 for preliminary survey), but this may have been focused on display rather than use. However, this supply might not have fulfilled all their needs for water and, even where a house had its own supply, water may have also been collected from a public fountain.

To turn to the spatial distribution of fountains in Pompeii, these were nearly always located at a street junction. Very few were located to supersede known sites of deep wells. What is most striking about the location of both fountains and water towers is the way in which they caused obstruction in certain streets. In some cases they even prevented access by wheeled traffic, and the fountain in Via delle Consolare obscured an altar of the *Lares Compitales*. The engineer who established the public fountains faced restrictions in their locations. Where there was space, they were located close to local shrines. However, in the narrower streets, they were placed in a manner that least impeded movement through the streets. In some cases, the fountain actually blocked the street, because the fountains were located so that they did not encroach upon private property (see Ling and Ling 2005: 173–4 for discussion of examples). This may suggest that their location was not sympathetic to the existing patterns of social activity and water collection. Indeed, the establishment of public fountains may have altered the existing pattern of social activity at a local level within the city.

People utilising a public water supply tend to draw their water from the nearest source, particularly if water in the city is of a standard quality. This can be illustrated with reference to Snow's study of an outbreak of cholera in Soho, London, in 1854. There were 500 fatalities in a period of ten days. Snow succeeded in tracing the source of the outbreak to a single pump in Broad Street. His method of locating it was simple: he plotted the mortalities on a map (see Map 3.3). This provided him with the spatial distribution of cholera victims, which was clustered around the pump in Broad Street (Snow 1965: 38–55; Pelling 1978). For our purposes, Snow's distribution map of fatalities from cholera provides an expected pattern of use of a water supply. Use was localised, with a number of people travelling to Broad Street from further afield to collect water, because the Broad Street pump delivered good-tasting water, unlike the pump in Carnaby Street, which no one used (Snow 1965: 46). In the case of Pompeii, such a discrepancy should not arise, because all fountains were supplied with water of the same quality, from the *castellum* of the aqueduct. If anything, the pattern of use should be more localised. To reconstruct the pattern of use for the fountains of Pompeii, each fountain was plotted on a base map; then the distance between each fountain and

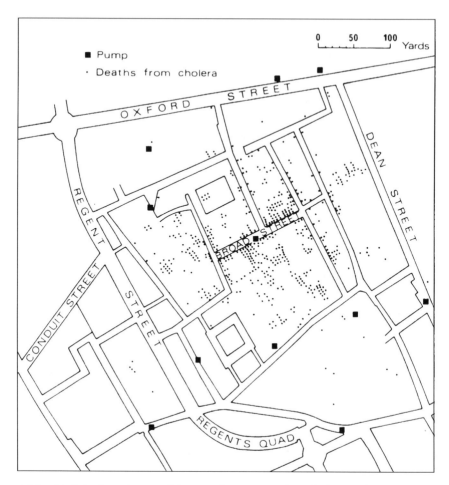

Map 3.3 John Snow's map of the Broad Street, London, cholera outbreak (1854)

the next was measured: the mid point of this distance was seen to be the edge of the area associated with those drawing water from a specific fountain. The assumption was that a person used the nearest fountain. This process was repeated for all fountains and was plotted as Map 3.4. The differently shaded areas on the map represent the local areas that utilised each fountain. The local pattern of water collection is similar to Snow's pattern of fatalities from cholera in 1854. Most people in Pompeii lived within 80 metres of a fountain. The local areas that used individual fountains would have been relatively small, with a number of exceptions to the south-east of the city. There were fewer fountains in this area of lower-density settlement, which might suggest that the density of fountains reflects the public demand for water in the city. Therefore, from the distribution map a series of very localised areas were established, where the inhabitants drew water from the same fountain.

50

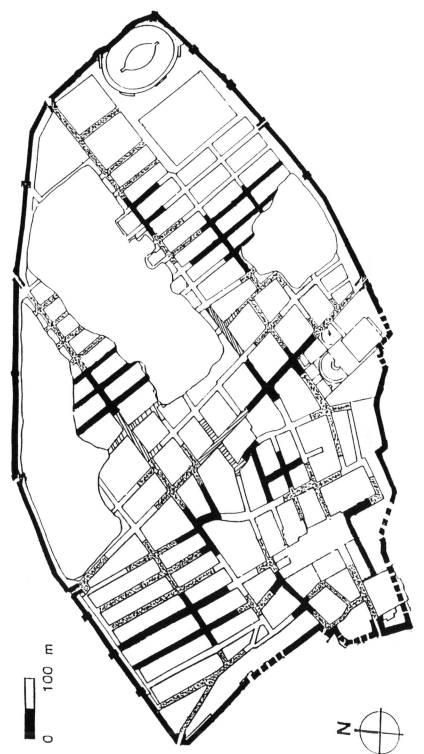

Map 3.4 Neighbourhoods in Pompeii based on distribution of fountains

These areas may correspond to the localised neighbourhoods in the city of Pompeii. This pattern of local divisions in the city would have been established by the manner in which the fountains were originally distributed. The pattern of neighbourhoods derived in this manner could be seen to have competed with the institutional neighbourhoods formed around the worship of the *Lares Augusti*, and the *vici* with their magistrates who policed violations of the public water supply in the streets of the city.

Another feature of the neighbourhoods of Pompeii was the ability to influence or direct the flow of traffic. Many of the streets were too narrow for two vehicles to pass and others would appear to have been closed to wheeled traffic altogether. Tsujimura (1991) identified thirty-five cases where access to a street had been blocked off within Pompeii. The locations of these interventions highlighted an interesting pattern. Access to the forum was blocked off from any form of wheeled access with the exception of the streets entering from the north. The amphitheatre and Large Palaestra, in the south-eastern part of the city, was accessed via a single street from Via dell'Abbondanza with the other five streets blocked. More than half of the streets leading to the south of Via dell'Abbondanza into *Regiones* 1 and 2 were blocked off to wheeled traffic. The overall effect of these interventions in the south-eastern part of the city was to create two north–south through-routes focused on the Porta di Nocera and Porta di Stabia with a north-east to south-west route running along Via dell'Abbondanza from Porta di Sarno to the junction with Via di Stabia. In addition there was another north-east to south-west route linking Via di Nocera with Via di Stabia (Map 3.5). The blocking of Via dell'Abbondanza to the west of the junction with Via di Stabia may have caused this second north-east to south-west route to gain greater importance as a traffic artery that connected *Regiones* 1 and 2 directly to the heart of the city in *Regio* 7. The blocking of streets in the south-west of the city was not confined to access into and from the forum: many of the *insulae* in *Regio* 8 were effectively isolated from the street network through the blocking off of streets to traffic from Via dell'Abbondanza. Not only was *Regio* 7 at the very centre of the city isolated from access to the forum, but the blocking of three other streets created a limited number of traffic routes connecting the region to Via di Stabia to the east and Via della Fortuna to the north. In contrast, *Regio* 9 focused on the north–south route would seem to have integrated the traffic of the city and could be seen to be the point at which traffic from the Porta di Nocera, Porta di Sarno, Porta di Vesuvio and Porta di Nola naturally coalesced. But, even here, the construction of the Central Baths was associated with the closure of streets, which would have disrupted the flow of traffic through the area or relocated that traffic to the major through-routes of the city. The north-western sector of the city, associated with *Regio* 6 and the borders of *Regio* 7, was defined by two traffic routes leading to Porta di Vesuvio and another leading to Porta di Ercolano, which were bisected by two traffic routes running north-east to south-west. The blockage of

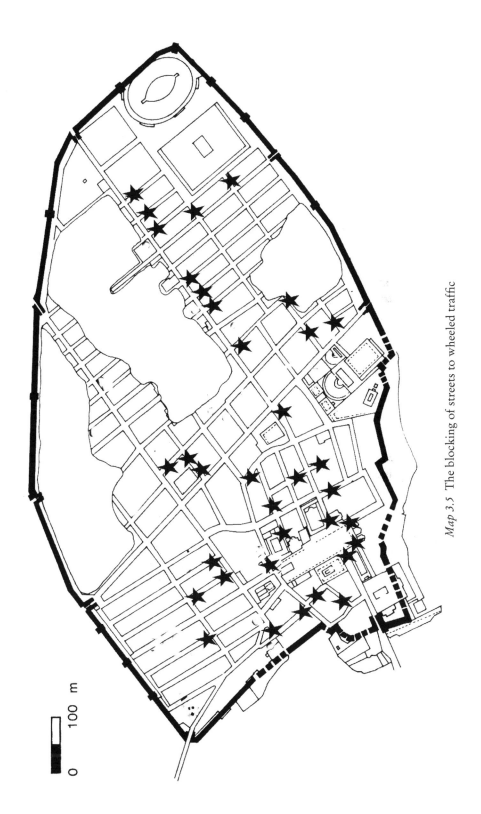

Map 3.5 The blocking of streets to wheeled traffic

streets can be seen to have effectively cut down the access between these routes (Map 3.6). The question remains: who was responsible for the blocking of streets? The aediles were responsible for the repair and maintenance of public streets and public buildings. Hence, we might suggest that the blocking of streets leading to major public buildings – the forum, amphitheatre and Large Palaestra, and the intersection close to the Stabian Baths (Wallace-Hadrill 1995), and the streets associated with the Central Baths – may have been actions sanctioned by them at a city-wide level. In contrast, the blockage of streets leading to the south of Via dell'Abbondanza between Via di Stabia and Via di Nocera would seem to have been the action of local interventions to prevent the movement of traffic down certain side streets. Some of these streets were even closed by gates and can be seen to have been private as opposed to public property (e.g. street between *Insulae* 1.6 and 1.7; *NSc.* 1927: 5). The blocking of streets in this way can be seen to reconfigure the street grid into streets that were integrated into the traffic system and those that were isolated from it (Map 3.6). This pattern is confirmed by Tsujimura's (1991) survey of wheel ruts caused by the incidence of traffic across the city (Map 3.7): the streets showing the greatest connectivity were those with the highest degrees of wear (note that there is a high degree of missing data from *Regiones* 1 and 2). It needs to be stated that the pattern of wear could also be reflecting the level of repair and intervention by the aediles in the replacement of paving. However, what is demonstrated is that there were streets that were integrated into the traffic system and areas of the street grid that were isolated from it as a consequence of the blocking of streets. Not surprisingly, the greatest degree of integration was on the through-routes leading to the gates of the city (note that wheeled access via Porta Marina was not feasible due to the gradient involved). The areas most isolated from the traffic arteries lay to the south-west and south-east of the city. The junction of Via di Stabia/ Vicolo di Tesmo with Via dell'Abbondanza and with Via di Nola/Via della Fortuna would seem to have been the heart of the traffic system and integrated the system as a whole, but was isolated from the south-western section of the city by the blocking of Via dell'Abbondanza on the south-west side of the junction with Via di Stabia. *Regio* 9 would seem to have been the heart of the city and the most integrated with all the through-routes of the city, and the flow of traffic through this *regio* was not disrupted by the blocking of streets leading on to Via dell'Abbondanza, in stark contrast to the neighbouring *regiones* (1, 3, 4, 6, 7).

The evidence of electoral notices or *programmata* that were placed on the façades of houses and public buildings such as the Large Palaestra, provides a further clue to understanding the competing concepts of neighbourhood in Pompeii. Henrik Mouritsen (1988: 47–58), in a systematic study of the evidence, highlighted first how the evidence in *Regiones* 6, 7 and 8 is recorded haphazardly (on the role of *programmata* in elections see the current debate: Biundo 1996 and 2003, Mouritsen 1999). However, from

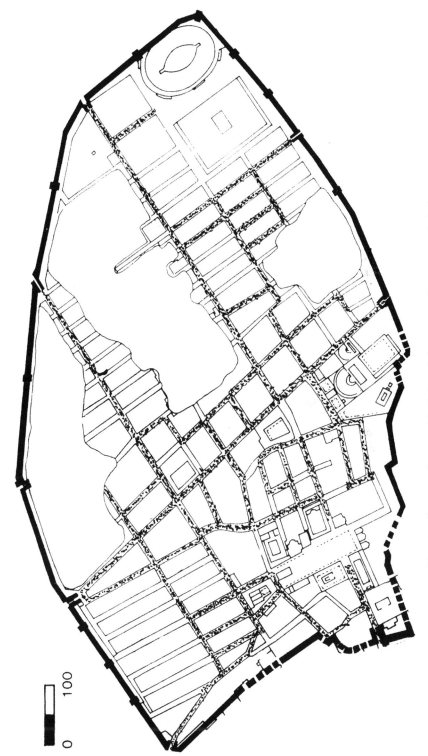

Map 3.6 Connected streets (shaded) and disconnected streets (unshaded)

Map 3.7 Streets and depth of wheel ruts

the rest of the evidence, it was possible for Mouritsen to define patterns of placement of the surviving *programmata* for individual candidates. This view should perhaps be amended to highlight the fact that the recorded *programmata* often survived in place year after year or were covered over by repainting of the façade of the house. Hence, what we see in the *programmata* of Pompeii is the preservation of some notices over a longer period. However, Mouritsen found within this evidence a normative pattern across the data, which was reflected also in the support of the candidate C. Cuspius Pansa (Map 3.8). In this case, the electoral notices were placed along the major through-routes of the city and were concentrated around their intersection: Via dell'Abbondanza, Via di Stabia, Via degli Augustali and Via della Fortuna. In contrast, Mouritsen found that the notices of a number of other candidates concentrated close to their place of residence in the city. For example, the house of A. Trebius Valens was located on the north side of Via dell'Abbondanza (3.2.1; Map 3.9). Mouritsen (1988: 56, on the basis of Cic., *Mur.* 73) suggests that the basis for the patterning was to win the vote in his own local constituency or *tribules*. Regardless of whether the shrines of the *Lares* positioned along Via dell'Abbondanza marked the centre or the boundary of *vici* (see above), the electoral notices of A. Trebius Valens cross over such institutional divisions and create a larger neighbourhood that extends not only down Via dell'Abbondanza, but also into Via di Nocera. Where electoral notices do not appear is in the side streets near Trebius Valens' house, and these were often closed to traffic (see above). Hence, the posting of notices was conducted with reference to visibility, and the decision to post notices would seem to lie with the candidate and his sign writers (Franklin 1978), rather than being a reflection of the support gained from the occupier or owner of a house. The view of neighbourhood seen here is centred on the house and the major roads linking it to the centre of the city, the amphitheatre and Large Palaestra. What is clear also is that the local magistrates of the *vici* or the aediles of the city did not regard the writing of electoral notices or other written material on façades of houses and public buildings to be out of keeping with the order of the city (Mouritsen 1988: 59).

There are a number of electoral notices in which the *vicini* or neighbours recommend candidates for office (Mouritsen 1988: 176). Mouritsen (1988: 67) has pointed out that there are thirty-two in total, which represent 7 per cent of all such recommendations. In the eight cases where a candidate's house can be identified with certainty, there appears to be some correlation between the place of a candidate's residence and the recommendation of that candidate by his *vicini*. However, only one commendation by *vicini* was posted close to a candidate's residence (Mouritsen 1988: 19). Therefore, the limited nature of the evidence of electoral notices referring to *vicini* does not enable us to define any particular local area with any certainty. However, the recommendation of a candidate by the *vicini* does highlight the fact that there was

Map 3.8 Locations of C. Cuspius Pansa's *programmata*

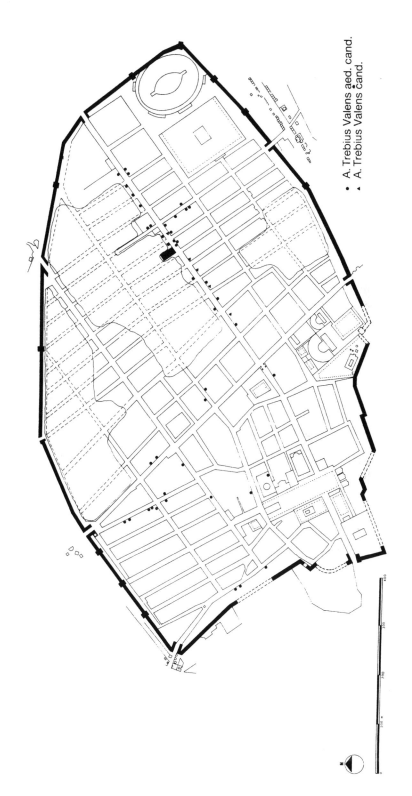

Map 3.9 Locations of A. Trebius Valens' *programmata*

a common identity amongst neighbours that was appealed to. These electoral notices play upon the loyalty of neighbours to act in unison. It should be noted that within the overall pattern of electoral notices, relatively few mention *vicini*, just as relatively few include named individuals.

Another feature of the electoral notices is the commendation of candidates by women as well as men. For the overall pattern of the election, these women did not vote and the number of notices is relatively small (Mouritsen 1988: 60–9), but there is an importance for our understanding of the nature of neighbourhoods. Women were involved in the formation of local opinion about candidates (Savunen 1997: 13–47; Chiavia 2002; Bernstein 1988). Liisa Savunen (1997: 17) points out that the average patterning of support (in named, rather than anonymous, commendations) was by ten men, two women and two groups (of professionals or other persons with a common interest). The electoral notices commending Gnaeus Helvius Sabinus demonstrate the nature of this pattern: one hundred commendations were anonymous, thirty were by men, nine by women and fourteen by groups of people (Savunen 1997: Table 2). Of those candidates not supported by women, Savunen found that they were also supported by very few named men (on average two) and very few named groups (on average 0.6, Savunen 1997: 22). Where supporters were named, the presence of women was significant. This is particularly so in the case of the candidature of Gaius Julius Polybius: eight named men, six named women, three groups and sixteen anonymous commendations (Savunen 1997: 39). This would suggest that the role of women in elections should not simply be dismissed out of hand. Although women were excluded from voting, their presence in electoral commendations, written in the same format as that of male *rogatores*, indicates a role or interconnection between the candidates and women across the city – an important connection between such humble persons as Caprasia, the innkeeper, and Gaius Julius Polybius: a neighbour and member of the *ordo* of decurions (see Savunen 1997 for further examples and discussion). What this implies is that within the neighbourhoods of Pompeii, there was an interaction between the elite candidates and their neighbours, both male and female (compare Cic., *Mur.* 73 for Rome in the republic). James Franklin (1986) in a piece of analysis of the graffiti, *programmata* and an advertisement for A. Suettius Certus' gladiatorial games, located near the shrine of the *Lares* at the junction of Via degli Augustali and Vicolo del Lupanare, integrates the three strands of evidence to suggest that the named individuals found in electoral notices were also prominent individuals from the locality. What we see at this location is the integration of neighbourhood competition in elections, in sexual boasts and insults that can make a linkage between the sacred site of the altar at this intersection and the large brothel located at the next street intersection to the south.

At Pompeii, we can identify competing conceptions of local identity: the institutional neighbourhoods that emerge with two magistrates and a focus on the religious worship at the crossroad shrines of the city; the collective activity of drawing water from the public fountains that created a structural division of the city into smaller cohesive units; the structure of neighbourhoods reconfigured via the blocking of streets to wheeled traffic; and finally the manifestation of neighbourhood found in the electoral notices that provides us with a wider perspective of human interaction locally within the city. Pompeii was not large enough to produce neighbourhoods as separate places or defended communities. Most of the manifestations of neighbourhood occurred in the streets with the highest incidence of activity and traffic (as we will see in Chapter 6). These were the streets in which local identity was paraded to others, rather than the secluded side streets. However, due to the sheer competition for use of space, the shrines of the *Lares* were often sited on the side streets close to the junction with the major routes of the city. Hence, the façade or space for display along the major streets of the city was extended at the crossroads to include the side streets, even if the latter were closed to traffic, and were isolated from the flow of people and goods through the city (for further discussion see Chapter 6). A further concept of locale can be identified by the provision of public water fountains, or their absence in the case of the area close to the amphitheatre and Large Palaestra. These competing conceptions of neighbourhood did not always fit neatly on to each other, and the boundaries could be seen to have been reconfigured according to the context in which a person spoke of neighbourhood.

4

PRODUCTION AND
CONSUMPTION

The excavations at Pompeii have produced tens of thousands of artefacts, many of them produced locally, but many also coming from other parts of the empire or even beyond. At the same time items produced at or near Pompeii found their way to sites elsewhere. Within the city itself there is plentiful evidence of workshops and market gardening. This raises the questions: what does all this evidence amount to and how should we characterise the economy of Pompeii?

The Roman city has been described as a consumer city (Weber 1958; Finley 1973; Hopkins 1978; Jongman 1988; Whittaker 1990; Morley 1996, 1997). In this model the city is represented as economically dependent upon the agricultural production of its hinterland. The surplus wealth from this agricultural production was displayed in the material and physical wealth of the city. The champions of the consumer-city model tended to minimalise the importance of trade and exchange. Recently, the orthodoxy of this model has been challenged by a revisionist onslaught, which for some conserves the sociological imperatives of that model, whilst opening up new questions, and for others reconfigures the model to a point of outright rejection (papers in Parkins 1997; papers in Parkins and Smith 1998, but especially Paterson 1998; Laurence 1999; Horden and Purcell 2000, especially 89–108, 143–7; papers in Lo Cascio 2000; Wilson 2002; papers in Scheidel and von Reden 2002). It is true that the Roman city did not mass-produce goods on a large scale for export to specific markets. Production, where it did occur, particularly in the urban context, was on a small scale and centred upon the workshop rather than the manufactory or factory. This small-scale production is dismissed as unimportant, because the exponents of the consumer-city model tend to define trade as the production of goods on a large scale for export (Jongman 1988; a view somewhat revised in Jongman 2000). The academic emphasis on the city as the consumer of wealth from its rural hinterland has marginalised small-scale production in the city, which served the needs of the surrounding rural population (see now Morley 2000; for the alternative of a 'service city' see Engels 1990, in particular 121–42). The macro scale of analysis taken by the exponents of the consumer-city model obscures many important features of Roman cities and, in particular, many of those which are strongly attested in the archaeological record from Pompeii, where there were a number of small-scale workshops that produced finished goods for sale to others in the city (La Torre 1988 surveys these; see earlier Mustilli 1950). Some of these products were traded over considerable distances. For example, the ceramic assemblage known as 'Pompeian Red Ware' (produced in Campania and Lazio, rather than specific to Pompeii itself) has a wide distribution in the western empire (Peacock 1977). The scale of individual actions of trade and exchange in the creation of this distribution was not necessarily all that large. Importantly, it is becoming clearer that the pattern of trade referred to here takes off only in the first century AD (Panella and Tchernia 2002; De Sena and Ikäheimo 2003). In this period, goods produced in Pompeii were traded over considerable distances, even though the producers of these goods need not have been directly involved in any form of production for export; whilst at the same time goods were consumed at Pompeii that had been produced in locations across the Mediterranean.

The nature of trade can be illustrated by a find of a box of imported lamps and bowls in Pompeii. In the *tablinum* of an *atrium* house (8.5.9) a wooden box was found which contained seventy-six *terra sigillata* bowls and thirty-seven lamps. The *terra sigillata* bowls were of south Gaulish origin. Fifty-four of the bowls were of form 37 and twenty-three corresponded to form 29. The thirty-seven lamps displayed a similar uniformity and were stamped with *fortis* and *communis*, which suggests that they were of a north Italian origin. Neither the bowls nor the lamps showed any sign of use. In fact, it seems likely that they had been delivered shortly prior to the eruption of Vesuvius in AD 79 (Atkinson 1914). The uniformity of the bowls and lamps suggests that they were not for domestic consumption in 8.5.9. Instead, it seems likely that they were destined for some form of trade, exchange or distribution by the occupants of the house. This box of bowls and lamps epitomises the small scale of trade (contra Harris 1980). The *terra sigillata* bowls had their origins in southern Gaul, but the lamps were from northern Italy. At some point between these points of origin and Pompeii, they were placed together in the box for delivery to 8.5.9. It appears strange that *terra sigillata* should be brought from Gaul to Pompeii when there was a source of this product on the Bay of Naples (Pucci 1981). Significantly, the majority of *terra sigillata* found at Pompeii was produced near Puteoli (Pucci 1977). Equally, to export lamps from northern Italy to Pompeii does not conform to the notions of economic rationality that underlie the Finley-based model/s of ancient trade (Harris 1980: 134). Lamps were produced locally in Pompeii, for example at 1.20.2–3 (Cerulli Irelli 1977; De Caro 1974). The imported products that found their way to Pompeii would have been subject to transport costs that local products would not have incurred. However, it would appear time and again, as we shall see, that an imported product could compete directly with a product of local origin. Such a situation contradicts the economic rationality underlying the consumer-city model. It would appear that there were a large number of small consignments of products, such as that found at 8.5.9, being traded or exchanged around the Mediterranean. The total production and consumption of these small consignments of goods formed an important part of the urban economy of Pompeii (for the scale of use of lamps for domestic lighting see Castiglione Morelli 1983). What the evidence points to is a fundamental shift in the nature of trade by the middle of the first century AD (see Saller 2003 for the institutional shift that facilitated this change), the effect of which would have transformed cities that may have conformed to a 'consumer-city' model in earlier periods into ones that were integrated into a network of trade and exchange, whose market was the numerous cities of Italy and its empire (identified also by Jongman 2000 with reference to the wool trade; see also Storchi Marino 2000 for regional centres of trade).

However, before we begin to analyse the local patterns of production and consumption in Pompeii, we must set the city in a wider economic perspective. Geographically, Pompeii was the *entrepôt* for the Sarno river valley (Strabo 247C = 5.4.8). It had good river connections with the towns of this economic hinterland. Also, it formed part of an economy based upon the luxury villas of the Bay of Naples and the wider Campanian economy, which was centred upon Puteoli (D'Arms 1970: 116–67). In fact, Frederiksen has argued that the towns of Campania, including Capua, Cumae, Neapolis, Pompeii and Puteoli, form a single socio-economic unit (Frederiksen 1984: 321). This socio-economic unit was not solely concerned with consumption of produce imported through the port of Puteoli (Frederiksen 1980/1). In fact, he goes on to suggest that the agricultural hinterland of Campania provided Puteoli with a wealth of produce that complemented its function as the port of Rome (Frederiksen 1984: 325). Pompeii's close proximity to Puteoli in economic terms meant that its pattern of trade with other parts of the empire mirrors that of Puteoli.

Pottery can be used as an index to establish the pattern, though not necessarily the scale, of trade between regions (Greene 1992 provides an introduction to pottery studies). Pottery, as such, was not normally the major product traded. It tended to be traded alongside other more important goods (Peacock 1982: 154). Pottery manufactured in the Campanian region has a distinctive red clay, which has been petrologically identified by volcanic elements from the region (Peacock 1977: 147). Equally, rigorous analysis has established the places for production throughout the empire of many types of pottery and, in particular, *terra sigillata* and *amphorae*. This evidence can be used to define the trading links of Pompeii and provide a wider context for production and consumption patterns in the city.

Products that were imported into Pompeii came from a variety of regions. Pucci's study of over 1,600 *terra sigillata* bowls provides a guide to the areas from which goods were brought to Pompeii (Pucci 1977): 29 per cent of the bowls were of Campanian origin, 35 per cent were produced in Italy, 23 per cent were manufactured in the eastern Mediterranean, 12 per cent came from southern Gaul and an insignificant number were of African origin. These figures provide illuminating detail about the nature of trade to Pompeii. Even though Puteoli was a centre for *terra sigillata* production, it does not dominate the assemblage found at Pompeii. There are a significant number of vessels produced outside the immediate locality. As Pucci argues, the importance of the east should not be underestimated. The material from southern Gaul may comprise 12 per cent of the total assemblage, but almost 50 per cent of the south Gaulish products come from the single box found at 8.5.9. Therefore, from this pottery assemblage, we can see that Pompeii had strong trading contact with the eastern Mediterranean as well as locally with Puteoli and other regions of Italy (see Slane 1989 for a Corinthian perspective). Such a pattern is mirrored in the assemblages of *amphorae* from Pompeii. Panella has forcefully argued in her study of *amphorae* that those bearing Greek *tituli* are also of a shape that is associated with wine production in the Aegean (Panella 1974/5; Panella and Fano 1974/5; Tchernia 1986: 240–1). The prominence of these *amphorae* in the assemblages from Pompeii suggests a strong link with this area of the Mediterranean. The nature and scale of trade are revealed in the *tituli* found on *amphorae* in Pompeii. If these *amphorae* had been traded in bulk, we could expect them to have uniform *tituli*. However, the recorded *tituli* in *CIL* IV on *amphorae* found at the same location in Pompeii seldom have the same format, which suggests that they were traded in small lots to individual buyers (Mouritsen 1988: 16–17; for an Aegean perspective on this trade pattern see Slane 1989). Again the scale of trade should not be seen as production for export, but as production that was exported.

Pottery studies can also provide an indication of the nature of exports from Pompeii. Pompeian Red Ware (produced in Campania, rather than specific to Pompeii itself) has been found at a number of locations. It should be noted that any pattern of pottery distribution is dependent upon the number of modern pottery studies. The intensity with which pottery has been studied varies enormously. It has been most strongly studied in northern Europe and least studied in the eastern Mediterranean: therefore, we see only part of the picture at present. Pompeian Red Ware fabric 1 has been found in Greece, north Africa, Italy, Germany and Britain (Peacock 1977). Therefore it has a fairly wide distribution, and further study may show that it probably had a very similar distribution pattern to *terra sigillata* produced in the vicinity of Puteoli (Pucci 1981). Pompeii, like Puteoli, was closely linked to Rome. One of the major products that was produced for the market at Rome was wine. This can be demonstrated with reference to stratified finds of *amphorae* from Ostia: the distinctive Vesuvian clays identify a group of vessels with the region of the Sarno river valley and the Sorrentine peninsula. The find of 180 *amphorae* associated with *terra sigillata* provided an early Augustan date for the total assemblage. This assemblage provides us with a representative sample of the maritime wine trade to Rome. The largest single group of *amphorae* were those of Pompeian or Sorrentine origin, which represented 28 per cent of the total assemblage (figures from Tchernia 1986: 153–4). This figure was rivalled only by north Italian *amphorae*, representing 23 per cent of the total assemblage. Thus, the destination for many products from Campania was the metropolis of Rome. As Jongman has so ably pointed out, the city of Pompeii did not produce manufactured goods specifically for export (Jongman 1988): there was neither a mass market nor the mass production of goods. However, goods were traded and exchanged for other products from other regions of the Mediterranean (maritime trade: D'Arms and Kopff 1980; D'Arms 1981; Rickman 1980; Garnsey 1988; Panella 1981). The scale of production was small, but there were a large number of products produced. This suggests that the producers were not a dominant element in the economy of the city, but their production was a social necessity for the city to function. It was the *negotiatores* (traders) who facilitated trade, by bringing goods from one location and selling them in another. The producers themselves seldom came into contact with the consumer at a distance. However, they sold products in the city to visiting traders in small lots. Secondary products, such as pottery, were traded in shipments of primary products, such as wine or oil, that had been produced to be exported. The pattern of trade indicated by pottery distribution does not follow the lines predicted by modern economics. In many cases, an imported product could compete with a locally produced product of a similar nature (see Peacock 1982: 12–52 for an ethnographic study of pottery production in the Mediterranean in the twentieth century). This is indicative of the complexity of trade in the Roman Mediterranean.

The urban economy was primarily based upon small-scale workshop production (see Andreau 1974 and Jongman 1988: 212–25 on the scale of finance). The workshop is a unit of production associated normally with a single specialised product. In pre-industrial cities, there tends to be specialisation in products rather than in the processes of production (Sjoberg 1960: 197). The form of production in the workshop differs from household production: the workshop is concerned with production on a full-time basis throughout the year, whereas household production tends to be a part-time activity supplementing other economic activities (Peacock 1982: 6–11, 25–41). The workshop, typically, produces a product using specialised equipment, which need not be widely available. Such specialised equipment appears in the archaeological record from Pompeii. The fact that this equipment is of a specialised nature allows for the identification of baking, metal production and cloth production. Significantly, the equipment involved does not tend to appear in domestic contexts. Thus, various forms of workshop define the place of production in Pompeii. Also, the fact that production took place in workshops rather than in any domestic context suggests that the producers formed a distinct group in the city. However, it should be noted that many workshops were located in converted *atrium*-style houses. Some groups of craftsmen appear in electoral notices (for example, goldsmiths: *CIL* 4.710). However, the absence of, for example, goldsmiths from the archaeological record is striking. In other cases, it is difficult to match up archaeologically defined workshops with craftsmen attested in the notices (Jongman 1988: 159–84; compare La Torre 1988). However, the operators of workshops did form a number of distinctive groups within the city, and we might expect certain streets or areas of the city to be associated with certain types of production. Therefore, in what follows, the position of archaeologically distinct workshops will be examined to evaluate the position of workshop manufacturing in Pompeii.

Bakeries can be identified by the presence of mills for grinding corn into flour or by the presence of a large oven (Mayeske 1972) (Plate 4.1). The distribution of bakeries in Pompeii is uneven: there are few in the excavated areas to the east of the city, and few in close proximity to the forum (see Map 4.1). However, there is a strong concentration of bakeries along Via di Stabia and also towards the north of the city. This might suggest that this general trend in the location of bakeries reflects the hinterland from where the grain was brought to the city (i.e. from the area to the north of the city). The only known *horrea* (warehousing) are located near the forum and underneath Casa del Marinaio in Vicolo dei Soprastanti (Franklin 1990). These would have been convenient for grain brought in from the north.

Those bakeries that do not have mills, and therefore did not grind their own flour, are concentrated in the central area (see Map 4.2). These bakeries only baked bread or other products in their ovens for sale on the premises. This type of bakery is found mostly in *Regio* 7 to the east of the forum. Indeed, it is in this area that we find the highest concentration of bakeries. In Via degli Augustali there are a total of seven bakeries. This would suggest that this street would have been associated with bread production and retailing by the inhabitants of Pompeii. In contrast, those bakeries without facilities for retailing were located away from the main through-routes of the city. This would facilitate deliveries of grain, without congesting a busy street. Also, bakeries that ground their own flour required a relatively large area for the mills. For example, bakeries with mills are sometimes found in converted *atrium* houses and the mills are located in the peristyle. Therefore, those bakeries involved in the grinding of flour and in production tended to be located in areas away from the through-routes of the city, where space was available for the location of mills. It should be noted that the mills were specialised equipment. These mills have been petrologically studied to establish the provenance of the stone: Peacock has successfully located the rock as predominantly Umbrian and has identified the quarry close to Orvieto (Peacock 1980, 1986, 1989; Williams-Thorpe 1988). The mills were transported over a considerable distance from Orvieto to Pompeii. It would seem likely that the mills from Orvieto were initially transported to Rome, where they were sold on to Pompeian buyers. It would appear from Peacock's series of studies of

Plate 4.1 Bakery: mill and oven

Pompeian mills that the Orvieto-quarried mills supplanted locally quarried mills (Peacock 1989). Therefore, the imported mills successfully competed with mills quarried in the vicinity of Pompeii. The mill trade provides us with an example of a bulky material being traded over considerable distances and competing with a local product of a similar nature.

The archaeological definition of a bakery by the presence of a mill or oven does not account for the total distribution and sale of bread and other bakery

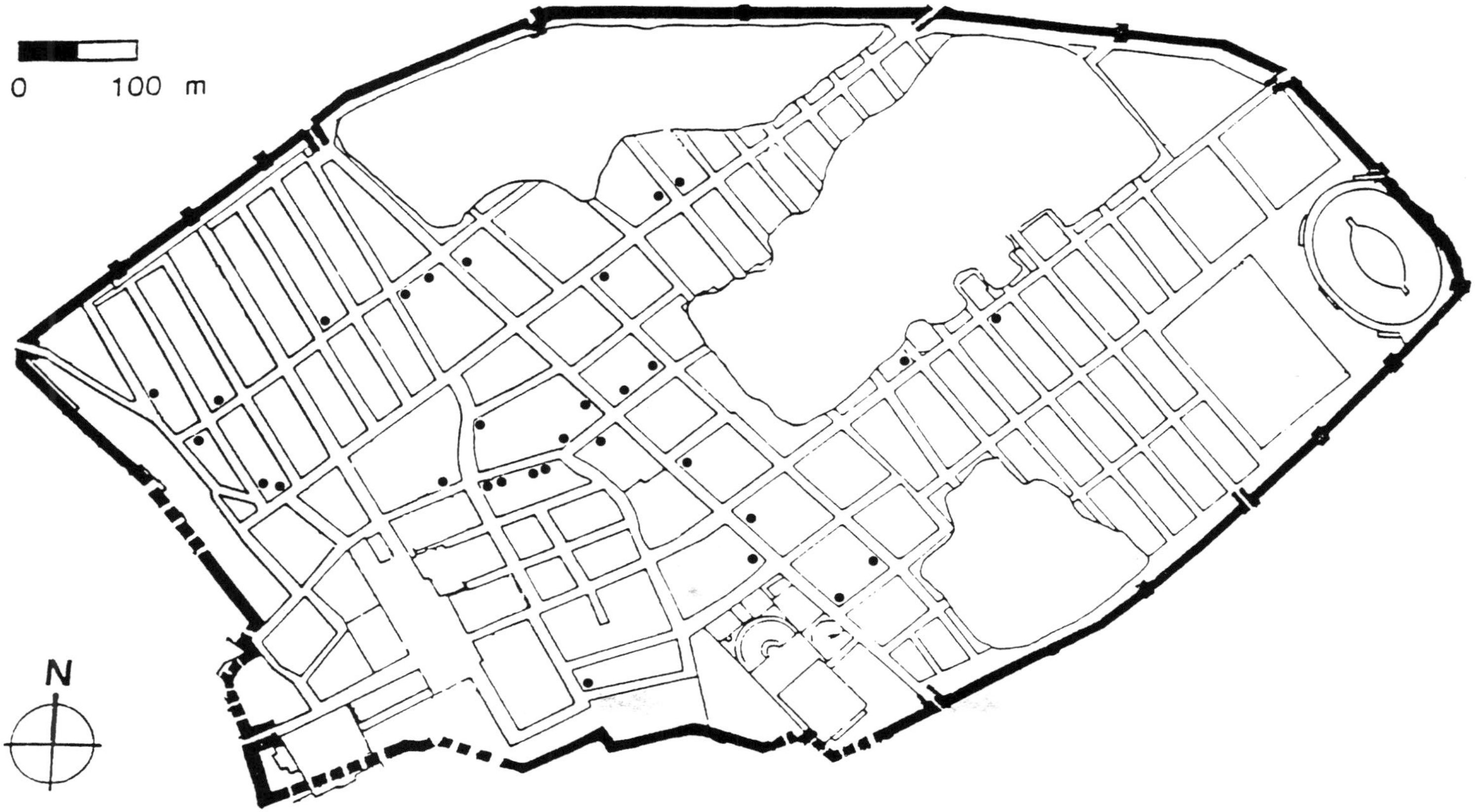

Map 4.1 Distribution of bakeries

Map 4.2 Distribution of bakeries without mills

products in Pompeii. Bread could be sold from other shops and stalls at other locations in the city. The data for such locations do not appear in the archaeological record. However, the distribution pattern of bakeries does suggest that bakery production in Pompeii was concentrated on the through-routes to the north of the city and in the central area to the east of the forum, with a strong concentration of bakeries in Via degli Augustali.

Moeller identified a number of archaeologically distinct workshops in his study of textile manufacture at Pompeii (Moeller 1976). Unfortunately, the available evidence for finds of loom weights is negligible (Moeller 1976: 39–41 mentions a total of fifty loom weights from a single location in his discussion of weaving. Jongman 1988 does not supplement this evidence). However, Moeller did identify a number of workshops in the archaeological record with processes associated with wool and cloth cleaning (for recent critique of evidence Bradley 2002: 26–7, needs to be read with Wilson 2003, and Flohr 2003; also Horden and Purcell 2000: 352–63). He supplemented this archaeological evidence with graffiti that mentioned fullers, dyers, felters and cleaners. In doing so, he attempted to link the position of the graffiti with neighbouring workshops. Such a methodology has proved to be unsound, because electoral graffiti were seldom placed in the vicinity of the place of residence or work of those mentioned in the graffiti (Mouritsen 1988: 18–27). Further, Moeller interpreted the evidence for wool production in Pompeii in terms of production for export. He suggested that this process of production was controlled by the *collegium* of the fullers. In his interpretation of the Pompeian evidence, Moeller overemphasised the scale of production. Jongman has thoroughly demonstrated that all of Moeller's conclusions about textile production were fundamentally flawed (Jongman 1988: 155–86), but in doing so, Jongman tends to minimalise the importance of Moeller's original fieldwork in Pompeii. What Moeller did succeed in doing was to define a number of archaeologically distinct workshops (Jongman 1988: 168–9 admits this). What Moeller ascribes as *officinae lanifricariae* are workshops that include vats and furnaces (Moeller 1976: 30–5); his *officinae tinctoriae* also feature vats and furnaces (Moeller 1976: 35–9). His *fullonicae* are defined by the presence of vats and treading stools (Moeller 1976: 41–51). It is the specialised equipment of these workshops that allows for their definition. Jongman concluded that textile production in Pompeii was for local consumption, because, in comparison with the textile industries of medieval and early modern Europe, production in Pompeii was on a much smaller economic scale within the individual city (Jongman 1988: 184–6); but the market for cloth in the cities of Roman Italy was on a far larger scale than in the medieval period (Jongman 2000). We need not concern ourselves with the economics of production here: our concern is with the spatial dimensions of production in the city. Were these archaeologically distinct workshops concentrated in particular areas? The *officinae lanifricariae* were concentrated in *Regio* 7 to the east of the forum (Map 4.3). The majority of these workshops were located in or

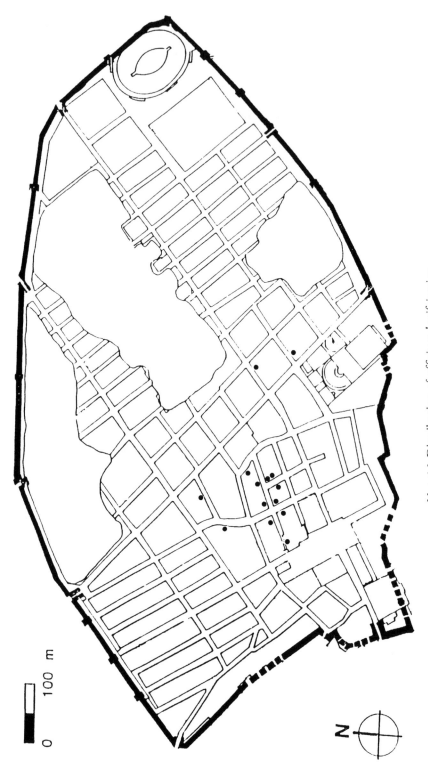

Map 4.3 Distribution of *officinae lanifricariae*

close to Vicolo del Balcone Pensile. Other *officinae lanifricariae* were located in Via dell'Abbondanza and Vicolo del Menandro. In contrast, *the fullonicae* were not concentrated in *Regio 7*, but were distributed throughout the city (Map 4.4). However, their distribution was not even, with a slight concentration towards the Porta del Vesuvio. Other *fullonicae* were located in Via di Mercurio, Via di Nola, Via degli Augustali, Via dell'Abbondanza and Vicolo del Menandro. There would appear to have been a tendency for *fullonicae* to have been located upon the through-routes of the city. The *officinae tinctoriae* have a similar pattern of distribution to that of the *fullonicae* (Map 4.5). These workshops occur on Via di Stabia, Via di Nola, Via dell'Abbondanza and in Vicolo degli Scheletri and Vicolo dell'Efebro. It is most noticeable that these three types of workshop were seldom located in *Regiones* 6 and 8 and, where they were located in *Regio* 1, there was a tendency for these workshops to have been located close to through-routes and towards the centre of the city, rather than in more isolated areas to the east of the city. This might suggest that these workshops were located in areas that were not dominated by the residential requirements of the inhabitants.

Workshops associated with metalworking can also be defined archaeologically. Gralfs (1988), in her study of metalworking in Pompeii, has six criteria for the definition of a metal workshop. These include: specialised tools, equipment, worked material, moulds and casts, worked clay, and inscriptions and shopsigns (Gralfs 1988: 11). From these criteria, she has identified thirteen locations for metalworking in the city (Gralfs 1988: 12–70). Most of these workshops were located upon the through-routes of the city, and do not appear to have been concentrated in any one area (Map 4.6). However, we do find workshops grouped closely together. There appears to have been a total absence of metalworking from the central area to the east of the forum and in *Regio* 8. Like the textile-producing workshops, the metal workshops avoided the residential areas associated with *Regiones* 1, 5, 6 and 8. Their location upon through-routes may reflect the need to transport raw materials to the workshop from outside the city, which is also reflected in the location of a workshop outside Porta del Vesuvio. This might explain why metalworking is not found in the central areas of the city associated with *Regiones* 7 and 9.

Pompeii was noted for its production of fine-quality *garum* (fish sauce), as recorded by Pliny (*N.H.* 31.94). To date, excavations have located a single *garum* shop at 1.12.8, which, as Curtis points out, was not a centre of production (Curtis 1979; see also his other articles on *garum* from Pompeii, 1983, 1984a, 1984b, 1985 and 1991 summarising earlier work). It would appear that the production of *garum* did not occur within the city walls. The most likely location for this production would have been at Pompeii's port facility on the river Sarno. However, although Pompeii was a renowned centre for *garum* production, *garum* and other fish-sauce products were imported to the city (Manacorda 1977). It would appear that *garum* imported from Spain could

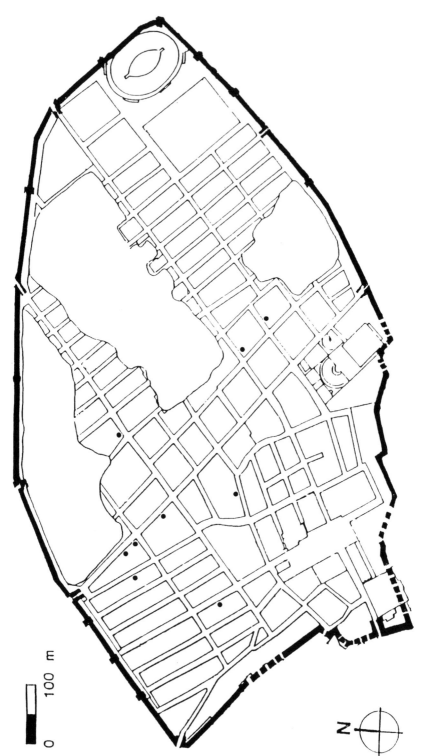

100 m

0

Map 4.4 Distribution of *fullonicae*

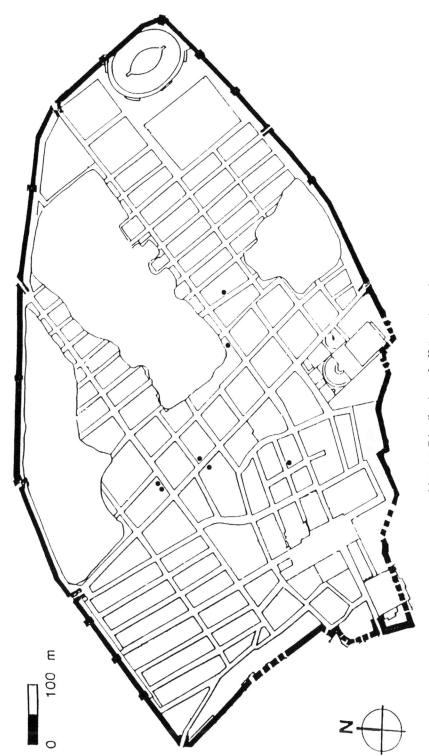

100 m

0

N

Map 4.5 Distribution of *officinae tinctoriae*

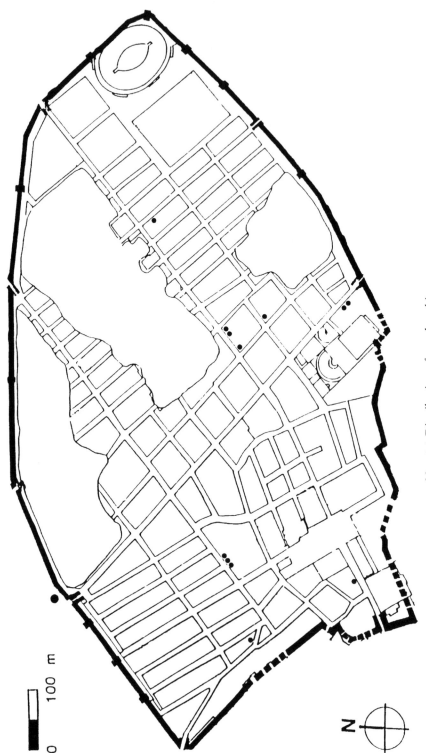

Map 4.6 Distribution of metalworking

compete with locally produced *garum*. This would seem to be one of the many economic contradictions associated with the ancient world: Pompeii produced, exported and imported *garum*. Curtis estimates from the *tituli* of *amphorae* found at Pompeii that 71 per cent were locally produced. It could be argued that *garum* varied in quality and was destined for different social groups accordingly (Curtis 1985: 215). However, any examination of the find spots of *amphorae* with *tituli* in Pompeii, published in *CIL* 4, suggests that *garum* was widely available to the population, from the rich to the customers at the *popinae* (bars).

Finally, we need to discuss the significance of agricultural production in the city. Jashemski's work was pioneering in the study of environmental data at the site. Her work concentrated upon excavating, and in many cases re-excavating, agricultural plots in *Regiones* 1 and 2 to the south-east of the city (for a full account see Jashemski 1979). Excavation and conservation in this area continued in the 1980s and 1990s funded by FIO (see reports in *Rivista di Studi Pompeiane*). Jashemski's excavations identified a number of large agricultural plots within the circuit of the city walls. In a large plot (2.5) opposite the amphitheatre, she identified 1,423 vine roots and evidence that olives were cultivated here (Jashemski 1979: 203). Clearly, wine was produced here and sold at a shop on Via dell'Abbondanza. There was also a small *triclinium* set up to serve visitors to the games at the amphitheatre (Jashemski 1979: 215). Other vineyards were identified at 1.20.1, 1.20.5, 3.7, 9.9.6–7 (Jashemski 1979: 228–32). A market garden was identified in the southern part of *Insula* 1.15. Greene (1986: 97) has argued that this garden produced far in excess of the needs for consumption at this location and that produce was sold elsewhere in the city. Produce included grapes, olives, nuts, fruit and vegetables. Jashemski observed that a similar planting pattern occurred in other parts of the city excavated in the nineteenth century (Jashemski 1979: 236: these include 6.6.1 and 9.1.20). She also identified an orchard at 1.22 and a number of sites associated with market gardening (Jashemski 1979: 243–50: 1.21.2–3; 251–65: 7.11.1, 7.10.14, 2.8.6; 171: 7.11.11/14; 188–90: 1.20.5). She argued that these locations could have utilised the Campanian soil and climate to grow at least three different crops each year (Jashemski 1979: 287). The location of these agricultural plots was predominantly in the south-eastern part of the city near the amphitheatre. This reflects not only the area in which Jashemski did most of her work, but also that in this area there appears to have been a lower density of settlement and hence less pressure on space for residential purposes. Also the *insulae* in this area are mostly sited upon a south-facing slope, an agricultural advantage which other parts of the city did not have (Colum. 3.2.6). However, market gardening was also conducted in the more densely populated areas of the city, including *Regio* 7 to the east of the forum (at 7.11.1, 7.10.14 and 7.11.11/14). This would suggest that the division between town and country was not as pronounced as we tend to expect. The soil in Pompeii was so productive that pressure to convert areas of the city from agricultural use into housing was resisted. Animal husbandry has been neglected in the study of Pompeii; but it was practised inside the city walls. For example, two skeletons of cows were found during the excavation of the Casa del Fauno (Jashemski 1979: 216; NS 1900: 31). Therefore, to date, we have only a partial picture of agricultural production in Pompeii (on market gardening at Rome see Carandini 1988: 339–57). However, productive gardens account for 9.7 per cent of the urban area, while ornamental gardens account for 5.4 per cent (figures from Jashemski 1979: 24). Thus, agricultural production was an important feature in the urban landscape of Pompeii. Produce from these agricultural plots would have been for local consumption, rather than for export to other cities and regions.

It would appear that the pattern of productive land use in Pompeii was not organised according to function. We do not find areas exclusively associated with craft workshops or productive gardens (see Map 4.7). The land use of the city was a mixture of functional categories: the residential areas were not separated from areas of retailing or production. Such a pattern of land use is similar to patterns established in the Adobe city at Mendoza in Argentina (Morris 1987). Morris' account of these is instructive for understanding land-use patterns in Pompeii. Virtually all of Mendoza was destroyed in 1861 by seismic activity. The city was rebuilt with buildings of two or three storeys, because the inhabitants feared the collapse of tall buildings during future earthquakes. The pattern of development in individual blocks is similar to that at Pompeii, because 'each house sought a street frontage and no alleys were made dividing the blocks, so that houses occupied the block periphery leaving a hollow centre' (Morris 1987: 66; for a similar process in Pompeii, see Ling 1983 and now Ling 1997 on *Insula* 1.10). Morris notes that the pattern of land use appears to lack logic, with housing mixed in with retailing, workshops, car-repair yards and wholesale establishments. To account for this disordered land-use pattern, so familiar to the Pompeianist, Morris (1987: 69–71) identifies a number of significant factors. First of all, a total lack of planning controls or zoning has prevented the creation of social or economic divisions in space. These would have caused certain locations to have been preferable for the location of certain enterprises. Second, the uniform chessboard colonial urban layout of houses and streets causes few points or lines to concentrate activity or intensify land use. Third, in the absence of municipal controls upon land use, the owners of individual properties have complete jurisdiction over it. This has resulted in the subdivision of property, which causes any developer to have to deal with a multiplicity of owners in the development of a single block. Finally, the low-density land-use pattern of the Adobe city in Mendoza, in itself, allows for a mixture of land uses, because the land is of high value, but the structures on it are of low value (Morris 1987: 70–1). The high value of the land in combination with a multiplicity of owners prevents the development of high-rise tenements in this zone of Mendoza. Therefore, in Mendoza, the combination of a street grid,

Map 4.7 Distribution of all known workshops

low-density land use and a lack of municipal planning results in a diverse land-use pattern similar to that of Pompeii. Significantly, the conditions for urban development in Mendoza and Pompeii were identical. Thus, it should come as no surprise that, in Pompeii, we find a diverse pattern of land use, which includes units of agricultural production and small-scale workshops.

In terms of production and consumption, the city of Pompeii produced materials for sale within the city, as well as being the recipient of goods from its agricultural hinterland. It needs to be noted that the importation of wine and other goods to Pompeii from beyond Italy was a relatively recent phenomenon, which was not present in the form outlined above prior to the first century AD (De Sena and Ikäheimo 2003). Some of the products from Pompeii and its rural hinterland were exported from the city region. At the same time, products were imported into the city by sea from other areas of the Mediterranean, many of which competed with local products, from the city and its hinterland. This economic reality is difficult to comprehend in the context of the consumer-city model, in which products incurring transport costs should not be able to compete with local products of a similar type (Jongman 1988: 138–41). It might be possible to explain this evidence away as an anomaly produced by the economic disruption caused by the earthquake of AD 62 (Andreau 1973). However, the AD 62 earthquake does provide an easy solution to any aspect of Pompeii that does not conform to our expectations of Roman towns. Alternatively, we might see these imports not in terms of trade at all. As Peregrine Horden and Nicholas Purcell (2000: 137–43) have suggested, much of this trade was in the form of cabotage, in which small ships acquire small batches of goods from numerous different ports. There is also the possibility that the movement of goods such as wine or *garum* may represent not trade but the concentration of a person's movable wealth, derived from their ownership of property in the provinces, to Italy. If these items are seen as representing trade, an alternative model can explain their presence at Pompeii: it can be argued that the goods imported to Pompeii were brought to the site along with more valuable cargoes. These cargoes would have contained products not available in Campania, which could incur large transport costs without making them uncompetitive. The more valuable cargoes would incur the transport costs of the whole shipment, and that part of the cargo associated with, for example, *garum* would have been priced without the addition of transport costs. In consequence, such products could have competed directly with locally produced *garum*. Therefore, in effect, the maritime trade in staples rode upon the back of a trade in luxury items (see Wallace-Hadrill 1990 on the spread of luxury). This situation would have produced the mixed assemblage of imported and locally produced ceramics. Equally, the demand and size of the mass market for wine at Rome allowed for the export of wine and other products from the Pompeian region. This is an important amendment to the consumer-city model set out by Jongman (1988) for Pompeii. Therefore, the urban economy of Pompeii does not conform to the consumer-city model. However, as Carandini has found, the correspondence between the Roman city and Weber's ideal types of the consumer and producer city is not an exact fit when the evidence for production and consumption is considered (Carandini 1988: 337–8). The Roman city was more diverse than these ideal types suggest, and was neither a consumer nor a producer city. However, goods were produced and consumed. Between the producer and consumer there was a network of traders that leaves no record of itself but is implicit for the production of the pattern of the ceramic assemblages available to the archaeologist, which have at best given us an indication of the complex patterns of trade and exchange to and from Pompeii. The economic complexity of this trade and exchange should not be underestimated (for discussion at length see Horden and Purcell 2000). Products manufactured in the many workshops of Pompeii competed with imported products from other areas. The workshops at Pompeii did manufacture goods that were exported; this export was not conducted with specific markets in mind, but it is more than likely that, initially, these products were exchanged in the markets of Puteoli, the port of Rome, from where they were taken to the markets of the capital. Traders in Rome and Puteoli would have diffused goods produced in Pompeii throughout the empire. However, it needs to be stressed that recent archaeological evidence from Pompeii has shown the development of such a pattern of exchange as beginning only in the mid-first century AD, rather than being a phenomenon of an earlier period (see De Sena and Ikäheimo 2003). What occurred can be seen as the proliferation of desirable goods over a wider space of the empire in the mid-first century AD. The new pattern took the products out of their locale of production and traded them, by some means – perhaps Horden and Purcell's (2000) cabotage – to produce a pattern of goods at any place of consumption, such as Pompeii, that drew on the produce of numerous parts of the empire. What is clear, however, from the archaeological evidence from Pompeii in the first century AD is that the pattern of consumption and production does not correspond with the tenets of the consumer-city model that has, until recently, dominated our conception of the Roman city and its economy.

5

DEVIANT BEHAVIOUR

In this chapter, Pompeii is examined to identify the areas in which deviant behaviour was tolerated, and those in which it was restricted. Deviant behaviour can be defined as behaviour that is condemned by a substantial proportion of the population, but is not considered to be beyond the limits of toleration by many people (Cohen 1980: 1). Deviant behaviour is delineated and created by those social groups that label this behaviour as abnormal (Becker 1987: 8; Rubington and Wennberg 1987; McGinn 2004 draws extensively on the history of brothels in the USA). In effect, the deviants in a society are those people who contravene the rules of that society (Goodie 1984: 3). Typically, deviant behaviour includes prostitution, 'excessive' alcoholic consumption and gambling. In the Roman Empire deviants were defined by the elite legally and termed *infames*. They were sharply defined by reason of numerous forms of wrongful or unseemly conduct, and were subjected to serious disabilities (see, e.g., *CIL* 1.593; Garnsey 1970: 185–91). The group included shameful trades: those of the prostitute, the brothel owner, actors, gladiators and the trainers of gladiators. Legally, the *infames* could neither act for someone else nor appoint someone to act for them (Buckland 1921: 92–3). However, the control of deviancy would not have been limited to its legal definition. It seems likely that deviant behaviour was policed or, at least, regulated by the aediles (Robinson 1991: 137–9; and Nippel 1984 on policing at Rome). This would have caused deviant behaviour to have been located in areas of the city that would have been tolerant of it. This constellation of measures facilitated the denigration of those who profited from such trades and also created the prostitute or gladiator or person serving in a bar not as a man or woman, but as a product (sexual or as a spectacle) to be consumed (Flemming 1999: 57). Like the products discussed in the previous chapter, prostitution was sold from or produced in purpose-built premises (workshops?) that can be identified archaeologically as brothels, as well as bars and other locations across the city (Wallace-Hadrill 1995 and McGinn 2004: Appendices 1 and 2). However, it is the construction of purpose-built structures or workshops that produced the commerce of sex that will be the focus of this chapter.

Brothels and prostitution

We need to understand at the outset that the sale of sex and the other activities of the *infames* were based on a market principle, in which profit could be gained from enterprises undertaken in the city (Flemming 1999 and McGinn 2004 on prostitution as an economic activity). The location of these activities in buildings that were designed for the sale of commercial sex forms a distribution pattern, quite distinct from that of bakeries or wool production discussed in the previous chapter (Wallace-Hadrill 1995 for discussion of evidence; as a result of delay in publication, this appeared after Laurence 1994a). These activities competed for space in the city with other interests. For example, the largest purpose-built brothel is not located on a major through-route but on a side street (for detailed description see Clarke 1998: 196–206). The forces that caused this location to be desirable for the building of a brothel need to be explained and understood. What I do not wish to argue for is any type of zoning based solely on morality or moral geography (this was not clear in the original 1994 version of this book, see De Felice 2001; McGinn 2002, 2004: 78–111; Ellis 2004). It needs to be stated that today the semantic and cultural meaning of 'zoning' varies from one Anglophone nation to another, and may imply quite different levels of segregation according to a person's normative experience in the modern world (the definition of 'moral geography' or 'moral zoning' attributed to the first edition might coincide with McGinn's [2002: 30] 'commercial-erotic synergy' in *Regio* 7). The explanation for the location of Pompeii's largest brothel and other archaeologically attested places of 'deviance' lies instead in the subtle interplay of regulation, ideology and socio-cultural coercion that the elite held over the free population and their enslaved dependents (see Wallace-Hadrill 1995). Prostitution was a necessity in Roman society for the maintenance of monogamy within marriage and the provision of sex for slaves (Clarke 1998: 199; Flemming 1999: 45). Although the entrepreneurs or slave owners of prostitutes were denounced, the customers or consumers of commercial sex were not. The shape of the distribution pattern of deviance, as defined in textual sources, was a product of those who controlled the city and dominated urban space – the elite (Ellis 2004 underplays this possibility, in favour of economic forces). From surviving evidence we can see, today, only a partial record of the ways in which the elite regulated these activities (McGinn 2002 highlights the limits of evidence, also Flemming 1999: 54), but the location of the main purpose-built brothel attests to the success of their activities in this field. What we do know needs further discussion.

The literary evidence of Latin authors provides a context for the definition and location of deviant behaviour and deviants. In literature, the location of deviance was in the brothels and *popinae* of the city, whose customers were the slaves, gladiators, drunks, thieves, gamblers, undertakers and bargemen (Hor., *Ep.* 1.14.22; Mart. 9.32; Sen., *Contr.* 1.2.10; Plaut., *Trin.*

1021; Juv. 8.171; Amm. Marc. 14.6.25; for discussion see Kampen 1981). In effect, this literary stereotype sees the location of the *infames* and their provision of services as suitable only for the undesirables in society. However, the reality might be rather different. The provision of services by the *infames* was a necessary feature of the structure of Roman society. Therefore, in what follows, the locations of prostitution, public drinking and gambling in Pompeii will be examined with reference to the literary and archaeological evidence to establish in which areas of Pompeii deviant behaviour was tolerated or restricted.

The prostitute was seen as the opposite of the Roman matron. The prostitute was easily distinguished by her short brightly coloured dress, elaborate hairstyle and make-up (Gardner 1986: 251), and the Augustan adultery law may have enforced a code of dress on prostitutes (McGinn 2004: 151–2). However, the prostitute should not be seen as the antithesis or enemy of the family and family values but, instead, as the preserver of those values (Goodie 1984: 151). Horace reported the remarks of Cato, when he met two young men coming out of a brothel. Cato commended their action in coming to the brothel rather than becoming involved in an adulterous affair with another man's wife (Hor., *Sat.* 1.2.30–7, 1.2.119–34). The possibility of an affair with an unmarried woman is not considered, because most women married for the first time at an early age (Rousselle 1992: 303–7; Saller and Shaw 1984; Shaw 1987, 1991). In contrast, men tended to marry later, in their twenties (Saller 1987). This imbalance in the age of marriage of male and female may have caused the prostitute to be a necessity for the maintenance of a society based upon monogamous marriage. Furthermore, as Rousselle (1992) points out, the purpose of marriage was reproduction rather than sexual love (see also Dixon 1992: 62–3). She stresses that sexual love between husband and wife was a disaster for the woman, because she would die from repeated child bearing. Rousselle sees it as equally disastrous for the husband not to find a sexual partner outside marriage, because again the wife would die from repeated child bearing (Rousselle 1992: 301–27). The need for the husband to have a sexual partner outside marriage was problematic, because the availability of such partners was limited by the norms of society. For husbands, adultery with a married woman, if discovered, would bring harsh penalties under the Augustan legislation against adultery (Gardner 1986: 127–31 provides a summary of the legal position; see Cohen 1991). An alternative could have been for the husband to have a sexual relationship with a slave in their household (Foucault 1984b: 73–80 points to this distinction). However, this might disrupt the structure of power relations in that household (Corbin 1990: 4–9). One alternative, for the husband, was a prostitute. The recognition of this need was reflected in Roman law: the husband's sexual activity with a prostitute was not recognised as a form of adultery. The adultery law was promulgated to promote the stability of marriage and the family. For that family to be stable, it would have been necessary to ensure the possibility of the wife/mother surviving. In any case, sex with a prostitute did not endanger the marriage or family structure of inheritance. In fact, prostitution promoted the stability of the family in Rome's patriarchal society.

However, the prostitute, as the total opposite of the Roman matron, was perceived as a threat to the majority in the Roman city, because she was a woman who did not fulfil the Roman ideal of womanhood. Thus, it was necessary for the prostitutes of the city to be regulated and controlled (cf. nineteenth-century Paris, Corbin 1990). Those deriving their income solely from prostitution had to present themselves to the aediles of the city to be registered (Tac., *Ann.* 2.85; Suet., *Tib.* 35; *Dig.* 25.7.1.2, 48.5.11.(10).2; Paul., *Sent.* 2.26.11; see McGinn 2004: 134–55 for full discussion of regulatory powers). This would allow the aediles to know who was and who was not a prostitute. We may assume that there was a penalty for non-registration. Presumably, registration included the place of residence or work of the prostitute. Women workers in bars or *popinae* were considered to be prostitutes, but did not need to be registered, because their income was not exclusively derived from prostitution (Gardner 1986: 251 citing Dig. 23.2.43). The prostitute, pimp or brothel owner was taxed at the rate of a single sexual act *per diem* (Suet., *Gaius* 40. Prices in Pompeii vary from 2 to 16 *asses*: Duncan-Jones 1982: 246; McGinn 2004: 40–55 on prices; McGinn 1998: 248–68 suggests there existed the power to collect the tax). This process of registration and taxation of prostitutes gave the aediles a powerful body of knowledge about prostitution in the city (Foucault 1977). How the aediles used this information is uncertain. Gardner (1986: 251) suggests that the aedile would have visited the brothels of the city as part of his duties. In contrast, McGinn (2004) argues for the collusion of the aediles in the trade. However, there might have been more to this process of registration than just finding out who was a prostitute. In any case, the prostitute was distinguished from other women by her dress and gesture. The point of registration of prostitutes may have been to control their activities and limit them to areas of the city in which the population would have been more tolerant of prostitution (McGinn 2004: 134–66 for discussion of evidence and suggestion of failure of the endeavour, but in contrast McGinn 1998: 248–68 argues for successful tax collection from prostitutes). Patriarchal societies tend to make prostitution invisible to women, children and the elderly, and it is young males who are normally more tolerant of the presence of prostitution in their neighbourhood (Cohen 1980: 5). If such a situation was the case in the Roman city, we would expect to find the prostitute located in certain marginal areas of the city, away from those areas where they might come into contact with women and children of respectable families of the elite.

The mechanics of getting a customer to the brothel in the literary sources are significant in the context of the spatial distribution of prostitution. These methods appear as a subtle part of a plot in the *Satyricon* by Petronius: a man visiting Puteoli could not find his way back to the inn he was staying at (see

Ling 1990 on the problems of strangers finding their way around Pompeii), so he asked an old woman selling vegetables from the country, where he lived; she answered that she did know and took him to a rather obscure part of the city, and then told him his home was behind a curtain that led into a brothel. The man's friend, Ascyltos, had also become lost and had asked a *pater-familias* the way. The *paterfamilias* took him to the same brothel not because he thought he was a customer, but because the *paterfamilias* had taken him to be a prostitute (Petr., *Sat.* 7–9). The important part of the story seems to be that the part of the city where the brothel was located was rather obscure.

At Rome, the location of prostitution was used by Martial to typify the Subura, which according to our literary evidence was an area of Rome that contained only a few aristocratic houses and was one of the areas within the city that was associated with people of lower status and many forms of deviant behaviour (Mart., *Ep.* 6.66, 11.61, 11.71). What is more, it was an area into which children of the elite would not venture. For the male youth, who had undergone the Roman rite of passage from childhood to manhood, the Subura offered a new-found fascination (Pers., *Sat.* 5.30–40). An informal part of this rite of passage may have included the sexual initiation of the sons of the elite with prostitutes in the Subura. Significantly, prostitution was invisible to the children of the elite and was seen only by adult members of this group. Other locations of prostitution were in the vicinity of public buildings of entertainment, such as the circus, the theatre, the stadium and the baths (S.H.A., *Elagab.* 26.3). Whether these buildings were being used for their main functional purpose at the time is uncertain. The public buildings not in use after dark would have been ideal spots for prostitution, because there were no inhabitants whose moral sensibilities could be outraged (Cohen 1980: 5). The baths were also a most suitable place for prostitutes to work from, for they would have been in contact with a high proportion of the male population (Foucault 1984a: 251–2). Martial also points out that the tombs and the walls were locations for prostitutes to work from (Mart., *Ep.* 1.34, 3.82; Gardner 1986: 251–2). These examples demonstrate that the prostitute was most prominent in those areas of the city that were isolated from other activities and, in particular, other women and children not involved in prostitution.

The location of the prostitute in the literary conception of the city was in the narrow alleyways, amongst the tombs, in the shelter of empty public buildings and under the walls of the city (compare Sen., *Vit. beat.* 7.3; Wallace-Hadrill 1995 for discussion). All of these places were isolated from passing observers, but their position would have been known to customers of the prostitutes and the city population generally. It is an important point that the city population would not have come into contact with prostitution unless they actively sought it out.

Evidence for buildings exclusively designed for the sale of sex has frequently been noted in the archaeological record of Pompeii. We need to be

clear that archaeology, even of better-documented periods, can only identify brothels as opposed to prostitution (Seifert, O'Brien and Balicki 2000:
118). The estimation of the number of brothels in Pompeii used to be as
high as thirty-five. However, recently, a certain amount of re-evaluation of
the evidence is in progress, and the most recent assessment suggests there
are in fact only nine purpose-built brothel sites, seven of which are single
cellae (Map 5.1; Plates 5.1 and 5.2; Wallace-Hadrill 1995; Clarke 1998: 195).
Their location is concentrated in the central area of the city to the east of
the forum. There are also two more sites in *Regio* 9. The brothels are sited
in streets that are not through-routes and were isolated from the main
areas of social activity (see Chapter 6 for definition). Also, they are located
in streets in which there are very few main entrances into large *atrium*
houses (see Chapter 6). This might suggest that the brothels were delib-
erately located out of sight of or away from the main activities of the city.
Thomas McGinn (2002, 2004) has reassessed the evidence for prostitution
across the city. He argues that there are forty-one possible brothels (2004:
78–84; Appendices A and B, see Map 5.2 here), of which he suggests he
would regard about half as 'more likely' as opposed to just 'possible' brothels. There is a distinction between his methodology and that followed here
(and by Wallace-Hadrill 1995). The establishment of purpose-built brothels
and *cella* (McGinn's 'cribs') presents us with locations at which prostitution was designed and a permanent activity; whereas his possible brothels
are locations at which prostitution may have occurred but did not display
the same level of permanency as the purpose-built brothel and *cella*. Hence,
I still remain inclined to view the permanent or purpose-built premises of
prostitution as having a greater diagnostic value for the spatial patterning
of Pompeii. Within McGinn's (2002, 2004) argument that the forces of law
and order with respect to prostitution were limited, he does not contest
that there was an ideology and legal basis for the restriction of prostitution,
but suggests such powers were limited and could not restrict prostitution
from reappearing in undesirable locations (but McGinn 1998 argues for
successful collection of tax from prostitutes). His list of 'possible' or even
his 'more likely' brothels in Pompeii are just such locations whose policing
by the aediles was attempted, but those attempts were thwarted through the
mobility of the trade itself to relocate in the face of opposition. However,
in examining the locations of McGinn's (2004: Maps 1 and 2, see Map 5.2
here) forty-one possible brothels and cribs (*cellae*), only six of this number
are located on the major routes of the city (as defined in Chapter 6 below).
Hence, even the location of 'possible' brothels follows that of the purpose-
built brothels and *cellae* discussed here and does not 'fatally compromise'
the results derived from an examination of purpose-built locations of prostitution (as McGinn 2004: 166 suggests).

The purpose-built brothels and *cellae* were constructed in locations
that may have been out of sight of the activities of the city. However, the

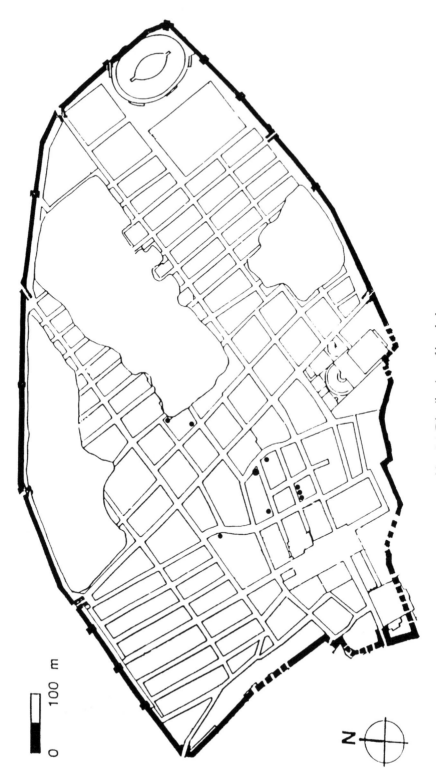

Map 5.1 Distribution of brothels

Plate 5.1 The large brothel at 7.12.18

brothels in most cases tend to adjoin large *atrium* houses, and most of the *cellae* were located in premises that were architecturally part of an *atrium* house. For example, 7.13.4 has two *cellae* located at the rear of the house next to its door in Vicolo degli Scheletri (Eschebach 1982, compare *Insula* 7.12; Nishida and Hori 1992). There is also another *cella* further down this street. At some point, the single cell associated with prostitution was divided off from the main house. What the relationship was between the owner of this

Plate 5.2 A *cella* at 7.13.19

large house and the prostitutes using these two *cellae* remains in question. At the front of this house, we find a perfectly respectable *fauces*, leading into an *atrium*. However, at the back of the house, the entrance is next door to two *cellae*, which had been constructed for prostitution. This seems to highlight the fact that the public face of the household was to be viewed from the *fauces*, rather than the door at the rear. Ideally, the *fauces* was located upon a main thoroughfare, rather than down an alley. Hence, on the main

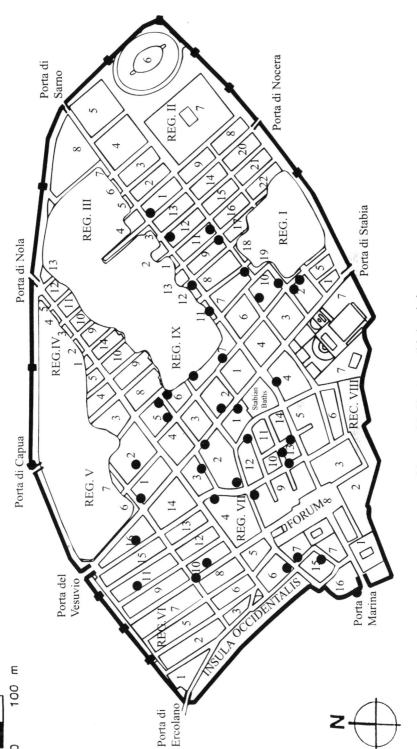

Map 5.2 McGinn's possible brothels

thoroughfares of the city we find the entrances of *atrium*-type houses competing for space with shops, bars, etc. It would have been particularly difficult for people outside the household to identify the other entrances, apart from the *fauces*, into an *atrium* house. Hence, in the example of 7.13.4, a stranger would not associate the doorway next to the *cellae* with the rather imposing *atrium* house they had seen in Via dell'Abbondanza. However, the person seeking the prostitute might note a series of phalluses on the road and walls of this *insula*, which would have guided that person from the wide thoroughfare of Via dell'Abbondanza, up Vicolo di Eumachia and into Vicolo degli Scheletri to the three *cellae* in this narrow street. Therefore, although prostitution was in very close proximity to the elite household, that household was structured to disassociate itself from the sites of prostitution. The physical distance between the elite and the *infames* in Pompeii was not great, but the elite distanced themselves from the *infames* through their social and economic control over urban space. In other words, the elite structured their environment to distance themselves from those associated with *infamia* without creating zones or what some interpreters have characterised as moral zoning (McGinn 2002 misses the distinction here), which created a perceptual distance between themselves and the rest of the population of the city. Instead, brothels in the city were situated in the narrower streets, in which there were few main entrances into *atrium* houses. This placed the prostitute out of sight of those arriving to dine with other morally respectable people, in particular wives and unmarried daughters, at the main entrance to houses. For visitors to arrive at the households of other members of the elite and to be confronted by the visibly deviant behaviour of the prostitute would have compromised the moral values of both the occupant of the house and the visitors. Therefore, brothels were situated in narrow streets, away from the gaze of the elite, in areas of the city that tolerated prostitution. These areas were, in most cases, the narrow streets of the central area to the east of the forum, but may at times have extended into other locations in side streets of a similar nature (McGinn's 2004 'possible brothels').

Bars and taverns

It was not only the brothels that had to be hidden from the view of women and children secluded from the realities of city life. The prostitute was a regular feature of the bars and inns of the city. The legal definition of a prostitute given by Ulpian reveals the male attitude to women working in inns and bars: 'we would say that a woman openly practises prostitution not just where she does so in brothels but also where she is used to showing she has no shame in *cauponae* and other places' (*Dig.* 43, *praef.*). This statement establishes a connection between the *caupona* (inn) and the brothel, which can be in close proximity at Pompeii. For example, a bill for a man bringing produce to market shows that he was charged at an inn for wine, bread, gruel, a girl, and fodder for a mule (*CIL* 9.2689; MacMullen 1970; Frayn 1993). The connection between women who served at *cauponae* (inns) or *popinae* (bars) and prostitution was strongly expressed. The cultural context expressed in literature does not suggest that there was a strong differentiation of places that served drink. The *popinae* were also associated with the sale of hot food, but the sources do not state that other places such as the *cauponae* did not serve hot food. The *cauponae* also provided accommodation, but it is possible that for the inhabitants of the city there may not have been a clear distinction between a *caupona* and a *popina*.

In the literary sources, there is a sharp contrast between the *popinae* and *cauponae* of the city and inns in the countryside. The country inns were respectable places where travellers stayed (Hor., *Sat.* 1.5). However, the city tavern, and particularly the *popina*, was attacked in literature as a place associated with drunkenness, singing, fighting and odious smells from the cooking of food to enable the drunk to drink more (Petr., *Sat.* 95; Hor., *Sat.* 2.4.62, *Epist.* 1.17; Propert. 8.19; Aus., *Mos.* 1.24; Sid. Apoll. 8.11.3.42). In reality, the *popinae* offered the facilities that aided sociability and conviviality. These features can be found in the archaeological evidence from Pompeii. The *popinae* at Pompeii were relatively small structures set up for the sale of food and drink. The *popina* at 9.11.2 highlights these features: at the front, there is a bar (see Plate 5.3), in which are set *dolia* from which wine was drawn (*NdSc* 1912: 112–20). At the end of the bar counter there is a small stove. In the oven a small pastry dish was found, implying that snacks were served. A number of vessels were found on the counter, and probably contained food; the walls were decorated simply with whitewash, and behind the bar a number of *amphorae* were found. The *popina* would have been lit by a hanging lamp to allow it to open in the evening so that the customer could drink through the night because the *popina* did not close (Amm. Marc. 14.6.25; Propert. 4.8.2; Petr., *Sat.* 92; Juv. 8.158). Fifty-seven bronze coins and five silver coins were found in the *popina* at 9.11.2. A dice box was found on the upper floor, which demonstrates the connection between this *popina* and gambling. In literature, the customer was made to fit the moral environment of the *popinae* and was assumed to have been the thief, the gambler, the hangman, the coffin maker, the *gallus* or the bargeman (Plaut., *Trin.* 1021; Juv. 8.171; Amm. Marc. 14.6.25: on this passage see Matthews 1989: 414–16). Some of these types appear upon the walls of *popinae* and *cauponae* at Pompeii (Todd 1939). Similarly, the proprietors' morality matches their environment and their customers' morals; often they sell diluted wine as undiluted, and the owner of a *caupona* often appears in dreams murdering the customers (Cic., *Divin.* 1.57; Petr. 95.8; Mart., *Ep.* 1.5.4, 1.56, 3.57). Thus, these drinking establishments were not places for respectable people even to set foot in (Hermansen 1981: 196; cf. Victorian England, Walvin 1978: 35–40).

In contrast, in the *Copa*, Surisca, a female server at a *caupona*, describes the facilities available inside to potential customers. To emphasise her points she gyrates to the noise of her castanets. Inside the *caupona* were the attractions of gardens, music, wine, garlanded rooms, a wide variety of food and, not least, girls (Pseud. Ver., *Copa*). Jashemski (1964) has highlighted how this image in the *Copa* mirrors the material evidence from Pompeii. For example, the largest *caupona*, at 7.11.11/14, displays many of these characteristics. There was accommodation for fifty guests; there was a small garden for the relaxation of guests, and to the rear a larger garden laid out for producing food for the *caupona*. A *triclinium* had been set up in what had once been the *atrium* of the house. On the ground floor and the upper floor were rooms for guests (Ruddell 1964: 105–6; Jashemski 1964: 344–6). However, the writer of the *Copa* still describes such a *caupona* as smoky. The large *caupona* at Pompeii was not located in the most morally correct part of town: its main entrance was opposite the city's largest brothel. However, it was located in close proximity to the *macellum* and forum, which would have been of considerable convenience for traders arriving for the weekly market in the city (Frayn 1993: 38–42). Therefore, if we penetrate the moral assumptions of the literary sources, it is possible to see in the *cauponae* many elements of popular entertainment available for the traveller: the provision of food and drink, singing, gambling, and a furnished place for social activity. That such places were centres for social activity is shown by Juvenal's comment that the *caupona* and *compitum* (crossroads) were both associated with gossip (Juv. 9.102; Hermansen 1981 notes that 20 per cent of identified taverns in Ostia were located on street corners). A further attribute, certainly of the *cauponae*, but also of the *popinae*, was prostitution. The *Digest* suggests that any woman working in or even entering a *caupona* was potentially a prostitute and that the laws against rape and adultery could not be implemented (*Dig.* 23.2.43, *praef.*, 23.2.9, 3.2.4.2). This suggests that the *popinae* were centres for male rather than female entertainment. Also, if a person was summoned to appear at a *popina* or a brothel, they could state that these places were unsuitable and refuse to appear (*Dig.* 4.8.21.11). This link between the culture of the *popina* and the brothel in Roman law should not be seen as accidental. There was a distinction between the morally good elite and the rest of the population. This is important, because the elite controlled, managed and enforced the law and imposed their will upon the population of the city.

The attitude of the elite to the parts of the city associated with the *popina* and the brothel is summed up in the way they attack their opponents. These people were characterised as deviant by individuals, who were, of course, morally correct. These attitudes appear in rhetoric: for example Cicero attacks Antony, in the *Philippics*, for wasting his life in brothels and *popinae*, in gambling and drinking. Aulus Gellius tells us that Cicero used such devices to indicate the sordidness of Antony's lifestyle (Gell. 6.4; Cic., *Phil.* 13.24; cf. Cic., *Pis.* 13 for an attack upon Piso emerging from a *popina* at the fifth hour; see also Suet., *Gramm.* 15). Again the connection between the *popinae* and the brothel is made. In the imperial period Nero and Vitellius were attacked by the historians for entering *popinae*. A general and a consul were also attacked by Juvenal for being resident in a *caupona* and a *popina* (see Suet., *Nero* 26; Tac., *Ann.* 13.25, 14.15; Dio 61.8; Suet., *Vit.* 13; Juv. 8.146–63, 171).

In the imperial period there was a concerted effort to control the form and nature of the *popinae* at Rome. The sources report an attack upon the *popinae*; however, the details are limited and only refer to the enforcement of restrictions on popular culture in the city of Rome. There is no record of a direct attack on the culture of the *popina* under Augustus, but Quintilian notes that when Augustus saw an *eques* eating at the games, he sent him a note saying 'If I want to dine, I go home' (Quint. 6.3.63). To eat in public was morally reprehensible. The first known restriction upon popular culture at Rome appeared under Tiberius, when in the context of other sumptuary measures, instructions were given to the aediles in Rome to forbid the sale of all food including pastries from the *popinae* (Suet., *Tib.* 34). These measures do not seem to have lasted, and under Claudius a series of measures were introduced: the *collegia* set up by Gaius were to be disbanded, some taverns were closed, and the sale of meat and hot water was prohibited (Dio 60.6.7; Philo, *Leg.* 311–12). Further, the butchers and *vinarii* were not allowed to sell cooked meat as they used to (Suet., *Claud.* 38–40). Nero extended these restrictions to include the sale of all food with the exception of vegetables and pulses (Suet., *Nero* 16.2; Dio 62.14.2). These restrictions on meat consumption appear to be part of sumptuary laws. Vespasian further restricted the food available to pulses only (Dio 65.10.3). Such regulations were probably never enforced in Pompeii. However, they do reveal the cultural values of the capital, which may have made an impression on the aediles of Pompeii.

The total distribution of *cauponae* and *popinae* at Pompeii provides a further indication of those areas that formed deviant street networks (Maps 5.3 and 5.4 for *cauponae* and *popinae*; Wallace-Hadrill 1995 for full survey; see Ruddell 1964; Kleberg 1957; Jashemski 1979; Packer 1978; and now Ellis' 2004 survey of the existing evidence today). The *cauponae* tended to be situated near the gates of the city, in particular Porta di Stabia and Porta di Ercolano. Other gates are not surrounded by such a concentration of places for the visitor to spend the night, which might suggest that communications through the city were predominantly by these two gates. The other major concentration of *cauponae* where visitors could spend the night was located in *Regio* 7 to the east of the forum. At the centre of this group of *cauponae* was the large brothel at 7.12.18/19. However, it would have been likely that the other *cauponae* were in close proximity to prostitution. The *cauponae* close to the gates of the city were not far from the tombs outside, a place of the prostitute in the literary sources, as we saw earlier. Other *cauponae* were close to the city walls, another place associated with the prostitute. Those *cauponae* located near the amphitheatre were near an ideal spot for the

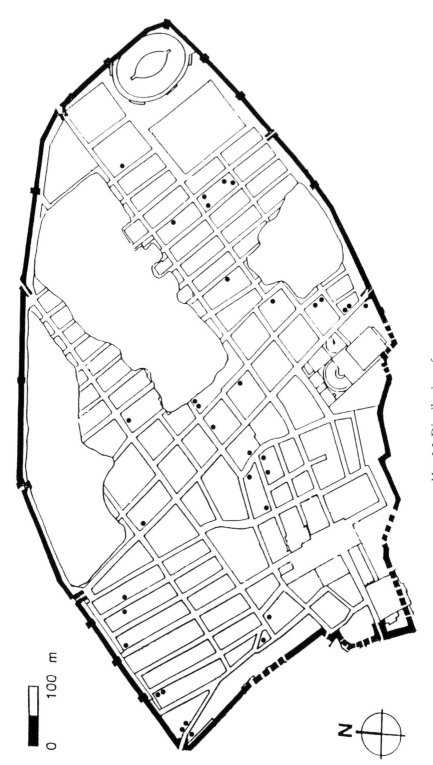

Map 5.3 Distribution of *cauponae*

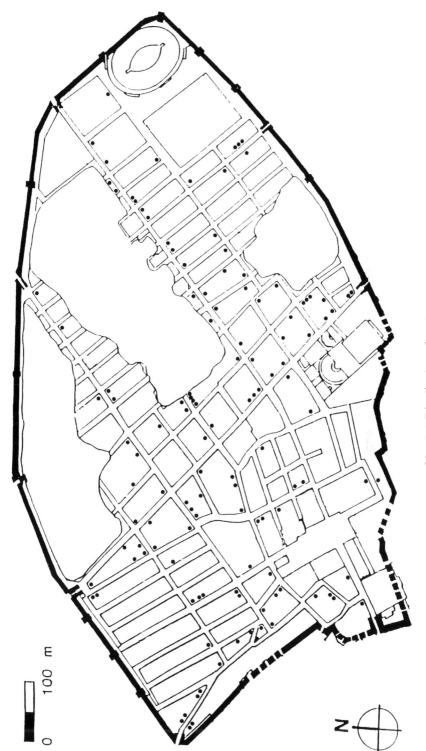

Map 5.4 Distribution of *popinae*

prostitute whilst the public building was not in use, under construction, or in a state of ruination. In fact, the *cauponae* of the city seem to have been located away from those areas that were predominantly residential. This would seem to place the visitors to the city at the margins, unless they were staying at the *cauponae* close to the city's main brothel.

The *popinae* appear to have been fairly evenly spread throughout the city. Andrew Wallace-Hadrill (1995) analysed the spatial distribution and presented an argument that it was uneven, with the *popinae* avoiding locations in the forum and in the stretch of Via dell'Abbondanza from the forum to the Stabian Baths. The absence and scarcity of bars continues from this street down to the Triangular Forum, which could be seen as a processional routeway. These conclusions have been disputed by Steven Ellis (2004), but he has not managed to marshal evidence to refute the specific observations of Wallace-Hadrill (1995). Instead, his survey of extant evidence of bar counters confirms the pattern detected (see Plate 5.3). The rhetoric of his argument depends on a rejection of the textual sources that point to the elite controlling the urban environment, in favour of one based on 'the forces of economic rationality' (Ellis 2004: 383). If this were the case, we would expect to see a far greater number of bars on the street connecting the Stabian Baths and the forum (Ellis 2004

Plate 5.3 A bar counter

ignores these inconvenient data). There appears to have been a strong preference for a location upon the through-routes leading from the gates of the city
and a clustering around locations at crossroads, which would also have been
the location of a water supply (see Map 3.2). There were some areas in which
there were relatively few *popinae* (Wallace-Hadrill 1995), including the forum,
most of *Regio* 8, the section of Via dell'Abbondanza from the forum to its
junction with Via di Stabia, those parts of *Regio* 6 that did not form a through-
route, a section of Via della Fortuna from the temple of *Fortunae Augustae* to
the junction with Vicolo di Storto, and parts of *Regio* 1 close to the amphitheatre and the Large Palaestra (the latter not mentioned by Ellis 2004). The
pattern is uneven and was produced by the intersection of three factors: the
proximity of the supply of water via water fountains in many cases; the proximity to customers; and the intervention of the elite. The latter could be seen
to have been undertaken by the aediles, or the economic ability of the elite to
buy up property and control its usage, or via patronage and social pressure to
restrict the use of a property.

The common factor delineating the city of the elite and the city of the
tavern or bar is determined by the location of elite residences and public
buildings, many of which were isolated from the *popinae*. This becomes relevant in the evening. At the ninth hour of daylight, the elite would have dined
with their guests. After dinner, there may have been some form of entertainment (Mart. 4.8). This could well delay the guests until it was getting dark,
when they would have departed into the street and been carried home in
a litter with an escort (Juv. 3.280–8). If this street had been associated with
popinae, the guests would have come into very close contact with this morally unacceptable *clientele*. For the elite, a home located away from moral
corruption was an advantage. Also in the evening, as it was getting dark, the
proprietors of the *popinae* would have lit lamps, which would penetrate the
gloom of the streets. Streets without *popinae* in them would have been dark
and quiet at night, whereas those associated with the *popinae* would have
been distinguished by activity. The streets with *popinae* and *cauponae* in them
were areas of the city in which social activity occurred in the late evening.
The areas outside this orbit of activity would have been dark and potentially
perilous to walk through without an escort (Juv. 3.268–301; Apul., *Met.* 2.32;
Petr. 79). However, these were also the areas in which members of the elite
entertained or visited in the privacy of the home. This marks a major difference in the lives of the elite: their eating and drinking took place in private
with a few selected persons, whereas for others drinking and eating occurred
in public at the *cauponae* or the *popinae*.

Gambling was a feature of the *popinae*, and was an activity in which
both the urban elite and others participated. Gambling was consistently
attacked by members of the urban elite. This attack appears in rhetoric, as
a means to discredit an opponent or their supporters. Typically, such an
attack would link gambling with drinking and passing time in *popinae* and

brothels (Macr., *Sat.* 3.16.14; Cic., *Phil.* 2.56, 2.67, 13.24, *Cat.* 2.10, 2.23). Juvenal (11.176, 14.4) contrasts the different attitudes to the gambler and states that if a man was a member of the elite his gambling was regarded as an attribute, whereas if he was poor and gambled it was regarded as shameful and deviant. The type of gambling is not explicit. If it was at dice or knucklebones the activity would be illegal except at the *Saturnalia* (Mart., *Ep.* 4.14, 5.84, 14.13; Plaut., *Mil.* 164), but betting on horses and chariots was legal throughout the year (see Balsdon 1969: 151–9). This law appears to have been disregarded. Betting on dice was particularly associated with the *popinae*. It was an activity that was regarded as a defect in a slave. The association of betting with drinking was common (Colum. 1.8.1–2; *Dig.* 21.19.1, 21.25.6; Tac., *Germ.* 24; Plaut., *Curc.* 355). In law, persons excluded from redress in the law of sale were gamblers, wine gluttons, impostors, liars and the quarrelsome (*Dig.* 21.1.4.2). Also, a person would have regarded himself as insulted if someone had taken his slave or his son into a *popina* or had played dice with him (*Dig.* 47.10.26). The gambler in comedy was associated with the criminal, and Plautus gives a fictional account of dice being played after a meal in a *popina*. The stakes were a cloak and a mantle; however, before the conclusion of the game one of the players passed out and was robbed by his opponent of his ring (Plaut., *Curc.* 355). A similar scene of dice playing appears on a wall painting in a *caupona* at Pompeii (*CIL* 4.3494; Todd 1939). An argument erupts over a dice throw, insults are exchanged, and the pair come to blows. The innkeeper removes the conflict to the pavement outside. Obviously, gambling often resulted in disputes of a violent nature. Roman law reflected this situation: a series of laws ceased to apply if gambling took place on the premises, and the owner or manager could not bring a charge of theft or assault if gambling took place. However, the gamblers themselves could bring actions for assault or theft, and thus gain redress in law (*Dig.* 11.5.1). More than anything, this seems to have been aimed at encouraging proprietors of *popinae* not to permit gambling on their premises. Therefore, a number of laws ceased to apply in the *popinae* or *cauponae*. These included the laws against rape and adultery and, also, those against assault and theft if gambling was allowed to take place. All these restrictions on the application of the law seem to have been part of an attack on the culture of the *popinae*, with the hope that women would not work in them and that gambling would be discouraged. In spite of these measures it seems that gambling continued as a feature of the *popinae*, and it was recognised that gambling was the activity in which some of the firmest friendships were made (Amm. Marc. 28.4.21). Given the restrictions in the application of the law, in the context of the *popinae* and *cauponae*, the distribution of *popinae* and *cauponae* reflects a male rather than a female pattern of leisure. Thus, the *popinae* and *cauponae* provided a social context for public interaction, entertainment and pleasure for men, with their emphasis upon drink, food, sex and gambling, as well as being a place to entertain friends. This public social interaction was frowned upon by the elite, with their emphasis upon entertainment in private. Therefore, the elite labelled the *popinae* and *cauponae* as deviant. However, in reality, social interaction at the *popinae* or *cauponae* would have been a normal experience in city life and a key characteristic of the city.

6

STREET ACTIVITY AND
PUBLIC INTERACTION

The doorway of a house had an important role in describing the resident's status and what was inside the house. This role was enshrined around the god Janus, associated with the beginning of events (Ovid, *Fasti* 2.51; Cic., *Nat. Deor.* 2.67). The doorway was thought to mark the division between two types of air, one inside the house and the other outside in the street (Lucr. 4.29). Also the door marked the division between private and public space, and could be guarded by a porter (Ovid, *Fasti* 1.135; see Wallace-Hadrill 1988 on the levels of privacy in the Roman house). The doorway was the entrance into the house not only for people, but also for curses and diseases (Plin., *N.H.* 32.44, 28.86). A door could also shut in rumour (Catull. 67) and was seen to protect the virtue of women from strangers' attention (Apul., *Met.* 9.5; Hor., *Carm.* 1.25). The doorways of the famous could reflect their glory. These doorways would have been decorated to emphasise a person's achievements. For example, Augustus' door posts were wreathed with bay leaves (*R.G.* 34; Juv. 12.80–102; Petron. 28–9), and the consuls of 509 BC were permitted to have their doors opening into the street (Plin., *N.H.* 36.112). It would appear that in Rome it was normal to keep the main doors of houses open during the day, with a porter to control access to the house (Liv. 5.13. 6–7, 6.25.9; Plaut., *Asin.* 273; Wallace-Hadrill 1988: 46). However, it is uncertain whether this was universal. It seems more likely that only the wealthy could afford the luxury of leaving their doors open. For others the door provided protection against burglars (Apul., *Met.* 1.11, 3.5). The ability to leave the door open allowed for the display of the status of the occupier. The onlooker in the street would have been presented with a visual narrative through the house, which would have provided information about the occupier's status (Watts 1987: 187). However, in times of crisis, even the wealthiest had to bolt their doors against attack (Cic., *Vat.* 22: Bibulus was driven from public spaces into the privacy of his house; cf. Cic., *Mil.* 18 for Pompey, or Cic., *Verr.* 2.69: Verres when governor in Sicily was besieged in a house; see Cic., *Cat.* 28 for Cicero; see also Tac., *Hist.* 1.33). The houses of the elite also had a side door that was not as strongly defended. During the looting of Cremona in AD 69, the Vitellian soldiers were particularly successful, because they knew where the side doors of the houses of the elite were (Dio 64.15). This suggests that the side entrances to houses were not easily identified. Equally, those doorways associated with shops or other retail outlets would have punctuated a person's journey through a street. Thus, the doorway was a noticeable feature of the Roman street. Also, the doorway marks the meeting point of space and the built environment, and the interface between public and private.

The placement of doorways and the use of street frontages would seem to reflect how the urban environment was used. For example, in a main street, there would have been a tendency for the maximisation of street frontages (see Plate 6.1). In contrast, in a side street, the use of the street frontage would have reflected the lower incidence of activity (see Plate 6.2). Therefore, the number of doorways opening into a street directly reflects the level of social activity and interaction that occurred in the street.

To analyse this phenomenon in Pompeii, a simple method was devised to measure the occurrence of doorways in a street. The number of doorways was counted in all streets. To allow for comparison between streets the figures for the number of doorways in streets had to be calibrated. This was simply done to reflect the occurrence of doorways in metres. The length of the streets was measured and the following simple formula was used:

$$\text{Occurrence of doorways} = \frac{\text{length of street in metres}}{\text{number of doorways}}$$

Some of the longer streets were divided into sections to gain a more representative sample that was of a similar size to the rest of the streets. For example, Via dell'Abbondanza was divided into four similar sample lengths: the first from the forum to the junction with Via di Stabia, the second from the junction to *Insula* 3.1, the third from *Insula* 3.1 to *Insula* 3.6 and the fourth from *Insula* 3.6 to Porta di Sarno. Via di Nola was also split, in this case into two sections: the first from Via di Stabia to *Insula* 5.4 and the second from *Insula* 5.4 to Porta di Nola. Similarly, Via di Stabia was divided into two sections: one from Porta di Stabia to the junction with Via dell'Abbondanza, and the second from this junction to the intersection with Via di Nola.

This methodology resulted in a measurement of doorway occurrence in all of the excavated streets from Pompeii. The range of values for the occurrence of doorways was between every 2.1m and 127.0m. The median occurrence of doorways was every 7.3m. For the purposes of data presentation, these data are divided into four groups. The first includes streets with doorways occurring between every 0 and 5 metres, the second with doorways occurring between every 6 and 10 metres, the third with doorways occurring every 11–15 metres and the fourth with doorways occurring less often than every 15 metres. This data set is plotted as Maps 6.1–6.4. If we examine the spatial distribution of streets with different incidences of doorways, we find a pattern emerging.

Plate 6.1 Via di Nola: high occurrence of doorways

Plate 6.2 Vicolo degli Scheletri: low occurrence of doorways

To deal with the first group of streets, with doorways occurring more frequently than every 6 metres (Map 6.1), this group can be divided into two sets. The first has doorways occurring more frequently than every 3.0 metres, and the second has doorways occurring every 3.1–6.0 metres. To deal with the first set of streets, those in which doorways occur between every 2.1 and 3.0m: these streets were found to be routes directly connected to the forum or major through-routes, or a combination of the two. Streets exclusively connected to the forum included Via del Foro, Via delle Scuole and Via degli Augustali with an extension to include the street between *Insulae* 9.3 and 9.2. Also within this group were the through-routes leading from the following gates: Stabia, Ercolano and Nola. Although its value is lower, we should also include Via Marina in this group. This is caused by its proximity to the basilica and the temple of Venus, which are public buildings and do not have doorways at the usual frequency. It is of particular note that the values in this group on through-routes tail off to the east, for instance along Via dell'Abbondanza, but not on Via di Nola. This group defines the major through-routes. Via di Vesuvio should also be included in this group, although it falls just outside our artificial division into categories, and the higher value may be due to the fact that two streets lead to the Porta Vesuvio, reducing the concentration of traffic on both those routes by 50 per cent.

If we now examine the group of streets with doorways occurring between 3.1m and 6.0m we find that these are located predominantly to the east of the forum and to the west of Via di Stabia. An exception is Vicolo degli Scheletri, which has a much lower occurrence of doorways. Its value is created by the fact

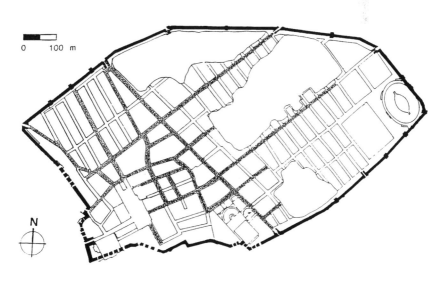

Map 6.1 Occurrence of doorways 1

that there was very high activity occurring in the streets on the other side of the *insula* blocks backing on to it. In other words, it is in Vicolo degli Scheletri that there were few entrances, because houses in these *insulae* were entered from other streets. This also made Vicolo degli Scheletri an ideal street for the location of prostitution, as we saw in Chapter 5. However, the rest of this area forms a zone of high activity, and should be associated with the central core of the city. This zone should be seen as an area that adjoins the forum, and therefore as a transition zone between the forum (CBD) and the rest of the city. After all, it is in this area that there was a strong concentration of inns, bakeries, workshops and brothels as compared with other areas of the city. Other streets with door-ways occurring between every 3.1 and 6.0m include Via di Mercurio, which can be seen to be a northward extension from the forum, and is a wider street than those found elsewhere in *Regio* 6 with a north–south orientation. There is another group of streets around the area of the theatre complex that has values in the 3.1–6.0m range, two of which form a route from Via dell'Abbondanza to a point on Via di Stabia near the theatres. It should be noted that higher levels of activity would have been expected here, because Via dei Teatri leads from Via dell'Abbondanza to the Triangular Forum, the Republican Bath complex, the temple of Isis and the theatres. The other two streets in this group are found adjoining Via di Stabia. These include Via del Menandro, which was associated with a number of craft workshops, and Vicolo del Conciapelle, which was in close vicinity to some of the city's inns. Thus, the streets with an occurrence of doorways more frequent than one every 6.0 metres are in the following areas: to the east of the forum, Via di Mercurio to the north of the forum, Via delle Scuole to the south of the forum, the through-routes of the city leading to gates, and the areas off Via di Stabia.

The next category of analysis consists of those streets with doorways occurring less often than every 6.0 metres, but more often than every 11.0 metres (see Map 6.2). This group includes the street leading from Porta di Nocera and the streets that form a direct route from the amphitheatre to Via di Stabia. The level of activity in these streets may have a direct relation-ship to the influence of the amphitheatre on the rest of the urban structure. The nature of activity in the amphitheatre was sporadic, with a high density of interaction occurring when it was functioning, and a low level of activ-ity when it was not. Thus, the direct routes to the amphitheatre experienced similar fluctuations in activity and, as a result, do not have the higher inci-dences of doorways found on the through-routes, in Via dell'Abbondanza, for example. Also in this category are those streets to the west of the forum and those streets not on through-routes to the east of Via di Stabia. It should be noted that the occurrence of doorways declines the further to the east the street is. A similar pattern occurs in the regions to the north and south of the central area. Thus, this group includes all of those streets that did not form through-routes, but were in close proximity to the through-routes or close to areas that were associated with high levels of activity.

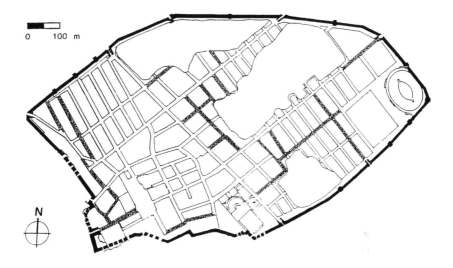

Map 6.2 Occurrence of doorways 2

The third category comprises those streets that have a doorway occurring less often than every 11 metres but more often than every 15 metres (see Map 6.3). These streets tend to be associated with areas in the west of the city with reasonably high levels of activity. However, because there was a preference for entering *insulae* from other streets, such as Via di Mercurio, the streets in this third category, for example Vicolo della Fullonica, did not have high occurrences of doorways. Equally, the level of social interaction in these streets was also much lower. It should be noted that one narrow street in this group, Vicolo di Tesmo, does form a route that joins Via delle Consolare with Via di Vesuvio and Vicolo dei Vettii. However, it did not develop as a route associated with high levels of activity, because it was isolated from the major areas of activity in the city.

The fourth category includes all those streets with doorway occurrences that are less frequent than every 15 metres (see Map 6.4). These streets are exclusively in the south-eastern part of the city, which was associated with a lower density of land use, which included agricultural plots, as we saw in Chapter 4. These streets were isolated from the social interaction associated with the rest of the city.

To allow for comparison of the pattern of social interaction in streets, as defined by the occurrence of doorways, similar analysis was conducted upon excavated streets from Ostia and streets on the *Forma Urbis Marmorea* from Rome (Rodriguez-Almeida 1980). The data from Ostia revealed a much higher occurrence of doorways in most streets, with a median occurrence of doorways at every 3.2m, whereas Pompeii's median occurrence of doorways was every 7.3m. The streets of the *Forma Urbis Marmorea* provide further data

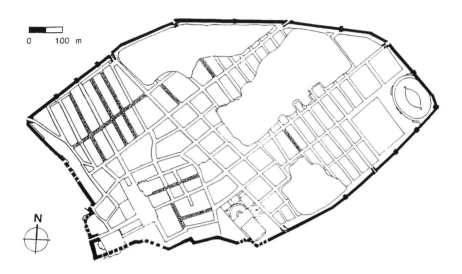

Map 6.3 Occurrence of doorways 3

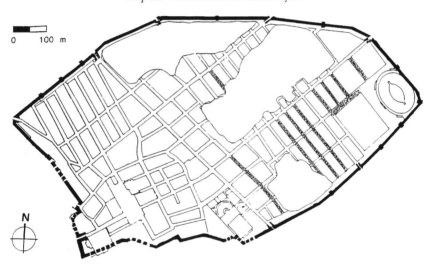

Map 6.4 Occurrence of doorways 4

for comparison with Pompeii. The three data sets include a similar number of streets. The number of streets within 1.0 metre categories of doorway occurrence is plotted for the three cites, as Figure 6.1, and this shows the extent of variation in the amount of interaction in the streets. The data from Pompeii display the widest degree of variation, which would suggest that the infrastructure allowed a degree of freedom in the types of human behaviour that could be achieved in the urban environment of Pompeii. In other words, there

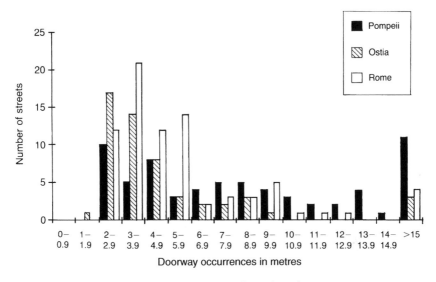

Figure 6.1 Streets in Pompeii, Ostia and Rome

were streets with intense social interaction and other streets with a less pronounced frequency of activity. In contrast, the data set from Ostia pointed to
very intense levels of social activity throughout the city. This is partially caused
by the nature of excavated streets at Ostia. They are for the most part through-
routes, which might suggest that activity would have been concentrated upon
them. The data from Rome, not surprisingly, pointed to a more intense level
of social activity in most of the streets. The lower intensity of activity in some
of the streets in Pompeii can be accounted for with reference to the density of
settlement in the city. Ostia, unlike Pompeii, was a city of apartment blocks,
which were designed to utilise space to the maximum. In contrast, the urban
fabric of Pompeii consisted of a form of low-rise housing that had been developed by the owners with little reference to the ideals of design so apparent in
Ostia (for Ostia see Meiggs 1973; Hermansen 1978, 1981; Packer 1971).

A second method of analysis was designed as a check on the assumption underlying the analysis of the occurrence of doorways, namely that the
number of doorways reflected the relevant levels of activity in a street. The
methodology is very similar to that for the measurement of doorway occurrences. The graffiti and electoral notices were counted and the length of the
streets was used to calculate the occurrence of messages in a street. The following equation was used to do this:

$$\text{Occurrence of messages} = \frac{\text{length of street in metres}}{\text{number of messages}}$$

The major problem with the second methodology is that it can only be
used in the analysis of Pompeii, and can be seen entirely as a function of the

unique data set available from Pompeii. However, even this data set is erratically recorded, and is dependent upon a variety of excavation and recording techniques (Mouritsen 1988: 47–52). For example, the excavations from the twentieth century pin-point the position of graffiti, but previous to this the graffiti and electoral notices were recorded erratically, with the result that the location of street messages in Via delle Consolare in many cases is unclear, even to the point where it is uncertain whether a graffito was written inside or outside a building. Nevertheless, the variation of recorded occurrences of messages through the city does not appear to be great. The data set has a range of graffiti occurring in streets from every 0.4m to every 258.0m. The pattern emulates the spatial distribution that was established from the examination of the occurrence of doorways in streets.

However, there are a number of significant differences. These highlight the interaction of those travelling through the streets rather than localised patterns of social interaction within the street (see above 52–61). Streets with graffiti occurring every 4.0m or less (Map 6.5) can be defined as the through-routes of the city, which correspond to the transport network. We should exclude from this transport network the section of Via dell'Abbondanza from the forum to Via di Stabia, because it was blocked to wheeled traffic. The rest of this group represents all those streets that lead to a gate, including the street leading north between *Insulae* 5.3 and 5.4 to the Porta di Capua, and the streets leading to Porta Ercolano and Porta di Marina (here the values fall outside our category; but this is likely to be a direct result of inadequate recording in early excavations). Also in this category are those streets that join two major through-routes, for example Vicolo di Mercurio, which connects Via delle Consolare with Via di Vesuvio. In our examination of the occurrence of doorways, these streets do not appear to exhibit high levels of activity, because the occurrence of doorways was not frequent. However, this fact is most revealing. These streets have a higher occurrence of street messages for the simple reason that there are fewer doorways in the street, which leaves a greater wall area on which to place messages. The placement of messages upon the walls of streets with few doorways suggests that these streets would form part of a network of streets in which movement rather than social interaction was emphasised. Others include the streets connecting Via di Stabia directly to the amphitheatre, Vicolo di Tesmo, Vicolo di Paquio Proculo, Vicolo di Nozze D'Argento, Vicolo delle Lupanare, the street between *Insulae* 2.3 and 2.4, the street between *Insulae* 9.1 and 9.2, and Vicolo di Balbo. The only street that does not connect up with a major through-route as defined by the occurrence of doorways is Via di Mercurio, which illustrates its exceptional importance in the urban form. It would seem likely that Via di Mercurio had a unique level of activity generated by its position in relationship to the forum, and that the properties on the street were mostly entered via a *fauces*.

Streets with values over 4.1 metres and under 8.0 metres form in most cases the streets of lesser activity and interaction, and generally did not lead to a gate

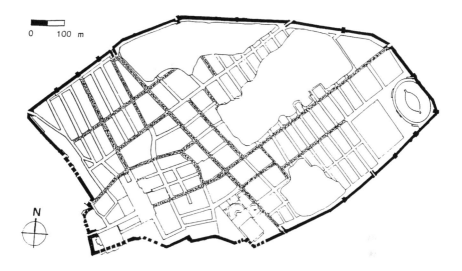

Map 6.5 Occurrence of messages 1

(see Map 6.6). However, many of these streets were primary transport routes. They include Via di Nocera, the north–south route through the central zone of the city to the east of the forum. The inclusion of Via delle Consolare, Via di Nola and Via delle Marina in this group can be accounted for because the graffiti in these streets were erratically recorded by the excavators.

The third category of streets, which has messages occurring every 8.1–12.0 metres, is particularly small (Map 6.7) and will be considered with the fourth category, composed of those streets with messages occurring less often than every 12 metres (see Map 6.8). A number of the streets in these two categories can be accounted for because they were poorly recorded by the excavators. However, those streets to the south-east of the city have been particularly well recorded, but do not display high incidences of street messages. These streets were isolated from the through-routes of the city. Significantly, on the through-routes in the south-eastern part of the city message occurrence was frequent. It would appear from Maps 6.7 and 6.8 that streets isolated from the main urban areas of activity were avoided by the painters of street messages. This, in itself, is for the simple reason that messages in these streets would not have been seen, because these streets did not experience high levels of social activity.

Therefore, from the above study of the occurrence of street messages it may be concluded that the position and frequency of graffiti in streets reflects the higher levels of activity associated with those streets. Unlike the previous examination of doorway occurrences, this methodology highlights the activity of people who used a particular street, but who did not necessarily live in that street. Parts of the region to the east of the forum have a significantly

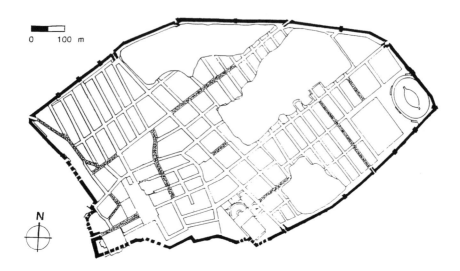

Map 6.6 Occurrence of messages 2

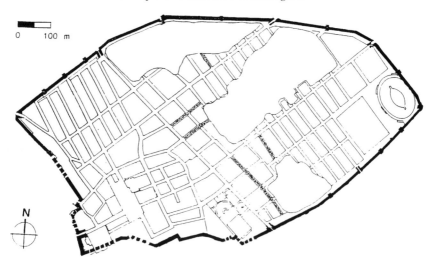

Map 6.7 Occurrence of messages 3

lower incidence of message occurrence, because the streets have consistently high occurrences of doorways. Thus, there was often limited space for the display of graffiti. Also, some of these streets do not form major through-routes and, in consequence, may have been less attractive for the placement of street messages. In contrast, the areas that form through-routes tended to have a high frequency of messages occurring in them, as well as a high occurrence of doorways. It was primarily the streets that were transport routes through the city

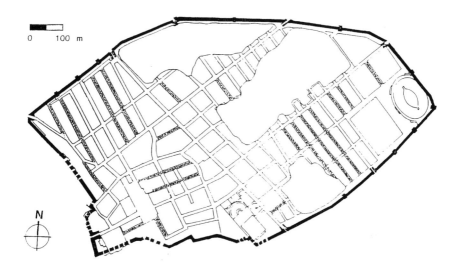

Map 6.8 Occurrence of messages 4

that were the most frequent locations for street-message placement. Such a pattern is also reflected in Mouritsen's distribution maps of the graffiti associated with individual candidates (see above 52–61) (Mouritsen 1988: 53–7). The graffiti were placed on walls without authorisation from the owner; therefore, their placement was at the discretion of their creator, and there is no conclusive evidence to associate the graffiti with the owners of property facing on to the various streets (Mouritsen 1988: 58–9). The fact that the graffiti tended to concentrate on the through-routes of the city suggests that these messages were intended to be read by people coming into the city, from the countryside, as well as people resident within the city walls. Thus, the distribution of graffiti reflects the incidence of inhabitants and strangers in the city of Pompeii.

To return to the study of doorways, we have already seen how some streets had higher occurrences of doorways in them. However, this methodology did not account for the variation of doorway types, or the variation in the use of street frontages. A doorway which was associated with a retail shop had a wide entrance looking on to the street. In contrast, the entrance to an *atrium* house was associated with a deep corridor, known as a *fauces*, that led into the house (see Plate 6.3). The *fauces* separated the *atrium* from the street, whereas the doorway associated with shops helped to integrate this part of the built environment with the street. Therefore, doorways can be categorised as either type 1, associated with the *fauces* of an *atrium* house, or type 2, associated with shops. To account for this variation in doorway type and use of street frontages, the two types of doorways are compared to ascertain whether some streets were dominated by shops or *atrium*-type houses. For the sake of comparison, this measurement is expressed as a ratio between type 1 and type

113

Plate 6.3 Two different types of doorway: type 1 leading into the house and type 2 associated with the bar

2 doorways. Because Pompeii was fundamentally a city of *atrium* houses, we might expect this factor to dominate the relationship between type 1 and type 2 doorways (Wallace-Hadrill 1990; Dwyer 1991). Ideally, this is characterised with a *fauces* flanked by two shops (see Plate 6.3). If this was the dominant pattern for the use of street frontages in Pompeii, we might expect a ratio of 1:2 (type 1:type 2). However, the ratios ranged from 1:1 to 1:9 (Via dei Teatri, however, had no doorways of type 1). The mean was calculated at 1:3 and the median was 1:4, which should be taken as the normal experience in Pompeian streets. This would suggest that the ideal of a *fauces* flanked by two shops was not the dominant type in Pompeii. The data range from 1:1 to 1:9 is not as numerically wide as our previous two data sets. Therefore, when we make comparisons between streets, we do not need to divide the data into four sets. For the sake of presentation this data set is divided into two, one group of streets with a ratio higher than the median and another with a ratio less than the median (see Map 6.9). Some anomalies do arise in streets that have very few doorways and lower levels of activity, for example Vicolo della Fullonica. These anomalies are most common in *Regiones* 1 and 2. In the category of streets with a ratio higher than 1:4 were the streets that were defined by method 1 as the central area and the through-routes in the western part of

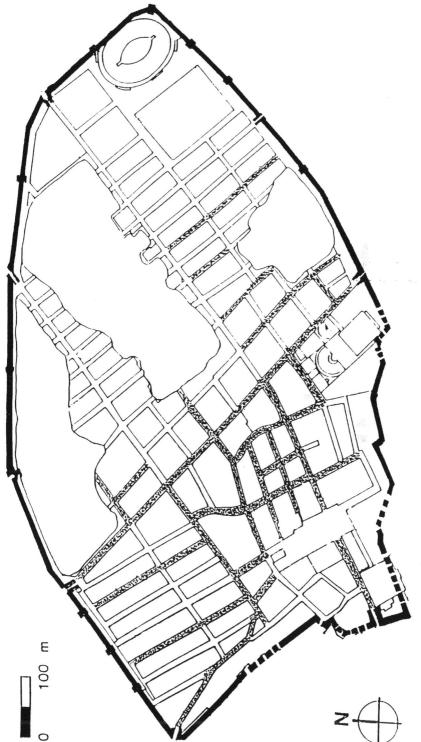

Map 6.9 Ratio of type 1:type 2 doorways (shading indicates those streets with a ratio lower than the median)

100 m

0

N

the city. However, the through-routes in the eastern part of the city are only partially represented in this group. In Via dell'Abbondanza, to the east of Via di Stabia, the higher ratio only occurs near the Porta di Sarno. In the case of the Via di Nola, a similar pattern is apparent. The lower ratios in the eastern part of the city would seem to reflect the dominance of the *atrium* house type in this area, with a *fauces* and flanked by two shops. These areas included *Regiones* 1, 2, 5, 6 and 9. We should also include the isolated parts of *Regiones* 7 and 8. It was in these areas that the *atrium* house was the more dominant housing type, whereas in the central area of the city and the through-routes in the western part of the city, other forms of urban fabric had a stronger presence. In this area, the retail shop took on a far more important role than in *Regiones* 1, 2, 5, 6 and 9. To see these areas, with their emphasis on the *atrium* house, as representative of all housing types in Pompeii is unrealistic (Wallace-Hadrill 1990 sees *Regiones* 1, 2 and 6 as a representative sample of the whole of Pompeii). There was a fundamental difference between the use of street frontages in these areas and the intensive use of street frontages in the central area of the city and through-routes of the western part of the city (this pattern is confirmed by a survey of wheel ruts undertaken by Tsujimura 1991). (See Chapter 3.)

To conclude this chapter, it would appear that the arrangement of streets in Pompeii had a certain logic which caused the variation in the number of doorways, message occurrence and the ratio of type 1:type 2 doorways. Emphasis was laid upon the through-routes as the streets with the greatest competition for street frontage. This suggests that interaction occurred at a higher level in streets that were major routes in the transport network. The fact that these through-routes led from the city gates towards the centre of the city implies that the social relationship between inhabitant and stranger was stronger than that between inhabitant and inhabitant, and that there was a high frequency of visitors to Pompeii. The through-routes with the highest incidence of usage were those that formed a north–south axis. This might suggest that Pompeii was placed on a north–south route for land transport, whereas the east–west route was dominated by water transport up the river Sarno. The major through-routes of the city were also marked by the shrines of the *Lares Compitales*, which defined the boundaries of the *vici*. It is notable that these through-routes were integrated at the core of the city in the area to the east of the forum in *Regio 7*. The separation of properties from the street was most pronounced in areas that were least integrated within the street network. These were also probably those areas in which the inhabitants had the greatest control over the internal space of their properties.

7

THE PRODUCTION
OF SPACE

In Chapter 6 a pattern of street activity was established from a study of the use of the interface between the edges of the *insulae* and the street. To begin to account for this phenomenon it is necessary first to identify the spatial generators which produced the pattern of doorway occurrences in Pompeii. In effect, what are being analysed are those local factors which imposed controls upon what would otherwise be the random occurrence of doorways.

One of the controls upon randomness which has been observed to be present in many Roman cities was the grid plan. This factor has been observed by numerous scholars, but seldom analysed in spatial terms (see Haverfield 1913: 14; Ward-Perkins 1974: 33–6; Owens 1989: 14; contra Mumford 1961: 246; Rykwert 1976: 41–67 for an alternative). It has also been recognised that an *insula* block can only be divided in so many ways to produce *atrium*-type houses (Maiuri 1942). The approach adopted here is somewhat different. An *insula* block is normally a quadrilateral form that is defined by the street grid. In Pompeii, these *insulae* vary in shape from square through rectilinear to rhomboid. Ideally the positioning of doorways upon these blocks would either be random or form an even distribution, but any brief observation of the distribution of doorways upon an *insula* block will reveal that this distribution is anything but even or random. For example the *insula* block *Regio* 7.14 has fourteen doorways on Via dell' Abbondanza, two doorways on Vicolo delle Lupanare, one on Vicolo degli Scheletri and three on Vicolo della Maschera. This would suggest that the dominant directional focus at a crude level was to the south on to Via dell'Abbondanza. However, in many cases such a procedure would not take into account the size of the street frontage. For example, some *insula* blocks have many doorways on their shortest side, but an equal number on their long side. Therefore, such a crude procedure of solely counting the doorways on each side of an *insula* block may not reveal the dominant direction in proportion to the amount of street frontage available. To avoid such distorted data the following method was adopted. Each *insula* block was measured, and the number of doorways was counted. Then this number of doorways was hypothetically distributed in an even pattern and the deviation of the real examples from this even distribution was measured. The exact controls which governed the siting and structure of Pompeian housing are far from self-evident: there would appear to be little overall planning of the forms of whole *insula* blocks, which might be attributed to the way in which these blocks have become subdivided over time.

However, there are two *insulae* that were planned as whole units, 7.5 and 9.4, which can be used as controls with which the other *insulae* can be compared. These two *insulae* contain respectively the Forum Baths and the Central Baths (Richardson 1988: 147–53, 286–9). By studying the layout of these two *insulae*, we see in their design a perception of use of the streets surrounding the *insulae*, and an appreciation by the designers of how these two *insulae* would be integrated into the extant street form.

The older of the two structures, 7.5, contains the Forum Baths. The faces of the *insula* are fairly evenly distributed round the circumference: 23 per cent face north, 18 per cent face south, 28 per cent face east and 30 per cent face west. If the building was designed to maximise use or to have an even pattern of use on all sides, these figures would be reflected in the proportions of doorways facing each direction. This is not the case: 28 per cent of the doorways face north, 14 per cent face south, 41 per cent face east and 17 per cent face west. The emphasis of the interface between the *insula* and its surrounding space is in an easterly direction, with another emphasis to the north. There would appear to be a designed directional pull away from the south and west. The main public entrances into the baths are also aligned on the north and east sides of the *insula*. Therefore, the person who designed the block was working within an already existing pattern of use of the areas around it, which emphasised the importance of Via delle Terme and Via del Foro. These are the major through-routes, whereas the other two streets performed a lesser role. It was these factors that were incorporated into the design of this *insula* block.

The *insula* containing the Central Baths, 9.4 (see Plates 7.1 and 7.2), has the following distribution of frontage around its circumference: 27 per cent face north, 23 per cent face east, 27 per cent face south and 23 per cent face west. The *insula* is approximately square, and if there was an even pattern of use, this would be reflected in an even distribution of doorways facing each direction. Again, this is not the case: 33 per cent of the doorways face north, 11 per cent face east, 6 per cent face south and 50 per cent face west. In this structure there was a strong directional pull away from the south and east to the west and the Via di Stabia, with only a minor positive deviation from the expected even pattern to the north. The building encroaches upon Vicolo di Tesmo on its east side and, as a result, this street is too narrow for wheeled traffic. This emphasises the lesser role played by this street in the structure of the building and the street pattern of Pompeii.

In these two examples, we see one of the fundamental structures of Roman urbanism being designed to utilise the space around it. This use of space is not a maximisation of the space available on all the frontages of the building,

Plate 7.1 Insula 9.4 from Via di Stabia

Plate 7.2 Insula 9.4 (right) from Vicolo di Tesmo

but only on those frontages through which people entered the structures. In both cases, these frontages coincide with the through-routes of the city, and the emphasis upon urban activity was towards the centre and the north of the city. The streets that were isolated by this emphasis of activity had a lesser role to play in the structure of the city; they were often narrower (compare Vicolo di Tesmo and Via di Nola), and were areas that would have been avoided by strangers, in favour of those streets that were wide and presented a vista into the distance. Thus the structure of even the most designed *insulae* took account of the extant patterns of street activity. These two examples of designed *insulae* set the context for the following analysis of the other *insula* blocks in Pompeii. All the *insulae* were examined to establish their directional focus, using the above methodology.

To unravel the considerable quantity of data generated through the study of the façades of *insulae*, a series of maps is used to highlight the main features. First, the side of each *insula* block with the highest proportion of doorways is plotted (see Map 7.1). This map demonstrates that in most cases the directional focus is concentrated towards the through-routes. Interestingly, there is a marked difference of emphasis between *Regiones* 6 and 1. Although both contain *insulae* that are rectangular and of similar proportions, in all but one case in *Regio* 6 the highest proportion of doorways in an *insula* was on a longer side, while in *Regio* 1 the emphasis is on the shorter north side of the *insulae*. This is particularly marked when the *insulae* come into contact with Via dell'Abbondanza. In this *Regio* some blocks do have their strongest focus towards a longer side, but in all cases these were related to contact with Via di Nocera. *Regio* 1 illustrates the standard influence of the through-routes. In contrast, *Regio* 6 does not conform to this local constraint upon randomness. This can be accounted for with reference to Via di Mercurio, which, although it is not a through-route, displays all the attributes of a through-route in spatial terms: a high occurrence of doorways and a frequent occurrence of messages. Its uniqueness is also highlighted by the presence of an arch at its southern end. However, this cannot account fully for the pattern of the other streets in *Regio* 6. In other areas of the city there is no marked deviation from the expected pattern, in which the random or the even distribution of doorways is modified by a greater emphasis upon the through-routes.

This method of analysis, although crude, has revealed certain factors. To resolve some of the anomalies, and particularly those in *Regio* 6, the percentage of the total number of doorways on each side of the *insula* block was calculated. In many cases, the proportional differences between sides of *insulae* were not very great. This is particularly true of the area of *Regio* 7 to the east of the forum. There would appear to have been a strong directional pull away from Vicolo degli Scheletri. Two *insulae* (7.4 and 8.4) had a virtually even distribution of doorways around their circumferences, and it would seem that this can be explained with reference to their position. Both *insulae* were surrounded by through-routes and streets that connected through-routes. Thus, these two

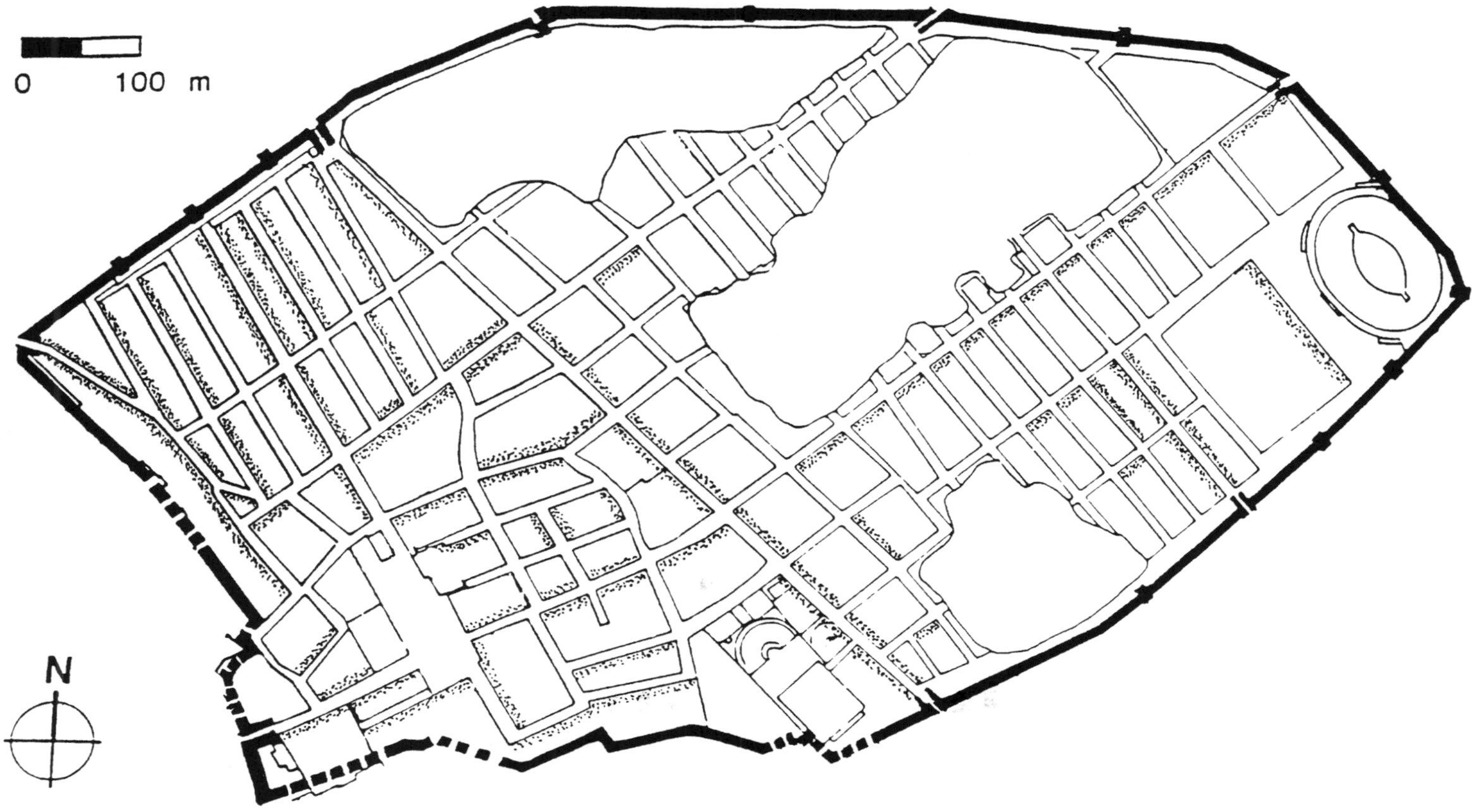

Map 7.1 Doorways in *insulae*

insulae were fully integrated into the street grid and maximised the use of their perimeter, whereas in all other *insulae*, certain sides had few doorways opening on them, and other sides were given a greater emphasis of use. Therefore, this method does not take us any further in attempting to understand the pattern of use of the façades of *insulae*. Instead, we have confirmed that the pattern of use was dominated by the relationship between the position of doorways on the sides of *insulae* and the location of the through-routes in the city.

To resolve this lack of definition, it was decided to plot positive deviation from an even pattern of doorway occurrence in *insulae*. This yielded some remarkable results (see Map 7.2). As expected, positive deviation from a random pattern was most marked when an *insula* came into contact with a through-route. This accounts for most of the positive deviation above 20 per cent. In *Regio* 6, *Insulae* 9, 11 and 14 approached an even pattern, for which it is hard to account. There was little positive deviation in *Regio* 7. However, the strongest positive deviation was shown in *Regio* 1. This seems to suggest that positive deviation from an even or random pattern occurs in areas in which the owners of property have the greatest control over how their property is entered from the street. In areas such as *Regiones* 6 and 7, where there is more pressure on space, the occurrence of doorways is less controlled by the owners of property. This would imply that there were a greater number of properties in *Regiones* 6 and 7 than in *Regiones* 1 and 2. This would appear to be one of the logical generators of the patterns of doorway occurrence identified in the previous chapter.

Therefore, the social relationship that would appear to cause the Pompeian spatial configuration was the relationship between inhabitants and strangers, or people from outside the city. This is demonstrated by the emphasis upon through-routes leading to the centre of the city. However, it would also appear that in some areas this relationship was suppressed, or masked by other relationships that were occurring. This is particularly true of the area of *Regio* 7 to the east of the forum and to a certain extent *Regio* 6.

The question as to why these areas mask the inhabitant–stranger relationship is not easily answered. Both areas are close to the forum. They have a significantly different arrangement of streets: *Regio* 6 has all the attributes of orthogonal planning, whereas *Regio* 7 is anything but regular in terms of street plan. Could the underlying logic of such a pattern be quite basic? Do regular and irregular street patterns in themselves produce very different spatial relationships?

We begin by examining the street plan (Map 7.3). Through-routes define the two areas of study. *Regio* 6 is defined by Via della Fortuna, Via delle Terme, Via di Stabia and Via delle Consolare. The second study area, the part of *Regio* 7 to the east of the forum, is bounded by Via dell'Abbondanza, Via di Stabia, the forum and Via del Foro, and Via della Fortuna. Thus both areas would appear to be integrated into a network of through-routes.

However, *Regio* 6 would appear to have a very linear alignment. The streets appear to promote movement in a north–south direction, from and

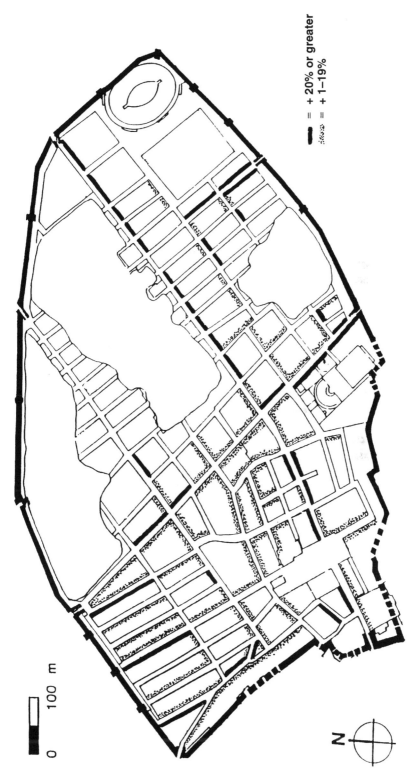

Map 7.2 Deviation from expected pattern of doorway placement

= + 20% or greater

= + 1–19%

100 m

0

N

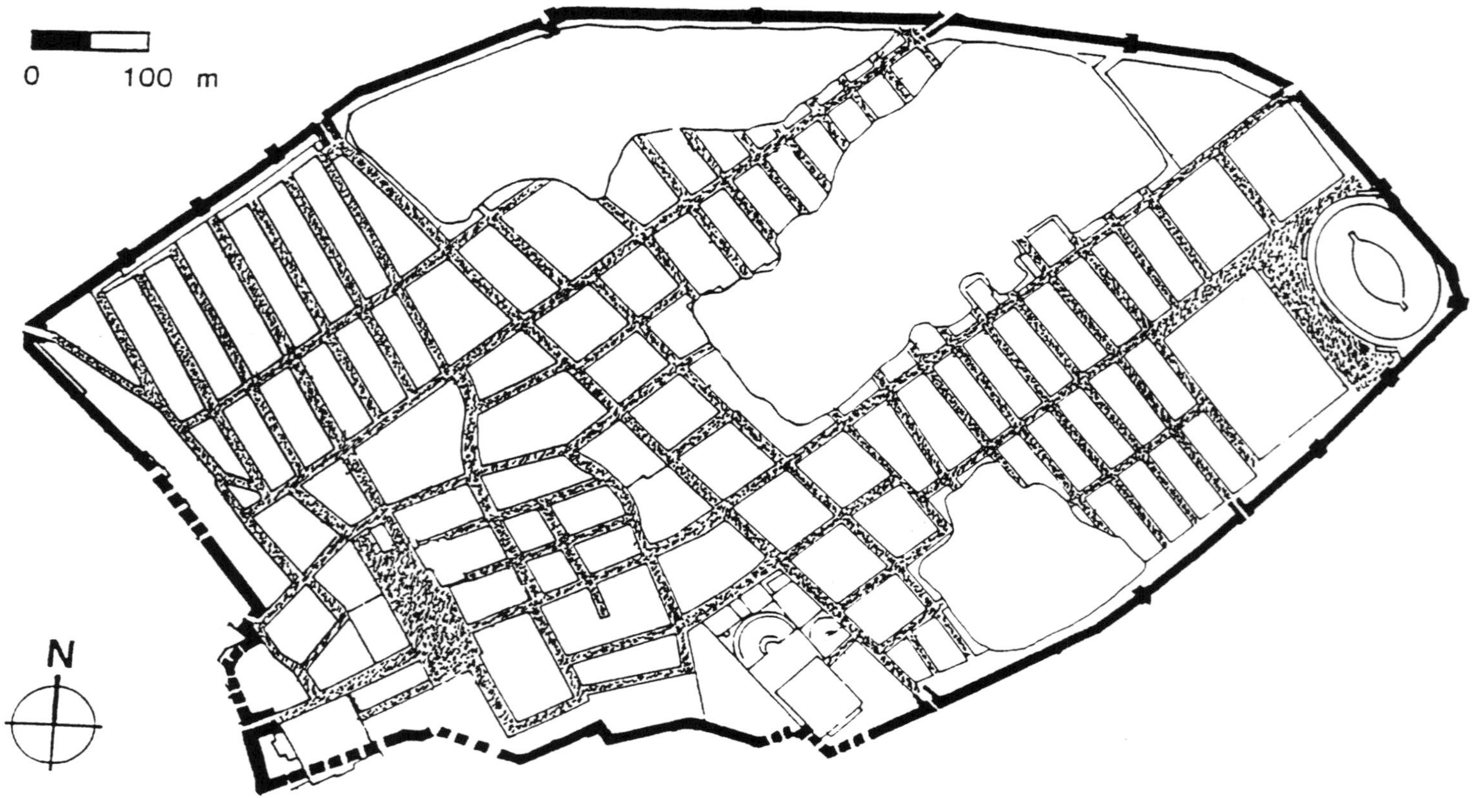

Map 7.3 The street network

towards the through-route of Via della Fortuna/Via delle Terme. This would appear to be caused by the physical structure of the street, which would have drawn people to its vanishing point, in those streets that lead from the south in a consistent northerly direction. The lateral street Vicolo di Mercurio would appear to play a lesser role, with a low occurrence of doorways upon it. However, its role as a communications channel is highlighted by the relatively high occurrence of messages in the street. The streets running north–south in this area are all dead ends beyond Vicolo di Mercurio. This factor in itself would isolate these areas from a stranger visiting the city. Few strangers utilise streets that do not connect with other streets unless there is a specific reason for them to visit that street, which is known in advance. This observation may be a key to comprehending the different spatial patterns displayed by *Regiones* 6 and 7. In many ways, *Regio* 6 is a non-distributive area, with the movement of people flowing around, rather than through, the area. This is illustrated further by the positioning of the arch at the southern end of Via di Mercurio. The arch would appear to be placed in such a manner as to form a boundary, but at the same time the arch draws a person's line of sight through it (MacDonald 1986: 75–87). The idea of a very permeable boundary is particularly significant, because there is a shrine of the *Lares* sited in Via di Mercurio (6.8.13). These shrines, as we have already seen, formed boundaries along the through-routes of Pompeii. Thus, *Regio* 6 would appear isolated from the inhabitant–stranger interface. Instead, the streets all lead into the central forum area, which suggests that an emphasis was placed upon the isolation of the area from strangers, and a greater emphasis upon the inhabitant–inhabitant interface.

Regio 7 is rather different. The streets and *insula* blocks are highly irregular in both size and shape. This would appear to reflect the antiquity of the area. It would also seem to reflect organic rather than planned growth. An alternative explanation is that a grid had been set out, but had become totally deformed because of pressure to build structures that expanded beyond the confines of the *insula* block. The form of *Regio* 7, upon destruction in AD 79, displays a mixture of orthogonal planning to the south with elements of informal growth to the north. For example, Vicolo di Storto and Vicolo delle Lupanare have pronounced curves. This mixture of informality and formality should not come as a surprise because, as Ward-Perkins (1974: 8–9) has pointed out, Roman cities usually display elements of formal and informal planning. As in the case of *Regio* 6 the through-routes tend to go around this area. However, as we saw in the previous chapter, there were high occurrences of doorways and street messages in this area. This suggests that the area was integrated with the rest of the city. An explanation for this might be that this area formed a central area within the city, which integrated the through-routes with each other, whilst maintaining a strong relationship with the forum. Via degli Augustali forms a link between the forum and Via di Stabia, with a side branch, Vicolo delle Lupanare, to Via dell'Abbondanza.

Vicolo di Eumachia and Vicolo di Storto establish a link between Via dell'Abbondanza and Via della Fortuna. Therefore, the central position of this area promotes movement through a series of rather complicated short cuts. For the total stranger such routes would remain undiscovered, but for the inhabitant or frequent visitor these routes provided rapid movement that avoided the circuitous through-routes. It is not so much the different street pattern of *Regio* 7 that marks it out as different from *Regio* 6, but rather its position within the city.

These observations in many ways return us to the question of zoning in the Roman city. Although, in Chapters 1 and 5, the concept of geographical zoning was dismissed as a useful tool in its pure geographical form, it would appear that two different zones have been identified inadvertently. There would appear to be fundamental spatial differences between *Regiones* 6 and 7 that could be explained by the fact that land rents in the centre would have been higher than those elsewhere in the city. This might be used to explain the level of street activity in this area. However, I would suggest an alternative explanation, which does not exclude the concept of economic zoning, in terms of centre and periphery (Champion 1989). The area to the east of the forum (*Regio* 7 and the western part of *Regio* 9) forms a central core that integrates the rest of the system. The fact that it does not rely upon orthogonal planning may be its greatest strength. Indeed, its role as an integrating core may be dependent upon its irregularity. Other areas that are orthogonally planned (for example *Regiones* 1 and 2) do not appear capable of taking on such a role. The combination of an irregular plan and centrality greatly increases the inhabitant–inhabitant interface within this region. Other areas of Pompeii do not reflect this relationship to the same degree, because of their position and their regular orthogonal plan.

The question of what was generating this pattern needs to be answered. The street pattern itself appears to have been partially determinate; also, the role of position within that street pattern has been addressed. The role of the internal structuring of *insula* blocks would appear to have been another factor. *Regiones* 6 and 7 were selected as areas in which the internal pattern of the *insula* blocks seemed to play a role in the organisation of external space.

The role of the *atrium* house type as indicated by the *fauces* might have had a determining role in the subdivision of *insula* blocks. This proposition was tested in the two study regions, *Regiones* 6 and 7, by plotting the number of *fauces* on each side of each *insula* (Map 7.4). From Map 7.4 it would appear that the variation in the number of *fauces* occurring was not large enough to support the conclusion that this was a primary factor in the structuring of external space. It was from such inconclusive data that it was decided that it was necessary to increase the resolution of study. The level that was adopted retained the street as the larger unit of study, but viewed the spatial configurations within the *insula* blocks as though they were seen by a stranger or a visitor. That is, the study looks at the spatial structures of

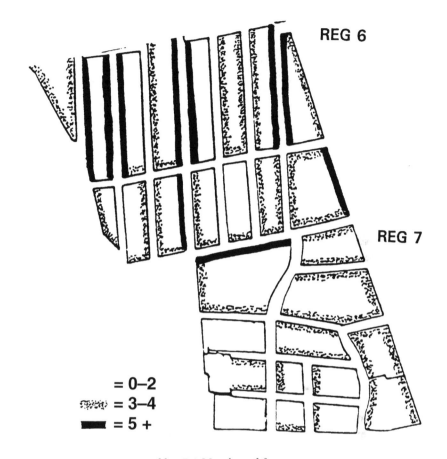

REG 6

REG 7

= 0–2
= 3–4
= 5 +

Map 7.4 Number of *fauces*

houses adjoining the streets from the point of view of a person in the street, rather than from that of the inhabitant or owner of the house. Each individual structure within a street was drawn in a morphic language of space (for a full account of the methodology see Hillier and Hanson 1984). This morphic language was made up of two components: dots and lines. The dots signify the existence of rooms, spaces or corridors and the lines represent the connections between the rooms, spaces or corridors. For example, in Figure 7.1, the morphic language of the House of the Vettii is set out. This methodology defines the spaces in a structure and emphasises the relationship between spaces. Therefore, an emphasis is placed upon the spaces or voids, rather than solids or walls, which are emphasised in the plans of houses. Once the houses have been converted into this morphic language, they can be analysed using the methods of Hillier and Hanson (1984). The number of spaces within a structure can be established: in our example,

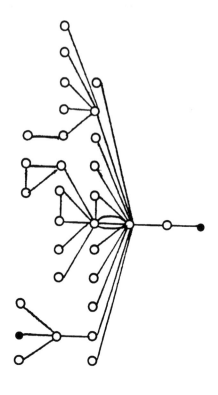

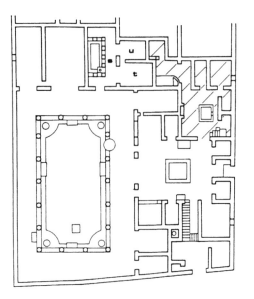

Figure 7.1 House of the Vettii in plan and as a morphic language

there are twenty-nine. These spaces can be seen to have varied in their depth from the street. For example, the *fauces* is the shallowest point, whereas the peristyle tends to be one of deeper spaces. To account for this variation the mean depth of the house was calculated. In our example, we find that the House of the Vettii has a mean depth of 3.6. This accounts for the overall position of the spaces in a house in relationship to the street. However, to account fully for the degree of integration or separation of a house from the street, it is necessary to utilise an equation devised for this purpose by Hillier and Hanson (1984: 147–55):

$$RA = \frac{2(MD - 1)}{K - 2}$$

where

> RA = Relative Asymmetry
> MD = Mean Depth
> K = Number of Spaces.

This equation results in the measurement of Relative Asymmetry, which summarises the arrangement of the house in numerical form. The results of this equation vary from 0.00 to 1.00. In our example of the House of the Vettii:

$$RA = \frac{2(MD - 1)}{K - 2}$$
$$RA = \frac{2(3.6 - 1)}{29 - 2}$$
$$RA = 0.19$$

Therefore the House of the Vettii has a Relative Asymmetry of 0.19, which can be compared with measurements of Relative Asymmetry in other houses. The figure of 0.19 suggests that the House of the Vettii is strongly integrated into the street structure. The main reason for this is the depth of the house in relationship to the number of spaces contained in the house. The usefulness of this method lies in its ability to examine and compare the variation in the structure of space that does not appear on the plans of houses.

However, our concern is not so much with the houses themselves, but with the variation in settlement types in relationship to the street structure of the city. Therefore, in each street the Mean Depth, the Number of Spaces and the Relative Asymmetry were calculated for each structure. Then the mean of these values was used as a description of the amount of integration or separation between any one street and its adjoining *insulae*. The number of structures that formed distributive units was also noted. For example, the House of the Vettii can be entered from Vicolo dei Vettii and Vicolo di Mercurio, so that it forms a distributive unit between two streets.

This process produced an array of data for the streets in the two study regions. The data highlighted the major differences and similarities between *Regiones* 6 and 7. The range of the Mean Depth in *Regio* 7 was from 1.0 to 2.4, whereas in *Regio* 6 it varied from 1.8 to 3.3. The mean number of spaces within buildings in a street varied from 5 to 11 in *Regio* 7, whereas in *Regio* 6 it was in the range of 5 to 15. The similarity between these figures is caused partly by the inclusion of the through-route, Via delle Terme and Via della Fortuna, in the *Regio* 6 sample. If these two streets are excluded from the sample the range is markedly higher, 12 to 15. Therefore, the properties in *Regio* 6 were considerably larger than those in *Regio* 7. We may also assume that as a result there were probably fewer properties in *Regio* 6. This might generate the pattern of doorway and message occurrence that was observed in Chapter 6. This would also imply that fewer people would have been encountered in *Regio* 6 than in *Regio* 7. Some of the properties in both *regiones* were defined as not having depth and were fully integrated with the street. Generally, in *Regio* 7 there were more properties in each street that lacked depth than properties with depth. In *Regio* 6, excluding Via della Fortuna and Via delle Terme, the majority of streets had more properties with depth than without. These observations need to be borne in mind in the following discussion of Relative Asymmetry. This was a measure of integration of properties with the street that can vary between 0.00 and 1.0. The lower the figure of Relative Asymmetry, the greater the integration of the building with the street. However, if the figure rises above 1 or cannot be calculated because of its lack of spaces or depth, it is said to be without depth and fully integrated with the street. The range of mean Relative Asymmetry was remarkably similar, from 0.24 to 0.49 in *Regio* 7 and from 0.28 to 0.50 in *Regio* 6. The highest figure for *Regio* 7 occurred in Via degli Augustali, whilst the lowest figure for *Regio* 6 occurred in Via di Mercurio. Both of these streets have high occurrences of doorways, but the relationship between the buildings and the street is completely different, as indicated by the figures for Relative Asymmetry. The reason for such a variation is that in both streets there were good reasons for siting property there, in competition with other property, but the way and the reasons for siting it there were rather different. In Via degli Augustali the larger houses insulated themselves from the street. The low figure of Relative Asymmetry for Via di Mercurio marks a desire to integrate the property with the street. This should come as no surprise, because the visual narrative from the outside would have revealed the structure of space through to the peristyle at the rear (see Plate 7.3). The reason that there was a high occurrence of doorways in this area is not that street activity was high, but rather that those requiring formality and separation from the street wanted to live in this street within easy reach of the forum.

In other streets the range of Relative Asymmetry was not significantly different (see Map 7.5). The similarity can be accounted for. The *atrium* house

Table 7.1 Summary of data for *Regio 7*

Street	Mean values			With depth (%)	Without depth (%)
	MD	SP	RA		
Augustali	2.0	6	0.49	33	67
Maschera	2.3	9	0.39	45	55
Scheletri	2.1	9	0.29	32	68
Balcone Pensile	2.4	9	0.39	37	63
Eumachia	1.8	5	0.34	26	74
Lupanare	1.8	6	0.34	38	62
Panettiere	2.2	11	0.24	50	50
Storto	1.8	7	0.33	45	55

Table 7.2 Summary of data for *Regio* 6

Street	Mean values			With depth (%)	Without depth (%)
	MD	SP	RA		
Mercurio (vicolo)	2.9	13	0.37	79	21
Fullonica	3.2	15	0.38	94	6
Mercurio (via)	2.7	15	0.28	67	33
Fortuna	2.1	8	0.37	38	62
Fauno	3.3	14	0.41	75	25
Labirinto	2.9	12	0.43	89	11
Vettii	2.7	15	0.39	81	19
Terme	1.8	5	0.40	37	63
Modesto	3.1	12	0.45	83	17
Narciso	3.1	13	0.50	86	14

would appear to have two different entrances: the formal one through the *fauces*, and an informal rear entrance. The rear entrance of these houses would appear to have been separated from the street, whereas the formal entrance was integrated with it. Another reason for this apparent similarity is inherent in the way the data are presented. Only those properties that had depth could have the level of their integration measured. This means that all those properties without depth are excluded from the analysis of Relative Asymmetry. Therefore, the similarity between the figures for *Regiones* 6 and 7 points not to a similarity between the two areas of study, but rather to a similarity of property type in the two study areas. The fact that there is a greater amount of property without depth in *Regio* 7 than with depth and that the opposite is true of *Regio* 6 points to the major differences between the two areas. In other words, the larger properties in *Regio* 7 have a greater tendency to be spatially separated from the street, whereas those in *Regio* 6 have a greater tendency to be formally separated from it.

The occurrence of similar property types in two structurally different areas of the city is most illuminating. In *Regio* 7, properties separated from

Plate 7.3 View from the *fauces* through the *atrium* into the peristyle (6.8.23)

the street to the same degree as in *Regio* 6 exist alongside properties that lack depth and are integrated with the street. This suggests that a hierarchy of space or economic zoning of space does not exist in *Regio* 7. Equally, in *Regio* 6 there does not appear to be a hierarchy of space or separation of groups, although it must be stated that there is conscious separation of property from the street.

Some general factors which produced the patterns of doorway occurrences do emerge from this study of Pompeii. Where the mean number of spaces is high, doorway occurrences tend to be low. Where doorway occurrences are high, Mean Depth tends to be low. Where doorway occurrences are high, the percentage of structures without depth is greater than the percentage of structures with depth. Where doorway occurrences are low, Mean Depth tends to be high. Where doorway occurrences are low, the percentage of structures with depth is greater than the percentage of structures without. It is this series of inverse relationships that would appear to be generating the spatial pattern of doorway occurrences. This would appear to be the spatial logic that generates patterns in Pompeii; it is related to the amount of activity and the density of settlement in an area. These two factors highlight *Regio* 7 as an area of intense activity not replicated in other areas of the city, where the density of the use of the urban fabric is not as great. In these areas, the urban

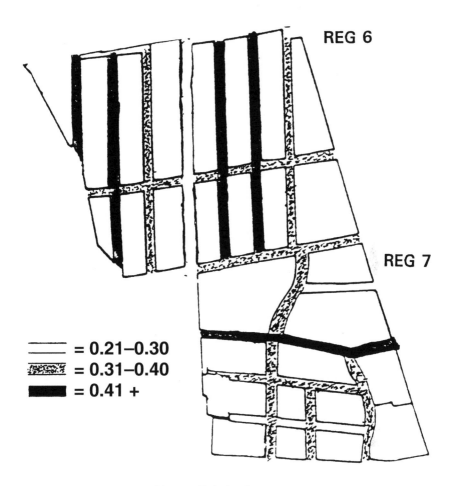

Map 7.5 Relative Asymmetry

fabric could have been designed to isolate a property from the street. This can only be done because the pressure upon space is not great. However, in *Regio* 7, the pressure upon the usage of the street frontage prohibited the isolation of property from the street.

8

PROPERTY OWNERSHIP AND URBAN LAND VALUE

The blocks of houses or *insulae* in Pompeii evolved over a period of more than three centuries into their final format as preserved by the eruption of AD 79 (Jones and Robinson 2004; Berry 1998; Fulford and Wallace-Hadrill 1999). There would seem to have been considerable variation to the format of the *insula* block across the city (Figure 8.1). We have seen in Chapters 6 and 7 that one of the factors that determined the use of the frontage of *insulae* was the position each block had with respect to the grid of streets and the flow of traffic through the city. This chapter moves the analysis a step forward towards a conception of the dynamics of urban land rent or variation in the value of property across the city. A key factor for understanding the city has been a recognition of the close proximity of those utilising a *domus* for urban living and their poorer neighbours using *tabernae* or workshops for their own economic survival (Wallace-Hadrill 1994). Parkins (1997) developed the thesis that the two were linked in a form of economic relationship between the major houses and the smaller properties that connected to them. However, in her work there is an implicit assumption that the inhabitant of the *domus* was its owner deriving rental income from the smaller properties rented to persons of lower status. There is an unspoken Anglophone assumption in the study of Pompeii that the *atrium* houses were owner occupied and the smaller units were rented out – even though our two pieces of evidence for rental at Pompeii refer to the rental of complete *insulae*. This chapter takes the opposite view: that *insulae* in Pompeii were created for the maximisation of rental income, by persons not necessarily living within the property themselves. The intention of this diagnostic assumption is to reverse the owner-occupied preference in the interpretation of Pompeian real estate. Behind this is not just an attempt to buck a trend in Pompeian studies. Parkins (1997) demonstrated that most property changed hands via inheritance and as dowry, rather than buying and selling. Properties forming part of a dowry often were not places of residence, but were investments to provide funds for children produced in marriage (Parkins 1997: 101). Property passing to those under twenty-five without a living father and into guardianship tended to be preserved or remain mothballed until the person came of age

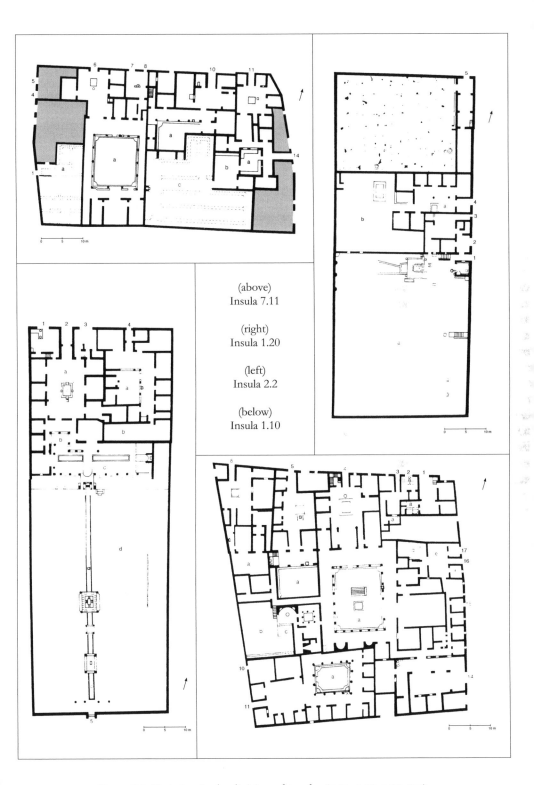

(above)
Insula 7.11

(right)
Insula 1.20

(left)
Insula 2.2

(below)
Insula 1.10

Figure 8.1 Variation in the division of *insulae* (7.11, 1.10, 1.20, 2.2)

(Saller 1994: 181–203). The same may have been true of a number of women in guardianship. These features of property holding would have impacted on the way in which property was held, rented or subdivided.

Rental income

The texts which are the basis for much of our understanding of city life highlight and emphasise the prominence of elite investment in urban as well as rural property. This material has been studied by Frier (1977, 1978, 1980) to understand the workings of the rental market at Rome. However, his findings, with a focus on the Roman legal side of rental, have shown that these factors were not confined to Rome itself but would have applied in other cities including those of Campania. Before we may observe the houses of the inhabitants as excavated, we must understand or set out the mechanics of the urban property market.

The observation made by Aulus Gellius (*N.A.* 15.1) that urban property was more profitable than its rural equivalent, yet at greater risk from damage by fire, is an important starting point for any investigation of the subject. Frier (1980: 21) calculated that an annual return from agriculture was likely to have been in the region of 5–6 per cent, whereas that from urban property was in the region of 8–9 per cent. The vagaries of agricultural yield whether from crops or from rental are displayed in Pliny's *Letters* (e.g. 9.37). It is clear from a number of texts that the elite owned extensive urban estates: for example Cicero had *insulae* in Rome in the Argiletum and on the Aventine, but also had inherited *insulae* in Puteoli. The return on the latter was in the region of 80,000 to 100,000 *sesterces* per annum (by comparison a labourer would have earned 3 *sesterces* per day, *Att.* 13.45.2–3, 13.46.3, 13.37.4). These were not atypical investments by a *novus homo*, and we can find similar investments by Atticus, Publius Clodius, Caelius Rufus and other members of the nobility (Frier 1978). However, the image of Crassus owning vast areas of Rome as created by Plutarch (*Crass.* 2.5) might have more in common with the biographer's moral imagination than with reality. As we read in Cicero's letters to Atticus, when his *insulae* rented out to tenants collapsed or were cracking, he saw a way to rebuild or subdivide the plots further to create greater profit for himself.

The extent of rented property should not be underestimated. From Pompeii, there survive two painted rental notices (*CIL* 4. 138, 1136 = H50, H44). The first is for the *Insula* Arriana Polliana (*Insula* 6 in *Regio* 6, Figure 8.2), which consisted of a *domus* (house), *cenacula equestria* (high-class apartments), *tabernae* with *pergulae* (shops with living quarters above) and was to be leased for a year from 1 July, via the slave of the owner Gnaeus Alleius Nigidius Maius. What is so striking about this rental notice is that the *insula* was made up of properties of quite different statuses – from the low-class shops with living quarters above, through the high-class apartments and then

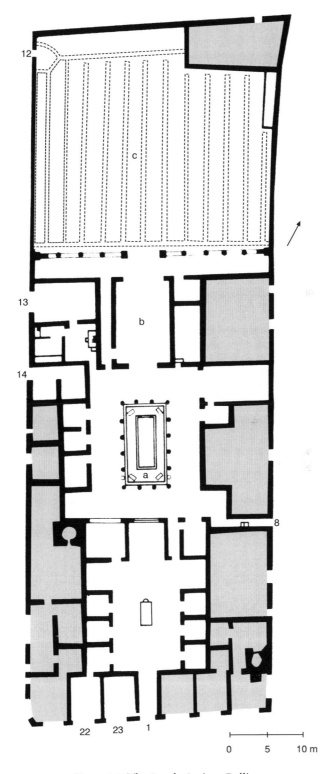

Figure 8.2 The *Insula* Arriana Polliana

finally the house itself, one of the largest in *Regio* 6 (there are thirteen houses of greater complexity) in the centre of the *insula* (see Pirson 1997 for analysis; Parkins 1997: 102–5) – and also that the whole block could be leased at once. Frier (1980: 34–9) demonstrates that the rental year began on 1 July, but negotiations began earlier, for example in the case of Cicero: at the end of March he wrote to Atticus to instruct him to interview lessees, and by April these had been arranged with payment of the whole amount due by June and certainly made by early July (*Att.* 14.9.1, 14.10.3, 14.11.2, 15.7.1, 15.20.4, 16.1.5; *Dig.* 19.2.7). The middleman is envisaged in Roman legal texts as subletting the property to tenants with a potential profit in the region of 20 per cent (*Dig.* 19.2.7–8). Hence, the person taking on such a lease was clearly in command of substantial capital but would make some considerable profit from letting the building to tenants.

The means of renting the property out and to whom varied according to the nature of the rental unit and the person to whom it was to be rented. It is clear that the upper classes rented property under certain circumstances: senators did not always own houses in Rome and needed to rent a high-status property, the young members of the elite moved out of home and rented *cenacula* (high-status apartments), freedmen often lived alongside these young men (Frier 1980: 39–47 for examples). It is the legal sources that deal with the upper-class rental patterns (and exclude those of the poor). Frier (1980: 46) locates the majority of references in the Digest that refer to the rental of apartments (twenty-two), with a significant number of references to the rental of houses (fifteen) and finally a much smaller group referring to the rental of apartments within houses (six). These are not statistics, but point to important factors in the way in which prestigious properties were laid out – they were independent of each other with their own entrance ways. We have to look beyond our legal sources to find the lower-class tenant. He appears alongside two travelling companions, in Petronius' *Satyrica* (81, 94), renting a single room that may be locked from the inside or outside. The rooms in the building are run by a procurator assisted by a staff and his family to provide rooms and cooked food to travellers as well as permanent residents. Often such places are referred to as *cauponae*, or *stabulae* – translated misleadingly as inns – but may have been formed by subdividing *atrium*-style houses. Payment in such buildings could be by the night and in advance. However, these tenants contributed to the overall profit of the middleman renting the *insula* block from the owner – the universality of such a structure of rental is proved by the presence of similar forms of lease in papyri from Egypt (see Frier 1977).

The variation in type of property to be leased was enormous. The second rental notice from Pompeii is quite different from that for the *Insula* Arriana Polliana. It is, for a start, a five-year lease of several parts of the *praedia* or property of Julia Felix, the daughter of Spurius, and it included the baths of Venus, first-floor apartments and shops with living space above (Pirson

1997: 179; see Figure 8.3). This does not exhaust the level of possible variation nor do the two notices account for all the rented property in Pompeii. They simply give two examples in the format of painted notices; other forms of rental evidence such as contracts do not survive. It is clear from legal sources that dedicated bath buildings, such as the Stabian Baths in Pompeii, were

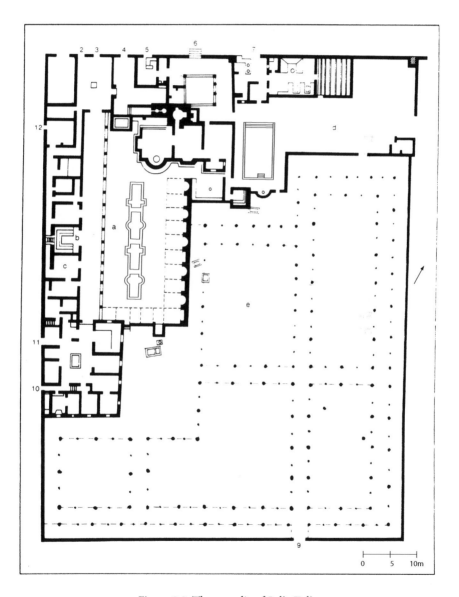

Figure 8.3 The *praedia* of Julia Felix

leased to the annually elected magistrates (aediles) to provide the citizens of the town with free bathing for the year (*Dig.* 19.2.30). This evidence suggests that large bath buildings often regarded by modern scholars as public buildings may in fact have been privately owned and profit was derived from their rental to magistrates in order to provide a service to the community.

Whenever we look at an *insula* block we need to consider its potential in terms of rental, as well as the possibility of owner-occupation. Factors that may have increased that rental were:

- the inclusion of high-class apartments (*cenacula*),
- the development of shops with living accommodation (*tabernae cum pergulis*),
- the addition of purpose-built workshops (e.g. bakeries)
- the subdivision of space to accommodate a large number of tenants in single rooms,
- the inclusion of baths for rent,
- the preservation of a large house (*domus*),
- the development of *atria*, and peristyle houses.

These seven factors were in a form of equilibrium according to: the place of the *insula* in the city – was it suitable for shops?; the nature of the rental market – was there a demand for large *domus*?; the demography of the city – was the population growing and causing a need to accommodate large numbers through the subdivision of space? It is clear from the archaeology of the major sites, such as Pompeii, that there were a variety of ways to manage urban property through the subdivision of space and the rental of that space to others (see Figure 8.1). What is clear from literary evidence, however, is that numerous people such as widows or freedmen, as well as the elite, might derive their incomes from a legacy that included the ownership of an *insula* that might form the main part of their income (*CIL* 6.10248, 29791; Petr., *Sat.* 95).

Ideology and practice

Ancient historians have traditionally been far happier reading texts than interpreting the use of space from archaeological sites or the reading of space in the city. It should be stated that until recently archaeology has not greatly concerned itself with this subject either. However, the remains from Pompeii have provided ancient historians and archaeologists with an opportunity to begin to interpret the social practice of living in the city in relationship to the statements found in the texts of writers from antiquity (see Laurence 1997). We need to understand at the outset that many of our texts (for example, Cicero's *De Officiis*) are not simply reports of the practice of urban living, but are instead recalling antiquated value systems and an ideology of the role of the elite within society (Garnsey 1976: 127). However, the elite, in many ways, were not only the owners of much property in the city but were also the managers of the public realm through their position on the *ordo* of decurions or town council or as clients of such elevated persons. Their views found in texts need not reflect what happened in the past, but demonstrate how they wished to articulate the form of the city and its material culture via language and in writing (see Moreland 2001 on the relationship of text and material culture).

The greatest problem for the discussion of life in the city is how we should view the only surviving treatise on architecture written by a single author. Vitruvius' *De Architectura* has become a source of great controversy. All today recognise that he was not simply reporting or describing the nature of, for example, the house. At this point, most scholars can take differing positions, from that of a rejection of the text altogether in favour of an understanding of houses derived exclusively from the archaeological evidence, later to be cross-referenced to Vitruvius and other literary evidence, to that of total acceptance. Wallace-Hadrill has developed an ever more sophisticated view of the role of Vitruvius that encapsulates both positions. He sees Vitruvius in the action of creating a distinctive 'Italian' architecture that is compared with the existing canon of 'Greek architecture' (Wallace-Hadrill 1997). In so doing, Vitruvius explains the nature of the Italian house form in relation to the functioning of the social institution of patronage (Wallace-Hadrill 1994: 10–11). In short, Vitruvius (6.5) argues that the common man (or client) does not need grand vestibules, *atria* and *tablina*, but a patron does. If the text of Vitruvius is aimed at the elite property owners, we see here advice on how to develop urban property for others – who might have been tenants rather than clients of architects, as some might assume. An equally important observation comes earlier in the same passage: there are those parts of the house that belong to the *familia* (the family, which includes all slaves living in the house as well) – the bedrooms, dining rooms and baths – and those rooms that are held with the *communia* or public – vestibules, covered *atria*, peristyles and other rooms of a similar nature. All might come into the latter, but only those invited could enter the rooms occupied by the *familia*. Again reading this as advice to those who own property for rent, we can see consideration of what needs to be provided for those who rent your urban properties. The communal areas open to the visitor, as Wallace-Hadrill observes in Pompeii, are defined or signified as public by the presence of elements of architecture found in buildings associated with the activities of the forum – most notably columns. The view from the door of the house – first of a covered *atrium* with columns, leading the viewer through the house (Plate 8.1) into the *tablinum* and beyond into the colonnaded peristyle to the rear – made the statement that this was a house of a man involved in the public life of the town. The space alluded to that of the forum and in a way recreated that space so that the man at home could continue to pursue his association with public life.

These syntactical associations between the public role of the elite in the forum and in their houses could, however, be appropriated by others. This

Plate 8.1 View from the *fauces* of the House of the Vettii

is demonstrated with reference to literary as well as archaeological examples such as the House of the Vettii (Figure 7.1; Plate 8.1) or more tellingly in Petronius' (*Sat.* 28–30 especially) beautiful and cruel parody, of the freedman – Trimalchio. This text creates the image of an *Augustalis* with a public role in his city attempting to demonstrate that role through the language of public architecture within his own house. What is clear here, elsewhere in literature and within the archaeological evidence from Pompeii is that freedmen consciously utilised the same language as the elite serving on the *ordo* of decurions from which all freedmen were excluded. Architecture is a social language that, as Wallace-Hadrill (1994: 60) notes, expresses ideology and aspirations better than reality, and could easily be appropriated by new citizens (freed slaves) to express their perceptions and their aspirations. This public architecture associated with the domestic setting could be developed within an existing property at great cost, acquired through the purchase of a property for sale, or simply rented for the period of time for which it was needed. The possibility of renting such a property to impress others can be found in literature (Petr., *Sat.* 124) and may have been a feature of those attempting to present themselves as aspiring to high status without incurring the expense of building in the manner of Trimalchio. Rental of a large *domus* might have been a first step towards acceptance or a domain to which the freed slave aspired.

This architectural language is prominent to all who visit Pompeii today, guided as they are to the very largest and most memorable houses. However, if we look at the distribution of public architecture statistically across all units of property we find a very different picture. Wallace-Hadrill (1994: 72–87) sampled houses in two parts of Pompeii and those of Herculaneum with a focus on the relationship between the size of a unit and its architectural format. The average size of a house (including its garden) was 271 m^2, but incorporated a vast range of sizes from the smallest shop to the largest house (see Figure 8.4). The overall distribution of units across the city was not by size, and large houses were not found significantly clustered into zones or even in specific streets. The overall pattern was one of a mixture of house sizes alongside each other. The sample was divided into four quartiles. The first broadly represented shops with a total absence of the forms of public architecture associated with the *atrium* and an average size of 25 m^2 (see Figure 8.5). The second quartile was also composed mostly of shops with back rooms and of a group of larger properties that included an *atrium*. The third quartile identified contained properties smaller than the average house size of 271 m^2 and a significant proportion (60 per cent) contained the functional characteristics of the smaller structures in the first two quartiles: shops or workshops within the structure. However, a far greater number (60 per cent) had attributes of public architecture including colonnaded gardens as well as *atria*. It is the fourth quartile that contained the largest units, and in it public architecture is prevalent, as are fully colonnaded peristyles. On average the units in this quartile contain nearly double the number of rooms of those units in

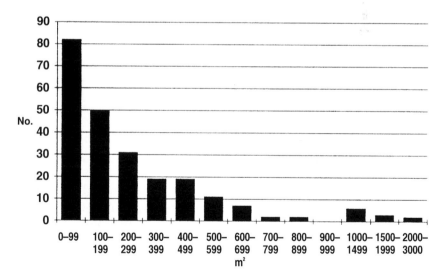

Figure 8.4 Distribution of houses in Pompeii and Herculaneum (Wallace-Hadrill 1994 samples)

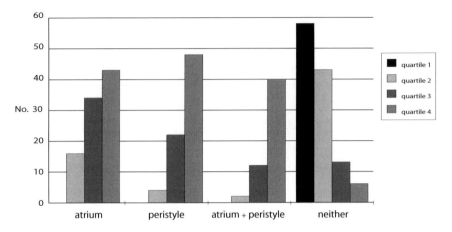

Figure 8.5 Distribution of *atria* and peristyles by quartile (from Wallace-Hadrill 1994)

the third quartile. Interestingly, a significant number of units in this quartile (19 per cent) contained large horticultural plots – the city block can include the productive countryside. The overall pattern is clear: the larger the unit, the greater the likelihood that it would contain the language of public architecture. However, it needs to be observed that this language could be utilised in units of habitation significantly smaller than the average (mean) and well below the median size of unit in the sample. The familiar large houses of the upper quartile, much studied and often visited by tourists, do not represent the experience of most living in Pompeii – their size combined with public architecture defined them as different and belonging to the world of the elite.

The relationship of even the largest houses in Pompeii and premises that were utilised for the sale of merchandise has been shown to be one that is quite distinctive and in many ways does not conform to the ideological statements made by Cicero (*De Off.*, 1.150–2) that the elite should steer clear of anything to do with retail sale. However, a cursory glance at the examples of *insula* blocks and houses in this chapter reveals a close relationship between the large houses and the smaller premises commonly referred to as shops or workshops. Wallace-Hadrill's (1994) sample of the city is again revealing (Figure 8.6). The houses that contain or were connected with a functional unit that can be identified as a shop or workshop were distributed across all the residential units regardless of size. However, it needs to be stated that there were also a large number of shops that were independent structures. There is also a tendency for workshops, e.g. bakeries, to have been located in larger premises above the lowest quartile of the sample.

Horticultural plots in the city needed considerable space generally with small houses attached to them (or in some cases without houses). This factor

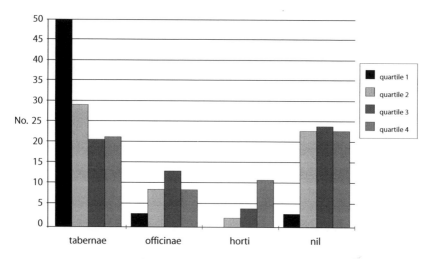

Figure 8.6 Houses with non-residential usage (from Wallace-Hadrill 1994)

places them in the higher quartiles of the sample. Those houses without any connection to retail or workshop premises are a significant number, but do not find a general pattern of greater separation from retailing and manufacture as the properties increase in size. For example, the Fullery of Stephanus on Via dell'Abbondanza was formed from a former *atrium* house to provide adequate space for the cleaning of cloth, which utilised large quantities of water, urine and ammonia (probably derived from pigeon excrement). The generation of this pattern in the sample demonstrates that the connection of a large residence with a structure that we associate with retailing was not determined according to size. Instead, it is location and economic opportunity that produce the pattern across the city that competed with the development of a large urban residence of a member of the elite. Where there was opportunity for subdivision and the rental of small units as well as larger *domus*, it was taken up.

The view of the house from the street is only one perspective of the domestic environment. When we enter today the *atrium* of a house, we feel ourselves within an empty architectural space enhanced by wall paintings of in some cases massive sophistication. It is hard to repopulate this central courtyard area of the house. This is partly due to the poverty of publication from the site in recent years and a neglect of the more mundane artefacts in the past. Penelope Allison (2004) and Joanne Berry (1997a) have sought to redress this situation through a thorough re-investigation of the day-books from the excavations preserved in the archives in Pompeii. What their work reveals is a pattern of artefact distribution that is of great complexity. But fundamentally, the house is full of material goods. Many items are simply stored in the *atrium* or the peristyle – for example wine *amphorae* are often found leaning against the corners of *atria* or empty in the *impluvium* (Berry 1997b).

Equally, even in the larger houses sampled by Allison, we find weaving and spinning taking place within the *atria* and peristyles (Allison 1997: 352–3, 2004: 146–8). This is a field where we could see development in the future. To date we have only Allison's sample of thirty *atrium* houses and Berry's sample of three *insula* blocks to guide us to conclusions that the artefact distribution reflects far more than a one:one relationship with the activities of the households that lived there. We do not know at present the distribution of artefacts across all property types across the sample of houses fundamental to Wallace-Hadrill's study. However, Allison's and Berry's studies reveal a variety of approaches to the use of artefacts within the houses of Pompeii that suggests an adaptability of the built form to a variety of types of display, segregation and functional activity. Questions remain: over what time period was this pattern of artefact distribution created? Can we determine different depths of time: between those houses only recently rented from 1 July to 24 August AD 79 to those that had contained families over several generations? What this material does reveal, however, is the level of adaptation of domestic space and the potential of such studies to identify rental property.

The House of Julius Polybius demonstrates the difficulties of interpretation of the artefacts in the context of Pompeian *insulae* (see Figure 8.7; for details of finds and discussion see Allison 1992c: 116–49). This house was associated with the decurion Gaius Julius Philippus by an internal graffito (Giordano 1974 nos 6 and 8), as well as a seal stamp with his name, and the presence of one – if not two – functioning kitchens points to active occupation by the ten victims of the eruption found in the rooms at the rear of the peristyle. However, the nature of habitation needs to be discussed. The house's façade included a shop, whose doors were found to be open, as well as the two *fauces* leading into the courtyards (A and C). In the western entrance way was found the skeleton of an equid, and the courtyards themselves revealed extensive building work being carried out with further rooms in the house utilised for the storage of building materials (Y and TT). There are also rooms that were simply empty (I, L, S and U). Penelope Allison (1992c, 2004) has suggested that these findings might suggest that the building was being 'downgraded' with the front courtyards of the house undergoing conversion to some form of 'commercial' purpose. It is difficult to posit the nature of this usage, but Allison considers the presence of a large number of *amphorae* as an indicator (it is notable that *amphorae* are not an uncommon find in *atria*). The picture of building work at the front of the house is complemented by a vista of storage. The rooms off the inner courtyard O that were not empty and out of use, apart from the kitchen, all demonstrate signs of storage whether simply shelves, or in the case of corridor R two *amphorae* and some iron nails, or the presence in room Q of a built-in cupboard containing pottery – but also a bird skeleton, iron nails, a jug and seven *amphorae*. Even sleeping and dining facilities were seemingly in storage: Room UU contained a bed in a recess and strangely a *dolia*, but was accessible only via a room (TT) that was uti-

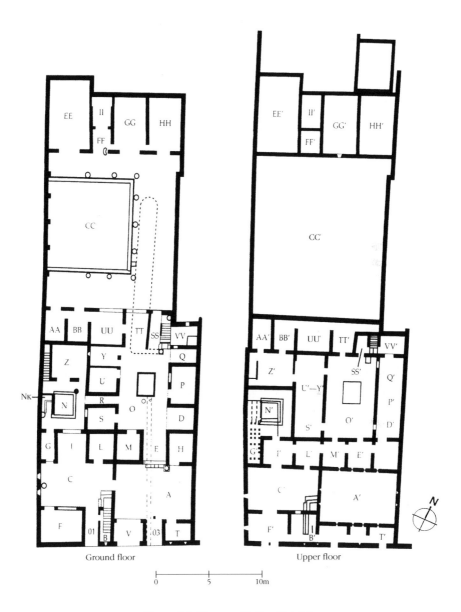

Figure 8.7 House of Julius Polybius

lised for the storage of building material. Moreover, at the rear of the house, the principal dining area (EE) contained elaborate couches alongside the storage of a bronze male statue and numerous other vessels (some of these items may have been moved here during the eruption, perhaps for safe-keeping). In contrast, the occupants of the house would seem to have been utilising

147

Room HH for eating and dining. This room and its neighbour, a storeroom, were where the skeletons were found. The picture of the upper floor contin-ues the theme of storage in most of the rooms. The question remains in terms of interpretation: how did the ten people (others may have left prior to the final phase of the eruption) found deceased occupy this building? The jour-ney of food from kitchen (in courtyard N) to dining room (HH) at the rear of the house, if marginally disrupted by the placement of two *amphorae* in cor-ridor R, was one that took food through the main areas of the house. To exit the house from the upper floors would have taken the occupants through the front half of the building undergoing some form of repair or change of use. There is the possibility that the peristyle contained the stable (BB, the open-ing to AA was blocked by a cupboard) for the equid found at the front of the house. Moreover, the five cupboards discovered in the peristyle contained an immense variety of domestic items – yet in some cases the cupboards simply contained four pottery vessels. The garden itself contained two fig and two fruit trees, as well as two other trees. The question remains whether the sum of all the elements identified in the house via attention to artefacts and their storage paints a picture of the normal or the exceptional occupation of the domestic environment. Do we go with Allison's (1992c) hypothesis that the house has been restructured for 'commercial' use, since it does not add up to the expected pattern of use we would assume for such a structure or its archi-tectural plan; or do we view this as normal and as what we should expect in terms of use based on the position of artefacts as found? In many ways, the question is unanswerable, since there is no normative pattern for comparison beyond the earthquake and eruption contexts of the Vesuvian sites. However, what the study of the finds does is to show that our assumptions based on the architectural plan or even a vision of that plan via the type of analysis utilised in Chapter 7 (or conducted by Grahame 2000) is subject to variation – wit-ness the blocking off of room BB by placing a cupboard across the opening to room AA. Moreover, the domestic environment of the city was subject to constant change in the final phase of Pompeii – building work may have been a continuous feature of urban life which affected the domestic realm. The *familia* could have been insulated from the work of construction by altering the nature of occupation of a building to facilitate both the needs of the build-ers and those of the inhabitants. Whether you could still conduct the ritual of the *salutatio* or impress diners whilst building work took place in the *atrium* is a moot point – would they be impressed by the owner's plans? However, redecoration and restoration were a fact of every building's existence in antiq-uity, and just as a hotel does not close today when the public areas are being renovated, the house in antiquity did not cease to have meaning for potential clients or *amici* due to a need for restoration.

The potential of examining the artefacts of a house in order to identify the spatial usage becomes more conclusive as we move down the social scale and towards a possible mapping of utensils with the lives of individuals in a smaller house. For example, far more objects are found in the part of the House of the Vettii associated with the service quarters than in the decorated house and statue-strewn garden. The Casa del Fabbro is a case in point, where Allison (1992: 199–211) has located finds in different rooms and there is a range of objects in all but one of the ground-floor rooms (see Figure 8.8). We might boldly suggest that the rooms of this property and their contents can be identified with individuals using those rooms. The absence of objects in Room 4 may indicate that this room was empty, perhaps even for rent. The house is entered from the street and immediately on the right is a latrine with a stairway leading to an upper floor. Finds included a hoe, an axe, a truncated *amphora* full of organic matter, bronze and pottery vessels and a bronze buckle. The next room on the right contained a cupboard without shelves, bronze vessels, a glass bottle, a hoe, a bone spoon, a large pot for washing, three glass *unguentaria*, a lamp and lampstand. Room 5 had a chest, a bronze jug, a small bronze *amphora*, an *unguentarium*, a bone awl and seven bronze needles. Now the variation from room to room may reflect a distribution of people through the house with rooms rented and the contents of each room reflecting the life of an individual. This, of course, cannot be proved and the lack of a bed (beds are very infrequent finds in Pompeii) needs to be explained away. The courtyard contains a series of four distinct cupboards with a mixture of domestic and non-domestic items that include a strigil, weights and bottles. Moving towards the rear of the house in Room 10, there was a cart, more than thirty tools and twenty hand tools and weights alongside domestic vessels. The mix of domestic vessels and professional tools is also found in Room 8. The storage of groups of tools, some identical to each other, in different parts of the house points to a number of individuals occupying the building and storing their possessions neatly in different areas of the house. They shared the kitchen and its *lararium* (11) and the dining room (9). The upper storey continued the theme of distinct assemblages associated with different rooms in the house: a wooden casket perhaps containing medical equipment, a chest containing bronze and pottery vessels, glass flasks, jewellery and coins plus an iron pick. The placement of objects in chests and cupboards, as opposed to on shelves, in distinct rooms points to a delineation of these objects as separate from each other and not to be mixed together. In other words, these are the possessions of people who are marking their ownership and ensuring that their possessions are kept separate from those of other people. Hence, I feel what we have here is a dwelling in which rooms are for rent.

Urban land value

It has become a common statement in the study of the modern city that cities are complex and difficult to understand. This chapter has sought to reveal some overall patterns to the city. In particular, rental of property has been

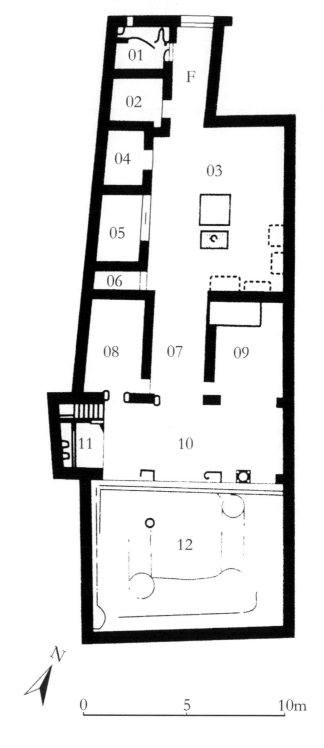

Figure 8.8 Casa del Fabbro

stressed in order to resist the tacit assumption that any or every *atrium* house was occupied by its owner and built or constructed with that owner in mind. The prominence of urban rental in legal texts and the two surviving rental notices from Pompeii suggest that this form of occupation was important, if not one of the determining characteristics of urban living. The division of *insulae* reflects a pattern of occupation that placed those with considerable space in a *domus* alongside those living in shops or workshops. Equally, any *domus* could be converted to provide workshop facilities, as in the case of the Fullery of Stephanus. Whether the owner of the property was the owner also of the production conducted here is unclear. There is the possibility or even the probability that the equipment was provided to the person renting the workshop (Bloomfield 2003: 48–9; *Dig.* 33.7.13, 33.7.15, 33.7.18, 33.7.23). Hence, we might consider rental not simply of the premises but also of the equipment it contained. Such a view of rental in the city would establish the elite as property owners and as the owners of the means of urban production. The fabric of the city also reflects the earlier histories of land division that have been studied by Salvatore Nappo (1997) with reference to the original division of *insula* blocks and their gradual mutation from the original format. Plots could be subdivided, parts joined to other properties in a constant symphony of change. What we see in Pompeii, whether in the House of Julius Polybius or in the Casa del Fabbro, is that process in action. The city is constantly being rebuilt: urban planners today see an advantage in having some derelict blocks ripe for redevelopment and it has been found in Coventry in the early modern period that a significant proportion of the houses of the city were uninhabited. For Pompeii, after the earthquake of AD 62, there may have been a greater emphasis on change and rebuilding; and those with capital may have been able to restructure the shape of the *insulae* for their benefit.

There is an overall pattern to the city of Pompeii. Streets shared a common identity that was expressed through the worship at the crossroad shrines, dedicated to the *Lares Compitales* or *Lares Augusti* (Chapter 3). There is an identifiable variation in the nature of streets in Pompeii that can be seen through the study of the intensity with which the frontages of the *insulae* were utilised (Chapters 6 and 7). Moreover, a number of side streets and a section of Via dell'Abbondanza were closed to wheeled traffic. This would suggest that some streets were far more intensively utilised than others – those leading out of or into the city via a gate were channels for traffic as well as social interaction of inhabitants and visitors. This was where the populations of the city and the countryside encountered each other. It was also where the urban inhabitants worshipped and collected their water from public fountains (not all properties were connected up to the water supply from the aqueduct). The cumulative number of functions and the intensity of use of street frontages on the streets and at the crossroads reflect the differences in use of the city. Parts of it, or in any grid of streets, would have become isolated from the major thoroughfares leading to the gates. This combination of gated wall circuit and grid of streets in most cities in Italy created or funnelled traffic and social interaction to certain key streets within the grid and isolated others from this intensity of *urbanitas*. The *insulae* of the south-east part of Pompeii converted to horticulture and viticulture were just such locations. Indeed, we might predict on the basis of the grid of streets and a wall circuit that areas within any city would become isolated from the dynamic of urbanism. This can be seen in the plans of other cities, for example Cosa or Faleri Novi. There is an almost inevitable spatial pattern for cities that have a grid and have a walled circuit under the further condition that competition to live within the walled circuit is not at its maximum. The presence in Pompeii of agricultural plots and even houses that were only partially in use points to a fragility of occupation in the final phase of the city's life. There would seem to have been a contraction of *urbanitas* from these areas isolated from city life. When viewing a city plan of *insula* blocks and walls, we can begin to predict where the greatest intensity of urbanism would occur. These observations would suggest that there were two additional factors that may have determined the level of rental of an *insula*:

- the position of the *insula* in the grid of streets and its associated circuit of walls,
- the intensity of competition for space in the city.

The first factor has already been discussed. The second needs some further elaboration. At times of population increase this competition would have increased, but it may also have been increased as a result of the disruption caused to other properties by natural disasters (fire, flood, earthquake); it should be noted that a decline in population may have been caused by the major earthquake of AD 62. In combination, these two factors explain an overall pattern of land rent across Pompeii. How that rent was extracted was in part determined by the position of a property in the grid – if at the centre, subdivision into shops with a large *domus* in the format of the *Insula* Arriana Polliana might have been a logical option; if at the edge of the grid but on the through-routes, the establishment of baths and leisure facilities focused on a garden area could be logical, as can be seen in the *praedia* of Julia Felix. Further away from the through-routes, even at the centre of town, the logic of location points to a return to horticulture or investment in viticulture as a means to gaining a return of some kind from these more peripheral urban properties (Figure 8.1). The investment was less than the full provision of a *domus*, workshops with equipment and shops found in the *Insula* Arriana Polliana, but the return in rental would also have been less. If competition for space was to speed up, these properties might have changed their usage with a view to greater profitability as the supplier reacted to the demand for accommodation. It should be noted, however, that a full understanding of this modern economic concept may not have been all-embracing. For urban densities to change, the owners of the *insula* needed to be willing to invest in subdivision and/or in the provision of more luxurious accommodation, and/or in equipment for the shops and workshops.

9

THE TEMPORAL LOGIC OF SPACE

Up to this point, the discussion has focused on space and the spatialisation of social action, whether the action of building new monuments, the collection of water from public fountains, the places of production, the provision of services, the organisation of private buildings. Now, in this chapter, attention shifts to the temporal aspect of social action, a subject that has entered into the debates and discussion by archaeologists with regard to understanding the materiality of human existence (e.g. Barrett 2004; Gosden 2004). The problem for understanding time and the temporalities in Pompeii is one of evidence. Essentially any study of time in the Roman world depends on the reading of literary evidence produced by the elite, who were mostly not born in Rome but tended to focus their attention on the temporality of the city of Rome. For example, Riggsby (2003) has demonstrated with reference to Pliny, a senator born in Como and expressing in his letters for publication the temporalities of villa and life in the city of Rome, that he utilised the same expression of temporality in both locations. What is implicit here is that the temporality of Rome was something that was shared by members of the elite across Italy and was also present in towns such as Pompeii. More importantly, in the Sulpicii Archive of legal documents discovered at Murecine, just outside the city of Pompeii, we find a convergence of the use of time whether at Rome or Puteoli on the Bay of Naples. As we shall see, the temporal framework also coincides with that found in literary texts (see Table 9.1; Camodeca 1999 for texts; Andreau 1999: 71–9 for introduction to the material). These factors justify the use of literary sources that chart the temporalities of activities in the city of Rome for our understanding of the temporal logic of space at Pompeii.

The Lund school of urban geographers developed a method for understanding human activity in both a temporal and a spatial context (Herbert and Thomas 1982: 362; Carlstein 1982: 38–64; Soja 1989; Giddens 1984; Harvey 1988). The underlying assumption of all studies of space in a temporal context is that each individual has a pattern of movement, which centres around the workplace, home, shopping and recreation. This arrangement of movement reflects personal preferences for certain types of activity, their spatial

154

Table 9.1 The use of time and place in the Sulpicii Archive

City	Place	Location	Time	Reference
Puteoli	Forum	Hordionian Altar	3rd Hour	*TPSulp*.1
Puteoli	Forum	Hordionian Altar	3rd Hour	*TPSulp*.2
Puteoli	Forum	Hordionian Altar	3rd Hour	*TPSulp*.3
Puteoli	Forum	Hordionian Altar	3rd Hour	*TPSulp*.4
Puteoli	Forum	Hordionian Altar	3rd Hour	*TPSulp*.5
Puteoli	Forum	Hordionian Altar	3rd Hour	*TPSulp*.8
Puteoli	Forum	Suettian Altar of Augustus	3rd Hour	*TPSulp*.9
Puteoli	Forum	Hordionian Altar	9th Hour	*TPSulp*.10
Capua	Forum(?)	Basilica	1st Hour	*TPSulp*.12
Rome	Forum Augustum	Statue of Gaius Sentius Saturninus	5th Hour	*TPSulp*.13
Rome	Forum Augustum	Statue of Gaius Sentius Saturninus	3rd Hour	*TPSulp*.14
Rome	Forum Augustum	Altar of Mars Ultor	4th Hour	*TPSulp*.15
Puteoli	Forum	Hordionian Altar	3rd Hour	*TPSulp*.16
Puteoli	Forum	Hordionian Altar	3rd Hour	*TPSulp*.17
Puteoli	Forum	Suettian Altar of Augustus	3rd Hour	*TPSulp*.18
Rome	Forum Augustum	Statue of Gracchus, on 1st step by 4th column	9th Hour	*TPSulp*.19
?	?	?	3rd Hour	*TPSulp*.20
Rome	Forum Augustum	Statue of Gaius Sentius Saturninus	3rd Hour	*TPSulp*.27
Puteoli		Octavian Chalcidicium	3rd to 5th Hours	*TPSulp*.35
Puteoli		Hordionian Chalcidicium	3rd to 5th Hours	*TPSulp*.36
Puteoli		Hordionian Chalcidicium	3rd to ? Hours	*TPSulp*.37
Puteoli		Hordionian Chalcidicium	3rd to ? Hours	*TPSulp*.38
Puteoli		Hordionian Chalcidicium	3rd to ? Hours	*TPSulp*.39
Puteoli	Forum	Hordionian Altar	3rd Hour	*TPSulp*.40
Puteoli	Forum	Caesonian Chalcidicum	3rd Hour	*TPSulp*.85

location, and the relative distribution and availability of these activities. Some activities have a fixed time and place, for example school. The movement to and from regular activities creates a pattern, which is dependent upon the availability of these activities in time and space (Herbert and Thomas 1982: 363). This regular pattern of availability creates a rhythmic pattern of movement, which in turn orders the urban environment. Significantly, it would appear that the temporal availability of any one activity is not independent of the temporal availability of other activities. In fact, they form 'a highly integrated and coordinated structure within which individual life patterns must be contained' (Herbert and Thomas 1982: 365).

Before we can begin to study the space–time solidarities of the Roman city, we need to understand the ancient conception and comprehension of time. It has been observed by modern historians that the Industrial Revolution altered people's conception of time from task time to clock time (Thompson 1967; see also the debate between Harrison 1986 and Landes 1987). Other variations in the conception of time can occur. For example, in a seaport time is dominated by tides (Thompson 1967: 60). Another factor is biological time, measured by eating and sleeping. There is also psychological time, associated with the amount of time spent on any one activity (Herbert and Thomas 1982: 365). Only by understanding the Roman concept and measurement of time can we begin to set up a model of space–time solidarities.

The Roman concept of time was dominated by a measurement of daylight and darkness. The primary division was between day and night (Gell. 3.2.9; Colum. 10.42; an equinox was naturally a time of equal day and night). Each day and each night were divided into twelve hours. The length of an hour varied seasonally (Ovid, *Met.* 4.199, Pont. 2.10.38; Lucan 10.218. The hour was not the sixty-minute hour of today). Balsdon (1969: 18) gives the variation of daylight in modern hours: the longest day was from 04.30 to 19.30 and the shortest day was from 07.30 to 16.30. Therefore, the length of a Roman hour would vary from summer to winter. At the winter solstice the Roman hour would have been forty-five minutes long, whereas at the summer solstice it would have been seventy-five minutes long. At the summer solstice the day was six hours longer than at the winter solstice. Figure 9.1 illustrates this variation in the day: the greatest differences appear at the extremities of the day; the central hours such as the sixth and, in particular, the seventh did not have such a wide variation. Significantly, the seventh hour began at the same point in real time, summer and winter. This was essential, because it was at the seventh hour that many activities recommenced after an hour of rest. The seasonal variation of daylight and, therefore, the length of the hours was understood, but there was no measurement of such a concept.

However, there were intricate devices for measuring time. These included accurate sundials, and water clocks which allowed for the measurement of time on cloudy days (see Gibbs 1976 on sundials; Plin., *N.H.* 7.212–15 on water clocks). Slaves were also employed to inform people of the time

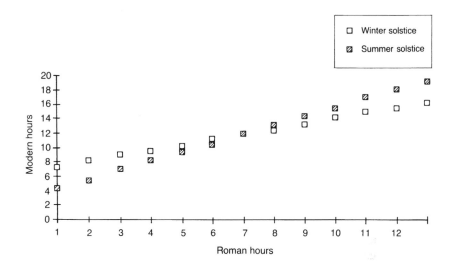

Figure 9.1 Variation in Roman time

(Juv. 10.216). Moreover, there was an understanding of time zones (Plin., *N.H.* 6.214 divides the world into time zones). This knowledge led to the development of sundials for travellers, which were adjustable according to the latitude people had reached (Plin., *N.H.* 2.182). The measurement of time varied from place to place, and so sundials were set up in public places in cities to tell travellers the local time as well (Vitr. 9.8). Pliny also noted (*N.H.* 18.133, 18.252) that in the countryside the time could be told according to the diurnal movement of the lupin. The interest in the measurement of time and the availability of timepieces in cities suggest that there was an important temporal dimension to public life and the use of space. This appreciation of time allowed for the arrangement of meetings at a certain hour of the day (Cic., *Quint.* 25; Verr. 2.2.91; Ovid, *Ars* 2.223; Sen., *Benef.* 1.23). In terms of documentation, someone's life could be measured in years, months, days and finally hours (see, e.g., *CIL* 6.2931). Thus, time was accurately measured to the hour.

Within this structure of time, the presence of certain activities or tasks was defined within the framework of 'clock' (or sundial) time. There are relatively numerous literary sources that refer to the activities of the city that were defined in this way. In Figure 9.2, the diurnal availability of activities at Rome is set out. Each activity will be examined in turn to present the temporal logic that structured the use of the city.

Public business, such as the meeting of the senate, could take place at any hour during daylight (Gell. 14.7.8). However, it should be remembered that prior to any public event the auspices needed to be observed. This would have required daylight. If the omens were bad, an activity could have been

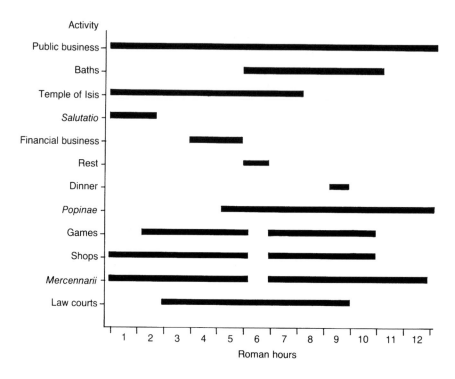

Figure 9.2 The availability of activities

delayed (see, e.g., Suet., *Nero* 8: on the announcement of Claudius' death, Nero did not go to the praetorian camp until the seventh or eighth hour, because there were bad omens). However, once public business was under way it could continue all day.

The baths appear to have been available from the sixth hour until at least the eleventh (Vitr. 10.1; Suet., *Dom.* 16.2; Juv. 11.205; Cic., *Att.* 13.52; Vitr. 5.10; Nielsen 1990: 112–38; Balsdon 1969: 28–9). In our sources bathing seems to have been preferred from the eighth hour (Nielsen 1990: 135). Martial notes that the baths were at their hottest at the sixth hour until about the eighth hour, when they began to cool down (Mart. 10.48.3). But he contrasts the patron bathing at the prime time and the client making his way to the baths late in the day.

The opening times of the temple of Isis emulated this diurnal structure. The temple opened at the first hour and closed at the eighth (Apul., *Met.* 11.20; Mart. 10.48.3), the eighth hour being the end of the public day. This might indicate a diurnal structure from the first to the eighth hour for the availability of religious worship (Solmsen 1979: 69–70 and 92).

The *salutatio* began at dawn (Hor., *Ep.* 2.1.104; Mart. 3.36, 10.70). The client in Rome might have made a long journey to visit his patron, perhaps more than two miles (Mart. 2.5). The *salutatio* would have lasted until the end of the second hour (Mart. 4.8). After the *salutatio*, the client might have followed his patron until the tenth hour (Mart. 3.36.5, 10.70). For both patron and client, the *salutatio* is expressed in terms of a task that needs to be undertaken, the duration of which was confined to the first two hours of the day. There are two conceptions of time at work here, that of the task and that of sundial (or clock) time (see also Riggsby 2003). The writer of the *Commentarium Petitionis* instructed Cicero to go down to the forum at regular times, so that people knew when he was going and they could easily follow him (*Comm. Pet.* 34, 36). This would suggest that time was widely observed by Cicero's followers and the population of the city in general. Therefore, the movement of clients to the *salutatio* and the regular movement of a patron followed by his clients to the forum created a spatial order that was temporally set to cause a senator's arrival in the forum, accompanied by some clients, by the third hour.

The courts were in session from the third hour in the forum (Mart. 4.8). The sessions could be lengthy: for example, at Milo's trial in 56 BC Pompey spoke until the sixth hour, and Clodius was still speaking at the ninth hour, when the meeting erupted in violence (Cic., *Q.F.* 2.3.2). If his patron was in court, a client would expect to be engaged until the tenth hour (Mart. 10.70; Hor., *Epist.* 1.7.46). There is here in the court-room a sense of time expressed in terms of duration (Riggsby 2003: 180–1). However, the court might be adjourned after only an hour (Mart. 8.67.1). The potential availability of court activity was between the third and tenth hours. The demands for the appearance of persons at a certain place and a certain time, found in the Sulpicii Archive, tend to place an emphasis on the third hour, in twenty documents of the twenty-five that provide a reference to time (Table 9.1). This is true of both Rome and Puteoli. However, orders could be given to appear at other hours: the first, fourth, fifth and ninth all appear. For arbitration, this was timed from the third hour to the fifth (*TPSulp.* 35–9). Other activities also began at the third hour, including the sale of slaves (*TPSulp.*85)

The fourth and fifth hours were associated with business and financial transactions (Mart. 4.8), and these were usually concluded by the sixth hour (Plu., *Q.R.* 84). The sixth hour was often associated with rest and relaxation (Mart. 4.8; Plin., *Ep.* 3.5, 9.44.2; Cels. 1.2.5; Cic., *De Orat.* 3.17). A similar siesta period can be seen in the countryside. In summer, animals would have been unyoked and flocks would be driven into the shade (Plin., *N.H.* 18.330; Mart. 3.67). Varro advised that a shelter should be erected for threshers for relaxation at the sixth hour (Varro, *R.R.* 1.51.2). There would appear to be some seasonal variation. Pliny the Younger (*Ep.* 9.44.2) had a siesta at the sixth hour in the summer, but not in the winter. In July 45 BC Cicero rested for three hours at Lanuvium on his way to Astura (Cic., *Att.* 13.34). It seems likely that much activity ceased at the sixth hour in summer for a siesta. This coincided with the time when the baths were at their hottest: the availability of the baths was designed to coincide with this rest period at midday.

Rather later, Ammianus Marcellinus (23.6.77) constructed a difference between the *urbanitas* of the Roman Empire and that of the barbarian Persians on the basis of eating habits and time. The Persians, he observed, had no fixed time for eating and their meal times were governed by their biological clock, rather than the sundial. From this remark, it is clear that the Roman conception of time structured eating habits. The hour for dinner was the ninth; dinner may have been followed by some form of entertainment, for example poetry (Mart. 4.8). However, it appears that the *popinae* were open by the fourth hour. Ampelius, city prefect in AD 371–2, gave orders that no *taberna vinaria* should open before the fourth hour. As we have seen in Chapter 5, the elite tended not to eat in public, and the *popinae* and *tabernae* were places that they did not enter (Cic., *Pis.* 13; Quinct. 6.3.63). The *popinae* might stay open all night (Juv. 8.158; Amm. Marc. 14.6.25). However, this does not imply that all *popinae* remained open, but rather that the activity of going to a *popina* was available throughout the night and most of the day.

The games began early in the morning, the crowd arriving at dawn or shortly afterwards (Suet., *Claud.* 34.2). There was a break at the sixth hour, for about an hour (Suet., *Claud.* 34.2; Dio 37.46.4). However, at *munera*, more humiliating killings continued during this hour (Suet., *Claud.* 34.2; Tert., *Apol.* 15.5; Coleman 1990). It is possible to determine the start of the games more precisely. Horace states that a theatre play would be four hours in duration (Hor., *Epist.* 2.1.189). If there was a break at the sixth hour, it would be necessary to begin the play at the second hour. The end of the games in the evening can also be deduced. The games would begin again at the seventh hour and continue for four hours until the eleventh hour.

The activity of workshops and shops began early in the morning (see Bloomfield 2003 for discussion of workshops and shops). Bakeries were open before dawn and workshops would have been open all day (Mart. 12.57). Shops appear to have opened certainly by the second hour (Plin., *N.H.* 7.182), and some stayed open until the evening, even up to the eleventh hour (Petr., *Sat.* 12; Aug., *Conf.* 3.7.13; Mart. 9.59; Hor., *Sat.* 1.6.113). However, this does not mean that all shops were open from dawn to the eleventh hour. Shops tend to be responsive to other areas of activity and open and close accordingly. For example, it is certain that the shops near the baths were open at times of activity in the baths (Sen., *Ep.* 56.1–2). At periods of inactivity in the baths, these shops may have closed.

The hired labourer (*mercennarius*) would have worked all day and was hired by the day for a set rate (Hor., *Ep.* 1.1.20; Matt. 20; see also Treggiari 1980: 51). In our sources, the *mercennarius* was associated particularly with various harvests. These naturally occurred in the longer summer days (Varro, *R.R.* 1.17). Night work was also known (Crook 1967: 196), and was made possible by artificial light. Working during the night may well have been normal in winter (Colum. 11.29.1).

In total this information, as presented in Figure 9.2, represents the temporal duration of activities in the city and surrounding countryside. Some of the activities follow on from one another (see Figure 9.3). Apart from bathing, all of these activities are associated by the elite with *negotium*. The temporalities of leisure or *otium* are not reported in the same way as either the duties of the elite, or the activities of the *plebs* in the *tabernae* and *popinae*, and by employees or slaves of the elite. The city for the elite was associated with a series of timed duties or hourly duration of tasks that ordered their

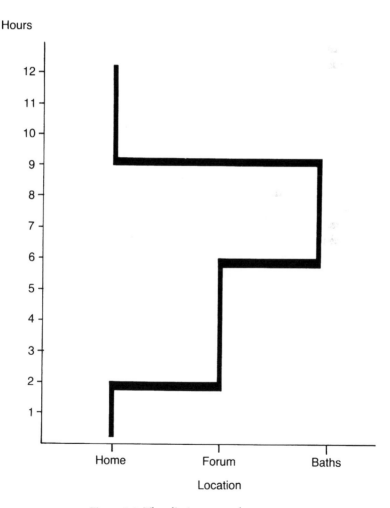

Figure 9.3 The elite's temporal sequence

days (Riggsby 2003 for discussion of the intersection of two senses of time). For example, we can posit a model of a member of the elite's temporal existence in the city. The day began with the *salutatio*. Then he left his house and went to the forum to take part in a meeting of the senate, a court case or other public business from the third hour. These activities could keep the senator or *eques* away from his house until perhaps the tenth hour, a factor which has important implications for the social structure of the households of the elite. For most of the day, the male members of the household were outside the house. Although there was no structural division of female and male space in the house (Wallace-Hadrill 1988: 50–2), there was a temporal division of this space. If the male member of the household was out from the second to the eighth or ninth hours, for half the day the house was a female space. Just as there is no expression of the temporality of male leisure in the city, there is no conception in literature of female temporalities. This may have been due to limited knowledge or the impossibility of applying a system of time based on the duration of activity either to female activities or to male *otium*. What is clear, however, is that the household space was male-dominated at the *salutatio* and at dinner at the ninth hour. Therefore, the beginning and end of the day were male-dominated, whereas the central portion of the day was female-controlled. This structural division emphasises male activity or duty outside the home, and even when male activity occurred in the home, it reflected the male world of duty and politics. In contrast, female activity was concentrated in the house and was spatially constrained. This division would produce completely different patterns of encounter for each gender. The male use of the household reflected a man's external self, as a politician and a man of duty to others. At the same time the household emphasised the external role of the male head of the household to visitors. The interior embodies the self and enhances the representation of the self at a global or city-wide level (Hillier and Hanson 1984: 260). The female self would seem not to have been represented, because it was subjugated to the external self of the *paterfamilias*. The female self was restricted in expression to the hours when the male member of the household was away for most of the day. For the elite, the spatial encounter patterns were divided by gender (see Hillier and Hanson 1984: 223–41).

To return to the male member of the elite in the forum, his day of duties or *negotium* would have been over by the sixth hour if he was not involved in public business for longer. This was the time when the baths were at their hottest (Mart. 10.48.3). If a person's leisure or *otium* commenced at the sixth hour, they could rest and then use the baths at the most desirable temperature. It is apparent that the owner of a shop or *popina* and the *mercennarii* could not utilise the baths at this point in the day, because of the need to attend to their work or business. Thus, the baths were utilised primarily by the elite from the seventh and eighth hours, when the heat was at its most desirable. It might be the case that the majority of the population did not experience hot baths, if they bathed after the tenth hour or later. When the female elite bathed is difficult to reconstruct, and in Pompeii two of the bath-houses featured segregated male and female bathing suites, which would have facilitated simultaneous male and female bathing. Others did not include segregation. It would have been possible to order male and female bathing at different times (as in *CIL* 2.5181), but there is evidence for male and female mixed bathing, suggesting that at least in Rome in the first century AD the timing of male and female bathing was congruent (see Ward 1992). For the elite, the bath was accompanied by exercise. Subsequently, they returned home or were invited to dine elsewhere at the ninth hour.

The activities or *negotium* of the elite affected the lives of others in the city and structured city space. Their pattern of movement established a routine. In the morning, they received their clients at their house; from there they went to the forum accompanied by their clients, from the forum they went to the baths, and finally they returned home. The temporal aspect of this routine articulated city space. Between the second and third hours the elite migrated to the forum, from all parts of the city. At the sixth hour, they went to the baths, unless public business delayed them, in which case they would go to the baths later, but before the tenth hour. Given the emphasis upon display, it would seem likely that the elite need not have bathed locally near their homes, but would enjoy the display of walking to baths further away. For example, the baths on the Campus Martius were not in a residential locality. At the ninth hour, there would have been a migration back to their houses for dinner. This regular pattern meant that the elite were seen at a certain time and place each day. The elite were mobile and visible outside their localities or neighbourhood. Their view of the city was one dominated by the duration of their duties: these took place in their home, and in the forum – the prime locations of elite display that largely excluded a public role for women or for males of a lower status (such as freed slaves or the plebians). The spatial separation of work and leisure was less pronounced in pre-industrial societies (Thompson 1967: 59). However, what we find in the case of the male Roman elite is that their vision of duty as a timed activity or duration is in complete contrast to their understanding of leisure. Their understanding of the city was a place of *negotium* or duty that was measured by the duration of specific events and expressed in this format. In contrast, the temporalities of work in the city for the rest of the population were expressed as a day of continuous labour, if employed by a Cato or a Columella, with the places of leisure, the shops and *popinae* open throughout the day for those who needed repose or were seen to have been idle (Laurence 1994b). It was the elite and their clients who were seen to have been mobile performing *negotium* within the city. This suggests that there were at least two sets of time operating (for the operation of contradictory sets of time see Salas 1966; Le Goff 1960): the structured day of the elite that took them away from their place of residence, and the unstructured day of the rest of the population, which was centred upon their place of residence.

The activity pattern of the elite undertaking *negotium* was contrasted to the *otium* of poets and other 'professional' writers. Horace suggested that his life was better than a senator's. His reasoning was simple: he did not have to get up early; he could lie in bed until the fourth hour, then get up and go for a walk. He might write or read something. At the sixth hour, he would go to the baths; then he would return home to his meal and idle the day away (Hor., *Sat.* 1.6.122). This alternative time scheme coincided with the elite's schedule at the baths and at dinner. This would give Horace the chance to encounter patrons from elite families.

The *otium* of the elite was described when they were outside the city in their villas. Interestingly, it is in this location that Pliny could transfer his conception of time from the city based on the duration of various forms of *negotium* to his day of *otium* (see Riggsby 2003 for discussion). Pliny (*Ep.* 9.36) says he kept to a routine when he stayed at his Tuscan villa. At the first hour he would get up; he then contemplated in the dark and called his secretary in order to dictate his thoughts. At the fourth or fifth hour, he would go outside on to the terrace and continue dictating, then he walked and read aloud or was read to by a slave. In summer, he would take a siesta at the sixth hour (*Ep.* 9.40.2); afterwards, he would walk and exercise. He then took his bath at the eighth hour and at the ninth hour had dinner with his wife and a few friends, after which they listened to a musician. Finally, he took a walk with his household slaves. This routine resembles city time: rest at the sixth hour, baths at the eighth hour and dinner at the ninth hour. However, the rest of the day remained unstructured, like Horace's day. The gender division of city time is also apparent. Contact between Pliny and his wife was only mentioned at dinner and afterwards. Country time for the elite resembled city time, except that their day was given over to *otium* and not restricted by the need to utilise the forum and transact public business.

The old had a different temporal pattern in their withdrawal from *negotium*. The senator Spurrina followed a temporal pattern of activities at his villa in the country (Plin., *Ep.* 3.1.8). He spent the first part of the morning in bed, and got up at the second hour. His first activity was a walk, whilst being read to. He then went for a drive in his chariot with his wife; after they had travelled seven miles, they walked for about a mile, and when they returned home, he studied and wrote. At the eighth hour in summer, the ninth in winter, he took his bath, and exercised by throwing a ball. Spurrina and his wife ate at the ninth hour, and at the tenth hour they watched a comedy. Again the day was structured, as in the city, around bathing and dining. The gender separation is not as great. Also, visitors, when they appeared, were controlled and restricted to the dinner hour or, if privileged, they stayed for a few days.

This rural pattern of *otium* did not exist in the towns of Italy outside Rome. Cicero visited Formiae in April 59 BC (Cic., *Att.* 2.14.2), and his activity pattern was quite different from that at Rome or the country villa. Cicero, as an ex-consul and senator, was in effect a celebrity to be seen, and in the morning many people visited him. He states that he was detained till the fourth hour, and even after that the *vulgus* continued to come. Indeed, it would appear that a senator spent his time meeting people in the towns of Italy: the arrival of a senator would disrupt the normal space–time patterning in the town. Outside Rome, a senator's space–time allocation to activities was quite different. In the towns of Italy, a greater amount of time was spent meeting people; less in a rural setting. This structure of time allocation would have affected the use of space, and the organisation of that space.

The pattern of elite space–time at Rome was coordinated around the rituals of decision making in the senate, the assembly and the law courts that were regarded as duties or *negotium* with a sundial-based duration. Similarly, the lives of the elite were dominated by the rituals associated with their role in decision making, alongside set hours for bathing and dining. There was a similar emphasis in the countryside upon bathing and eating at a set hour that should be seen as universal to elite culture across Italy, whether in town or country. For the rest of the population, including the female elite, the space–time pattern was localised in city and country, with a concentration of activity closer to their place of residence.

Can we apply this temporal framework to Pompeii? The elite in both Rome and Pompeii devoted a considerable amount of their time to public business and political decision making in the forum. The emphasis on the rituals of reception and dining in the houses of Pompeii has been stressed by a number of scholars (Wallace-Hadrill 1988; Clarke 1991). The major differences were in size and scale in the lives of the urban population in the two cities, rather than any major dissimilarities in the underlying structure of urban life. The temporal framework outlined above would appear to have been standard for most cities in Italy, which would suggest that such a temporal sequence can be applied to the spatial structure of Pompeii.

The houses of the Pompeian elite were in no way separate from those of the less privileged; they did not cluster round the forum, baths, temples or other prestigious buildings. However, there might be a logic behind the location of an elite household. This logic might not be spatial but, rather, a temporal arrangement of the elite's lifestyle. By using the example of M. Obellius Firmus, one of Caecilius Jucundus' witnesses, who had held the offices of aedile and *duumvir*, we can begin to understand the temporal dynamic that structured urban life (Jongman 1988: 207–30). At dawn, clients probably gathered at Obellius Firmus' house (9.14.4) in Via di Nola, from where they departed at the end of the second hour for the forum in procession. Presumably, Obellius Firmus spent time in the forum until the sixth hour, when he may have departed with his clients to the baths. After spending time at the baths, he returned home for dinner at the ninth hour. His life would have been structured around the need to be at a certain place at a certain time each day. A key part of elite display was the movement through the city with an entourage of clients. To fulfil this need, the place of residence needed to be a short distance from the forum; the baths needed to be a short distance from the forum and the place of residence, to create the possibility of people, going about their daily lives, seeing the passage of a member of the elite through the city. Also, for much of the day members of the elite would have been out of the house. This would cause a gender division of space in time. In the first two hours of the day the house would have been utilised by Obellius Firmus for the purpose of receiving clients. From the end of the second hour until just before the ninth hour it would be dominated by the activities of the household without the adult male presence of the *paterfamilias*. At the ninth hour, the house would revert to the role of receiving guests and emphasising the position of the *paterfamilias* in Pompeian society. Therefore, in the Pompeian house, gender divisions, which are spatially indistinct, were emphasised temporally. It is such a temporal logic of elite activity that locates the public buildings and, in particular, the public baths. Also, the need for the elite's place of residence to have been separate from the place of social activity distributed the elite throughout the city, rather than concentrating them in any one area.

However, for the majority of the population such a temporal structure did not apply. The *mercennarius* worked from dawn to dusk with a break at the sixth hour (Hor., *Ep.* 1.1.20; Matt. 20; Treggiari 1980; Varro, *R.R.* 1.17), the shops opened from dawn until the eleventh hour (Plin., *N.H.* 7.182) and the *popinae* opened from the fourth hour and might not close until late into the night (Cic., *Pis.* 13, *Quint.* 6.3.63; Juv. 8.158; Amm. Marc. 14.6.25). Thus for the rest of the population, such temporal concerns were less relevant, and it was the nature of the street structure that organised their lives spatially. For the *mercennarius*, the place of work was often his place of residence. The break for an hour at midday for rest would have punctuated the day. It should also be recognised that the pre-industrial concepts of time associated with work were far more task-orientated than our own conception of work, as we have seen in the discussion of the elite's conception of the duration of tasks that they understood as *negotium*, yet this was associated with a set number of hours per day (compare Thompson 1967). The day of the *mercennarius* would have been orientated and punctuated by the arrival of customers and deliveries, rather than the ritualised time sequences or duration of the elite's business, which was orientated towards the reception of clients, public business in the forum, bathing and dining at set times each day.

By understanding the temporal sequences of the elite, we can account for the dispersal pattern of elite houses, which needed to be separate from one another to facilitate separate processions of clients to the forum during the first and second hours. Also, the separation of the forum from the baths was important to allow further processions of the elite and their clients later in the day. Finally, the baths were located at a distance from the homes of the elite because there was a final procession from the baths home. In this context, zoning was neither desirable nor possible without restructuring the nature of elite display.

10

URBAN SPACE AND THE PRODUCTION OF ADULT CITIZENS

The previous chapter discussed the conception of time and the arrangement of space at Pompeii. Our concern in this chapter is also with temporality, in particular the transformation of the child into a citizen and the distinctive learning of the city, and the role of the spatial structure of the city in the learning of Roman citizenship. Age distinguished the way in which people utilised the city: for example, children did not bathe in the same way as adults (Celsus 1.3.32; Galen, *De Sanitate Tuenda* 1.10) because of a belief regarding the role of heat in their constitution based on the Hippocratic conception of the humours. Children were constructed as different from adults due to their age, and became a particular type of adult, a *iuvenis* or youth, on the assumption of the *toga virilis* in their mid-teens. Later, in their early to mid-twenties this phase or stage of life was seen to have passed and they were viewed as adults with few of the traits mapped on to their childhood remaining (see Harlow and Laurence 2002 for discussion). Youth was a transitional stage and can be understood as a time in which the young were free (from the constraints associated with childhood) to experience the city, and became subject to the city as a force in their own development (see Persius, *Satires* 5.30–8). In other words, at this time of life they experienced and were shaped by the institutional structure of the city and its spatial form. What we are concerned with in this chapter is how that spatial structure (and alteration to it over time) may have facilitated or hindered the development of a youth's sense of citizenship and/or *urbanitas*.

Youth was seen as a time in which the individual was faced with two paths: one leading to vice and the other to virtue (see for example Cicero, *On Duties* 1.118; Harlow and Laurence 2002: 69–71 for further discussion). The freedom to reconnoitre the city presented the youth with this challenge: after all it was Seneca's (*De vita beata* 7.3) conception of the city, as characterised by a forum as a place of virtue and the alleyways as associated with vice (Wallace-Hadrill 1995). Tacitus would later adapt this conception of urbanism to explain the adoption of the city in Britain (*Agr.* 20–2). He saw a division between the new fora, new *domus,* and the learning of Latin rhetoric as symbols of virtue, but with these urban features came others: the *porticus* (we might read palaestra), baths and elegant dining that would lead to vice. The Britons learned or adopted both the virtue and the vice associated with the Roman city; the two sides of urbanism went together and formed a conceptual whole. In a similar way to the provincials' adoption of Roman practices, the youths of the Roman city were seen to be malleable and always open to the corruption of vice (see Harlow and Laurence 2002: 69–71). The view of urbanism with its twin poles of vice and virtue is a construction of the authors in question, but, as we have seen, it can be plotted across the city. For Seneca or Tacitus, to accept urbanism as a conquered barbarian, or enter into urbanism as a young adult male, was to enter a matrix of virtue and vice. But what was also learned was a sense of identity via an induction or training in citizenship. Thus, out of the matrix of virtue and vice, citizens were produced and gained knowledge of the sense of place associated with the city of Pompeii. Hence, what we are looking at is the way in which the city's identity was transmitted from the current generation of adults into the future generation of adults, which also was a system by which citizens were produced.

Iuventus and sacred space

Iuventus was both the time of life and the name of the social institution that transformed *iuvenes* (young men) into adult citizens (Della Corte 1924: 11). The origins of the institution may lie in either the Greek *Ephebia* or the Italic *Vereiia*, which came to be translated into Latin as *Iuventus* (Della Corte 1924: 7–11; Jaczynowska 1970). This social institution was for those adults, mostly from the elite, who had just taken up the *toga virilis*, but were not yet of an age to hold a magistracy. It had a focus on the palaestra or the gymnasium (or Tacitus' *porticus*), and the building of the body for battle, as well as having a mental side that assured the development of thinking and the mental consideration of action to be taken. The institution has been found in thirty-nine cities in Italy and seventeen cities of the Western Provinces (Della Corte 1924: 11). It can be seen to have been an institution of some antiquity back into the fourth century BC (Liv. 9.25) and continued to be present in Italy into the third century AD (SHA *Gord.* 4.6). *Iuvenes* or young men of the elite were the persons who stood for the aedileship in elections and were described as *iuvenis* (e.g. *CIL* 4.317). In some cities (but unknown in Pompeii) the holding of an earlier *magister iuventutis* formed part of *cursus honorem* (Jaczynowska 1970: 268). Once in office as aediles, they would have taken care of the streets and sacred buildings of the city, and would have needed to have an understanding of the sense of identity and culture of the city. What transformed the young elite of Pompeii at the end of the first century AD was a social institution that had caused the cultural reproduction of *urbanitas* in Italy for more than four hundred years. The organisation of the institution varied from city to city, sometimes a *corpus* or a *collegium*, at others connected to divinities or *locales*. However, the name of the institution did not exclude a presence of older men as procurators, curators, patrons or fathers within these institutions, as well as a junior level of boys at a younger age attached to the institution or organisation of *iuvenes*. Such organisations of youths were led or inculcated into the culture of their city by other older men, whilst perfectly capable of articulating their identity, in the case of Pompeii, via the full-blown riotous attack on visitors from Nuceria watching the games in the local amphitheatre in AD 59 (Tac., *Ann.* 14.17 = D34; for evidence of *Iuventus* in other cities see De Ruggiero 1948–58: 4.317–20).

However, it is in the transmission of identity and understanding of sacred space that the institution may have been at its most effective. For Pompeii, the linkage between the transmission of the culture of *urbanitas* and *Iuventus* has been clearly articulated by Filippo Coarelli (2001). He suggests that the public buildings close to the Triangular Forum constituted an area of the city that was fully integrated, via the training of young men for citizenship prior to the establishment of the colony. The buildings featured in this region of the city were the temple of Isis, the temple of Aesculapius, the theatre, the Samnite Palaestra, the Republican Baths and the 'barracks of the gladiators' (see Figure 10.1). The last of these and the theatre are linked to the Triangular Forum by a ramp or monumental staircase (later altered after the earthquake of AD 62). Within the confines of the Triangular Forum itself, there was a running track, a Heroon or founder's tomb and a temple of Hercules and Minerva (de Waele 2001: 211–14 on the dedication of the temple to Minerva and 328–33 on the zone as a *Campus*). There is also another public building located in *Insula* 7.6, just outside the main entrance to the Triangular Forum from the city, as well as a set of baths in *Insula* 7.5 attested in the second century BC, known in the modern literature as the Republican Baths. The combination of features in this part of the city is rather overwhelming, but there is logic to it. Coarelli (2001) suggests that the entire complex is based around the celebration of the mythic hero Hercules, who named the city after the *pompe* or *pompa* (procession) of the cattle of Geryon that passed in triumph through the city as he led them from Spain to Greece (Solin. 2.5; Isid. 15.1.5; Mart. Cap. 6.642; Serv., *Aen.* 7.662 = A2, A3). Coarelli goes on to hypothesise (on the basis of Dion. Hal. 7.72) that the youths of Pompeii processed up the ramp from the 'gladiator barracks' to the temple of Hercules and Minerva within the Triangular Forum. The presence of the palaestrae points to the training of youth, as does the presence of a copy of the statue of Doryphorus by Polyclites in the Samnite Palaestra and the inscription on the statue base of Marcellus, the nephew of Augustus, in the Triangular Forum who is identified as patron – what is not clear from the inscription is whether Marcellus is patron of the colony or *Patronus Iuventutis* is referred to (*CIL* 10.832 = F101; Coarelli 2001: 100; Della Corte 1924: 57). In short, this was the place in Pompeii where the youth of the city trained in the shadow of the city founder: Hercules and his sanctuary complex formed by the Triangular Forum and the adjacent theatre.

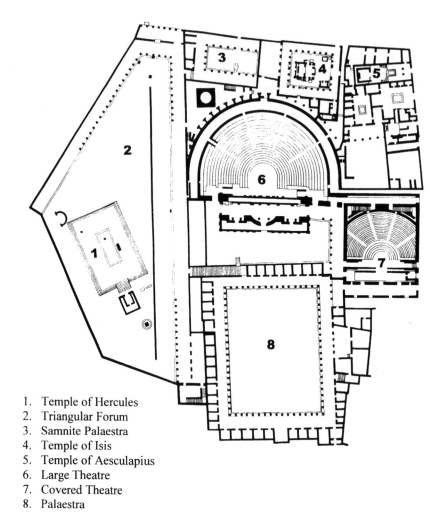

1. Temple of Hercules
2. Triangular Forum
3. Samnite Palaestra
4. Temple of Isis
5. Temple of Aesculapius
6. Large Theatre
7. Covered Theatre
8. Palaestra

Figure 10.1 The Triangular Forum and associated public buildings

It was not just the place to recall the deeds of Hercules and the foundation of Pompeii in mythology as a place of procession, but also for the young
men to develop strength of the body and an ability to endure exercise. These
exercises took place in the palaestrae and may also have included training of
the mind via philosophy and rhetoric. Other buildings followed this theme:
a set of baths in an adjacent *insula* block, as well as the area being close to
the larger Stabian Baths. There is also an emphasis on the maintenance of
health as can be seen from the presence of the temple of Aesculapius, and

votive deposits, including anatomical elements, have also been found within the Triangular Forum (D'Alessio 2001). The games and processions would have given meaning to this landscape, just as they did at other second-century BC sanctuary sites (compare Praeneste: Quilici 1980, 1989; Coarelli 1987, 1989). Importantly, this was the place in which young men were trained to become citizens, through a training for warfare and also, for the elite at least, a training for public office holding. At the heart of both of these features of youthful development was a mythology of the foundation of the city, which was integrated into the survival of the city to their present, and seen to endure in the future via the training and good health of the young men of the city.

This neatly configured and defined urban landscape of the second century BC was altered by the arrival of the colonists in the first century BC and the construction of new bath buildings, the Odeon or covered theatre, the temple of Venus and the amphitheatre. However, the institution of *Iuventus* adjusted to the new spatial arrangement. The building of the Odeon can be interpreted as enhancing the facilities around the Triangular Forum (*CIL* 10.844 = B9). However, the placement of this structure cuts off the monumental staircase leading to the Triangular Forum from direct access to the Via di Stabia (later shops were built in the palaestra of the theatre to further compromise this access). The placement of the Odeon may explain a cause of conflict between the colonists and the Pompeians over *ambulatio* (Cic., *Sull.* 60–2 = B15; Berry 1996: 254–6). There was further disruption to the institution of *Iuventus*: the new bathing complex to the north of the forum, as well as improvements to the Stabian Baths (*CIL* 10.829 = B11), both included a palaestra creating new competing centres for the training of youths. By the end of the reign of the Emperor Augustus, a swimming pool had been added to the Stabian Baths and, adjacent to the amphitheatre, a vast new palaestra incorporating the equivalent space of six *insula* blocks with a much larger swimming pool had been constructed. A response to the development of this *Grande Palaestra* may have been the construction of the baths in the adjacent Praedia Julia Felix in the mid-first century AD. The baths included well-lit (by window glass) bathing in contrast to the darker Stabian and Forum Baths. Access to the new palaestra and amphitheatre via streets leading to these new facilities was controlled: only one of the six streets leading from Via di Nocera and Via dell'Abbondanza was open to wheeled traffic – comparable to the level of access into the forum itself (Map 3.5).

The Large Palaestra and amphitheatre constituted an integrated space devoted to *otium* that was physically set aside from the traffic of the city, just as the forum constituted a landscape of *negotium* set aside from the traffic of the city's streets. If anything, the new spaces of the Large Palaestra and amphitheatre were more successfully set apart from the activities of the streets, due to the absence of water-fountains and, in consequence, the establishment of numerous *tabernae* and bars was hindered or even prevented (see Ellis 2004 for absence of bars in this region). The former civic centre of

Iuventus located around the Triangular Forum was not set aside from the traffic of the city's streets in this manner. Indeed, evidence would suggest that it was in these streets that the incidence of wheeled traffic was fairly high (Map 3.6). What we are seeing in the first century AD, after the death of Marcellus, is a spatial shift of the culture of *Iuventus* from sites adjacent to the theatres to the south-east of the city into spaces that were re-developed to create a new urban landscape of *otium* characterised by lighter and wider spaces, with the inclusion of aquatic swimming as well as the traditions of the Italian bathhouse, Greek gymnasium and gladiatorial *munera*. In this new configuration of space for the learning of *urbanitas*, the games of the theatre were still present but now detached from the central areas of youthful recreation that had shifted to the Large Palaestra, Forum Baths, Stabian Baths and those of Julia Felix. This factor is confirmed by evidence for a school-teacher working from the Large Palaestra (*CIL* 4.8562, 8565 = H45, H46). There was a change in the training given to young men, which included not just those features of the Greek gymnasium, such as javelin throwing, but also full training in beast hunting or even gladiatorial combat (Rostovtzeff 1900); the emperor Titus seems to have had a first-hand knowledge of gladiatorial combat (Suet., *Tit.* 8). The spatial shift from the Triangular Forum and theatres to the amphitheatre and Large Palaestra reflects a cultural change in the focus of the training of young men for adulthood and the incorporation of matters gladiatorial into this informal or cultural curriculum of *otium* for life. This new environment for learning for life was situated at a distance from the bars of the city and away from what the elite may have seen as a culture of pleasure or vice. It was in the new Large Palaestra that the culture of virtue in leisure or *otium* could have been enacted. Just as virtue was seen to categorise the *negotium* found in the forum, so virtue could characterise the *otium* found here in the new setting of colonnades and trees set aside from the bustle of city traffic and the culture of drinking in bars.

The amphitheatre and Large Palaestra located at the south-east of the city were spatially separated from the rest of the city through distance and also via the blocking of streets to wheeled traffic. However, in other ways, this area was integrated into the city's consciousness. Eighty-two advertisements or *edicta* alerting the population to gladiatorial shows survive right across the city. There is a greater concentration of these notices in the vicinity of the amphitheatre (fourteen), along Via dell'Abbondanza (eight), close to the forum (six) and in the palaestra to the rear of the large theatre (six). The greatest concentration of these notices was in the Porta di Nocera *necropoleis* (twenty-six), where notices were set up not just to games at Pompeii, but also to those held at Nuceria, Nola, Puteoli, Herculaneum, Cumae and Baiae (Sabbatini Tumolesi 1980 for full listing of the evidence for these notices; Cooley and Cooley 2004: 49–57). The notices did not just advertise a future event, but after that event had passed the notice continued to exist for up to twenty years. Notices to the various games of Gnaeus Alleius Nigidius Maius remained posted on walls located across the city that included the court-yard of the Forum Baths, the rear of the large theatre's *scaenae frons*, in Via della Fortuna and in Via dell'Abbondanza. Tiberius Claudius Verus' notices survived on the north side of the Large Palaestra itself, and another notice acclaimed Gnaeus Alleius Nigidius Maius here as the giver of games, and in Via della Fortuna. What is apparent from the distribution of these notices is that the activities of this area were advertised and preserved in other parts of the city. The coincidence between *Iuventus* in the Large Palaestra and the proximity of the amphitheatre did not mean the area excluded others. The survival of notices advertising games at various locations across the city points to the integration of the games into the city's identity. However, when the riot occurs in AD 59, it is the *iuvenes* of Pompeii who are seen as the ini-tiators of the ambush on the visitors from Nuceria (Tac., *Ann.* 14.17; Moeller 1970). The scene was commemorated in the famous wall painting now in the Naples Archaeological Museum (Cooley 2004: 62: D37a, D37b), but found in the peristyle of a modest house, out of sight of the casual visitor to the house (1.3.23; discussed by Clarke 2003: 152–8 = D37a, D37b). The scene of rioting did not just show the action in the amphitheatre but included in this vision of turmoil the Large Palaestra as well, and even the details of the edicts for the giving of games are legible from the northern side of the Large Palaestra (*CIL* 4.2993x, 2993y; compare actual examples *CIL* 4.7988a, 7988b, 7989a = D37, D39). In the fresco, the two buildings are bounded by the walls of the city in the background, and the trees and stalls of sellers in the foreground. The fresco celebrates the violence of the *iuvenes* of Pompeii in their triumph over their Nucerian foes, who lie being beaten on the ground. Clarke (2003: 157; follows Fröhlich 1991: 247) identifies the owner of this house as participating in the riot and celebrating the Pompeian *iuvenes'* victory (similar sentiments can be found in *CIL* 4.1293 = D38). The size of the house makes it a suitable location for a youth, living apart from his *paterfamilias* or tutor. The modesty of the house within the reading of it belonging to a young man would have contributed to his uprightness as a young man approaching the possibility of election to the *ordo* and a person who prominently rejected any form of *lux-uria*. Alternatively, the house could be read as that of an impoverished youth from the elite. The image of the riot was flanked by two images of gladiatorial fights to the death (see Clarke 2003: 155 for sketches). The unique imagery from this house attests to the integration of the Large Palaestra, amphi-theatre and riot into the domestic setting.

From home to bathhouse: learning gender and sexuality

The houses of Pompeii should in theory be a place to locate the distinctions and meanings both of male and female and of age. However, in an objec-tive or processual sense, this has been found to be impossible. Allison (2004: 155–6), working from artefact assemblages from thirty houses, found that it was not possible to identify clear gender divisions across the sample. Similarly Wallace-Hadrill (1996), working from a selection of texts and visual imagery, found the subject equally difficult, if not impossible. Of course, men and women of different ages were present in the houses of Pompeii, and we have to consider the compelling possibility that women as well as men were the owners of these houses. What we find difficult, if not impossible, is to identify gender from the surviving three-dimensional spaces and the artefacts associated with those spaces (Berry 1997a, 1997b). This does not mean that the houses are gender neutral and represent both male and female equally or not at all. The problem of reading gender in the houses of Pompeii reflects the under-theorised nature of our expectations of this type of evidence: we expect it to tell us the answer; when in fact we might be looking at an arena, the house, as a place in which the normative rules of society were formed (i.e. the house was a cultural form for the production of gender). Children were born into houses that were the spaces of a society, within which power and agency were learned (Wallace-Hadrill 1994). What surprises us, viewing these houses today, is that the images of sex were not hidden from the view of children (Wallace-Hadrill 1996). This is in contrast to the secrecy or seclusion of the *cubiculum*, the place in which sex took place (Riggsby 1997). Wallace-Hadrill has argued that the representation of male and female adults in mythological contexts, such as Pasiphae and the bull in the House of the Vettii, can be seen as part of a system of thought that categorised female chastity as a surrender to male sexual violence (Wallace-Hadrill 1996: 114, a view also developed by Koloski-Ostrow 1997; contra Elsner 1995: 62–87). Children inhabiting houses in which there is a presence of mythologised sexuality grew up with knowledge (as opposed to innocence) of normative sexual practices derived from these gendered figures in mythological settings. These images categorise and eroticise the female body as powerless and pale, in contrast to the male body as young, heroic and tanned (Wallace-Hadrill 1996: 114). The bodies of the men and women in mythological scenes tend to be those of young adults, especially if naked. The representation of the child or the old seldom takes place, or occurs as an exception to the norm (e.g. Hercules as a child). The result is the creation of an ideal, in which the active or even violent male becomes a paradigm of virtue. Other themes of wall painting, including dining, tend to focus on the youthful male and young females within the same set of visual signifiers. Although these images need not represent actual dinners or drinking sessions (Dunbabin 2003: 52–68; Clarke 2003: 223–33) they portray male and female roles at these occasions that would in turn influence the construction of gender and sexuality. What is clear from the presence and format of these paintings is that gender is present in the houses of Pompeii and, like the house itself, is active in the learning or reproduction of gender norms over time. The age of those represented in wall paintings coincides with that of first sexual encounter and can be viewed from a child's perspective as an expected future, or from a young man or woman's perspective as their current state of becoming, and from an older adult's viewpoint as a past experience. What is apparent in both these sets of domestic imagery, however, is that the gender roles, however idealised or derived from Hellenistic imagery, were ones that had resonance for viewers in the first century AD. For those males reaching adulthood or youth, the penetration of another for the first time may have been an important moment of departure from one life stage into another (Celsus 2.1.18–22). The house and its imagery may have had an important role in determining the cultural reproduction of male sexuality.

The house or home was not the only place in which sexuality was learned. The act of bathing in public, on a regular basis, was undertaken in the situation of nudity. Youths, unlike children, bathed with other adults (Celsus 1.3.32; Galen, *De Sanitate Tuenda* 1.10). The visibility of the body would have varied from bathhouse to bathhouse and we can identify a change over time (I am indebted to A. Asa Eger for discussion of sensory perception at the baths). The older bathhouses, the Forum Baths and the Stabian Baths, tended to be much darker and spatially segregated men and women, whereas the bathhouses constructed in the first century AD with the benefit of window glass, such as the incomplete Central Baths or that of Julia Felix, were not (the change can also be found in literature: Mart., *Ep.* 1.59, 2.14.11–13; and discussion by Fagan 1999: 20–1). The development and adoption of window glass in the first century AD coincides with a greater number of references to mixed bathing (Ward 1992 for texts referring to mixed bathing). The change in technology, which made people more visible, and the social change to nude bathing may go together to underline not so much a fear of the gaze in the new well-lit baths, but a fear of sexual assault in the more gloomy confines of the older baths (*CIL* 4.10678 points to how mixed bathing and sex occurred in the Suburban Baths at Herculaneum). There is clear evidence in literary texts, in particular Martial, of a mixing of ages at the baths, the nudity of the participants and the presence of both men and women, which facilitated the viewing of the young and old bodies and suggested that slave attendants of the opposite sex could have been present (Mart., *Ep.* 2.14, 2.48, 3.20, 7.35, 11.52, 11.75, 12.83; Plin., *N.H.* 29.10, 29.96, 33.153; Quint., *Inst.* 5.9.14; see Ward 1992; Fagan 1999: 24–9). The emphasis on the shaping of the male body, including the penis, in childhood only makes sense if the body was on view at the bath (see Gleason 1995: 70–3). It might be significant that the mosaics from private bath suites in three houses in Pompeii display naked male 'Ethiopian' bath attendants with erect penises (Dunbabin 1989: 43–4; Clarke 2003: 119–42). This is a fashion that Dunbabin considers to have been short-lived, but coincides with the emphases in literature of male bathers viewing the genitalia of male slave attendants and other bathers regardless of sex. In terms of age, in the previous century, fathers and sons bathed separately due to the situation of nudity (Fagan 1999: 48; Cic., *De Or.* 2.223–4, *Clu.* 141, *De Off.* 1.129; Plu., *Cat. Maj.* 20.7). The change towards a mixing of ages and genders would seem to have been a phenomenon of the first century AD, even causing Quintilian (*Inst.* 5.9.14) to discuss the possibility of an accusation of adultery against women who bathed with men, which he rejected on the same grounds that women were permitted to dine with *iuvenes* without the possibility of an accusation of adultery. The linkage to the dinner party and mention of the *iuvenes*, as opposed to men in general, is striking, since as we saw at the start of this chapter, Tacitus was to see the baths and dining as two aspects of the world of vice adopted as part of an urban package by the Britons. Equally, the *convivium* was often held in rooms with paintings of nudity and sexual suggestion, such as those from the House of the Chaste Lovers in Pompeii (Wallace-Hadrill 1996: 110). The connection between bathing and sex was made more explicit following the discovery in the 1980s of a series of scenes of sexual gymnastics in the changing rooms of the Suburban Baths. The images represent sexual intercourse between men and women, men and men, women and women, cunnilingus and other forms of sex beyond the normative sex roles found earlier in the discussion of imagery from houses in Pompeii, which emphasise an active male and a surrendering female. These have provoked a rethinking of the viewer and erotic painting. Clarke has argued that what is shown is the graphic or laughable humiliation of male sexuality that might have appealed to male and female viewers (Clarke 1998: 212–40 includes colour plates of the images). Their location high up above the alcoves for the storage of bathers' clothes created a different perspective on these images from those of sex found in houses across the city. The relatively small images at a height of well over two metres would have prevented children from examining these intricate images until they had grown to a height from which they could be seen (i.e. that of the adult viewer). At the point at which children would have achieved this height, female teenage girls might be betrothed or married, whereas teenage men would have been in a position to view the dangers of or deviance associated with uninhibited sexual congress and humiliation. The images have also been found to coincide with a type utilised to achieve arousal by Tiberius in old age (Suet., *Tib.* 43–4; Clarke 1998: 224, 234), and hence can be seen to have been included in the changing rooms of the baths to stimulate male sexual arousal prior to bathing. This might imply that men at the baths were seen with an erection, just as male bath attendants were represented with erect penises in mosaics (Clarke 1998: 120–42). The baths were a location in which the body, male or female, was on display and knowledge of normative male sexuality was learned. The representation of humorous humiliation in the changing room of the Suburban Baths enhances the normalisation of sex between men and women, and penetration by an active or erect man. Moreover, it has been argued that the Suburban Baths, like the brothel, was a location that could contain such seemingly transgressive imagery without disturbing the normative social relations such as marriage in the *domus* (Elsner 1995: 86). However, in time, these scenes were painted over and the images of transgression were removed – perhaps proving the limitations or inappropriateness of these images found uniquely in this location in this particular bathhouse in Pompeii.

The discourse of sex was also, quite literally, written across the city in public places, where it could be read. Graffiti from Pompeii that refer to sex and, in particular, the celebration of the penetrative male with female and male partners have been thoroughly catalogued (Varone 2002). There is the possibility within graffiti for women to celebrate their sexual prowess, as well as that of men. However, the dominant mode of discourse is penetration by men of others, alongside the denigration of men who had been penetrated by other men or gave pleasure to women. This is primarily a discourse on masculinity and, if read, was a means by which sexuality was celebrated or became normative. The accusations of other males being *cinaedi* or practitioners of cunnilingus or of fellatio indicate a discourse which established or assassinated the character of others in the city (it coincides with the discussion of masculinity based on literary texts, see Gleason 1995: 55–81; Corbeill 1996: 143–69; Parker 1997; Williams 1999). Sexuality, in this context, is not just about humour, but about the revelation of deviance and the delineation of normative sexual practices. The graffiti, of course, highlight sexual variation, even empowering a female voice, but by doing so this only goes further to reinforce normative practice. Hence, the reading and writing of graffiti in Pompeii would have been a form of introduction into the culture of sex for young adults, in which masculinity was constructed around penetration of women and of men. The latter were seen as wholly lacking the masculinity which was achieved by penetration. Equally, the celebration of sexual conquest indicates a culture in which masculinity and penetrative sex were linked (Varone 2002: 65–86).

To have learned the city

Numerous young men went on to become members of the *ordo* of decurions and join the elite of the city in adulthood and entered into the world of duties and *negotium*. The tomb of Gaius Vestorius Priscus (Plate 10.1) provides a vision of such a young man who had learned the city and the imagery that represented his short life curtailed by death at the age of 22. The tomb was built by his mother, Mulvia Prisca, at her own expense, on a site to the north of the Porta Vesuvio given to her by the *ordo* of decurions (Mols and Moorman 1993–4 provide a thorough description of the tomb; also *AE* 1911: 72; 1913: 70 = F88). Gaius Vestorius Priscus died young, whilst in his aedileship in AD 70–1. The tomb and its associated paintings allow us to see a representation of this young person's life. Entering the tomb, the viewer (one of his relatives) would have encountered a scene on the opposite wall of a young man, in the toga of a magistrate, entering a room that contained scrolls, writing instruments and a slave attendant (my interpretation of the role

Plate 10.1 Gaius Vestorius Priscus from his tomb outside the Porta Vesuvio

of the viewer differs from that of Clarke 2003: 187–203). On the opposite wall stood an image of a shrine and to the left was a wall painted with a large pomegranate. Moving to the viewer's right, there were scenes of a victorious Thracian gladiator standing over his vanquished foe, a banquet scene placed opposite a scene of hunting; beyond this there were images of a magistrate in a curule chair surrounded by togate figures, and on the opposite wall was a garden scene, flanked by an image of silverware displayed on a shelved table, and another image of the ingredients for a meal. Not surprisingly, these images are open to a variety of interpretations (see Mols and Moorman 1993–4). However, it is clear that the images within the tomb compound or create an overview of a young person's identity as a magistrate undertaking *negotium*, dispensing justice, perhaps, providing a gladiatorial combat and a new shrine, amid a world of *otium* seen in the garden, hunt and banquet scenes. The representation of Gaius Vestorius Priscus' life and identity within this world of *negotium* and *otium* was constructed to be viewed not by a public audience, but by his relatives and in particular his mother, who acts alone in building the tomb and hence must be considered to have been a widow – a factor underplayed by many commentators on the iconography of the images represented (e.g. Dunbabin 2003: 88). It is her son's public achievements in the male arena of competitive politics that are celebrated, and this goes some way to explaining the support of candidates by male and female *rogatores* in the *programmata* from Pompeii (Savunen 1997: 13–47; Chiavia 2002; Bernstein 1988). The presence of a representation of silverware points to a very specific meaning, rather than a generic expression of *luxuria*, and may even represent the acquisition of these prestige items by Vestorius Priscus during his lifetime. They are as much a part of the commemoration of his contribution to the world of the living as the banquet scene, the image of him surrounded by writing materials, and the garden and hunt scenes. There is a general intersection of the public world of the magistrate and the landscape of leisure. The inclusion of this display of material culture locates its parallels in the precious metal hoards from the House of the Menander and from a villa at Boscoreale (Painter 2001). Such collections of silverware, if similar to those of the House of Menander, were composed of a variety of items that varied considerably in date and were valuable in their own right. Hence, a collection of silverware in the tomb painting needs to be explained as a symbol of acquisition of wealth rather than in relation to the other painted panels. We can assume that, if a real collection, it was in the possession of Mulvia Prisca. She is also the tomb builder and the person who can be identified as the viewer of the images on the internal walls of the tomb. These images represent the achievements of her deceased son, but also reflect her own achievements as a mother introducing such a man into the world. There is also a sense of loss of her status achieved via the association with her son, whilst he was alive. The tomb and its images have replaced his presence. Her identity as a mother of a son who had achieved high status and magisterial office, whose presence was known and seen across the city, has been transformed into that of a bereaved mother, whose son will only be known in the future by this prominent tomb beyond the Porta di Vesuvio and whose *urbanitas* was revealed only to those who entered the tomb.

The freed slave and urbanism

For those sold as slaves and entering Pompeii for the first time or born into slavery, the city was learned in a different way. As Parkins (1997) has demonstrated, their knowledge or urban experience was thoroughly curtailed to a far greater extent than that of a freeborn child and their lives were restricted to service in the household. However, a question arises: how did the slave who was freed gain knowledge of urbanism? Did the spatial and institutional structure of Pompeii create a different type of citizen out of slavery in contrast to the citizen produced out of childhood? The freed slave was, of course, excluded from the *ordo* – a fact that is reflected in the exclusion of the commemoration of freed slaves, even if *Augustales* or public priests, from the forum. Moreover, it would seem that the transition into freedom from slavery was not characterised by the process associated with the institution of *Iuventus*. What would seem to have been learned was an understanding of commemoration in death via tombs that were on a grander scale and located in close proximity to the city, in contrast to those set up by the freeborn population often at a distance from the city (Mouritsen 2005). A consciousness of the imperfect learning of the symbols and signifiers of refinement or *urbanitas* is what creates amusement in the text of Petronius and the character of Trimalchio, who simply gets the signs and symbols of refinement wrong to create an absurd image of *luxuria* in his home and on his tomb (Wallace-Hadrill 1994: 3–6). Lacking an experience of *Iuventus,* both institutionally and in terms of age, these ex-slaves are seen as unable to learn the urban format and, in consequence, are excluded from office holding. In contrast, their sons will experience freedom from birth, and the ability to learn urbanism as a child and to experience *Iuventus* with the consequence that they might hold magistracies and become members of the *ordo* of decurions. This exclusion points to the importance of *Iuventus* in the learning of urbanism: freed slaves, like resident aliens, were not fully integrated into the local urban culture that reproduced citizenship through time. For them the transition into urbanism or into citizenship from slavery was only partial and was only complete in the next generation with their children born as free citizens. This is not to say that the freed slave did not have an impact on the nature of urbanism (Løs 1995). The tombs of Pompeii adequately demonstrate their adoption of the cultural symbols of the city. For example, the monument created for Gaius Munatius Faustus by his wife, Naevoleia Tyche, includes reference to the duties performed by her husband. The inclusion of a scene of togate officials making some form of distribution to people dressed in less formal attire may have referred to a distribution by him of food or to some ritual or *munera* performed by him. The very fact that the *ordo* of decurions with the consent of the citizens of Pompeii awarded him the right to a *bisellium* or honorific chair, mentioned in the inscription from the tomb and an image of it engraved on one side of the monument, identifies him as a man of *negotium* (*CIL* 10.1030 = G47). The *bisellium* was awarded for generosity (*CIL* 10.1026 = G37) and was a symbol that pointed to the wealth and ability to distribute largess. In a similar way, the prominent tombs confirmed the place of the freed slave as an individual of value to the city. Yet, the honours voted to freed slaves were transitory and they were recorded not in the forum but on the tomb of the individual in question. This confirms their acceptance into the world of *negotium,* but also their simultaneous isolation from and recognition of their *virtus* – achieved via these acts of munificence. Slavery was felt even after success during a lifetime that included duty to one's fellow citizens and, as Mouritsen (2005: 57) suggests, there was a 'distinct freedman community' within the city. There were two reasons for its existence: the freed slaves shared a common experience of slavery and transformation to citizenship (Mouritsen 2005: 57) and were inexperienced in the learning of the city via the institution of *iuventus*. Their epitaphs reflect an exclusion from the city, as well as recognition of their achievement as former slaves (Mouritsen 2005: 60). This highlights the importance of youth and the institution of *Iuventus* in the construction of the free citizen and for the acceptance into the institutions of the city of Pompeii.

11

URBANISM IN ROMAN ITALY

It has been repeatedly argued in the preceding chapters that models such as the 'consumer city' or 'service city' do not provide a full explanation of the Roman city. This chapter seeks to view the Pompeian evidence in the wider context of Roman urbanism, and to define the nature of the Roman city. Models such as the 'consumer city' rely upon the analysis of economic production. Although the city is seen as the consumer of produce from the countryside, the economic nature of consumption is never explained. Equally, the opposition of city and countryside, such a prominent aspect of these models, may not be as relevant in pre-capitalist societies (Giddens 1981: 117). However, we should not focus solely upon the economic aspect of the Roman city. David Harvey (1988: 22) sums up the problem: 'The city is manifestly a complicated thing. Part of the difficulty we experience in dealing with it can be attributed to this inherent complexity. But our problems can also be attributed to our failure to conceptualise the situation correctly.' The models used by ancient historians have oversimplified the Roman city. These models tend to be based upon Weber's explanation of the evolution of the Western city. Weber's intention was to account for the formation of the capitalist city, rather than to explain the ancient city. In any case, Weber's work has been strongly criticised by urban theorists (e.g. Saunders 1986: 28–38). The adoption of Weber's ideal types of city by ancient history was only problematised at the beginning of the twenty-first century. The debate around the consumer-city model was based upon agreement or disagreement with the propositions of Moses Finley's argument, and about whether that argument was substantiated by the ancient evidence. No theoretical debate about the nature of urbanism was conducted. Thirty years on, the consumer city can still be viewed as the best model we have, but most authors express their dissatisfaction with it (e.g. Whittaker 1990). There are other models available. These tend to be put forward by urban theorists working on the city in the modern world. However, some of their models can be applied to urbanism, capitalist or non-capitalist.

An alternative to Weber's analysis has been presented by David Harvey (1988; for a critique see Deutsche 1991; Massey 1991; Wolff 1992, to be read with Smith 1992). This should not be seen as a rejection of Weber's work but, rather, as a more sophisticated analysis of the relationship between cities and surplus. Surplus in this context is seen as being social and/or economic. Harvey (1988: 238–40) makes a series of propositions:

1   Cities are built forms created by the mobilisation and geographic concentration of significant quantities of a socially defined surplus product.
2   Urbanism represents a pattern of individual activity which forms a mode of economic and social integration that mobilises and concentrates a socially defined surplus product.
3   A surplus product of a social nature is produced by all societies, and it is always possible to create more of it. The concept of this surplus may change as conditions of consumption, production and distribution change.
4   Urbanism is more likely to occur in the following circumstances: (a) there is a large total population; (b) this population is settled and immobile; (c) there is a relatively high density of population; (d) there is potential for high productivity; (e) there is easy communication and access.
5   The mobilisation and concentration of a social surplus in cities on a permanent basis implies that the circumstances in (4) existed.
6   Urbanism necessarily arises with the emergence of a market mode of economic integration and its associated social stratification.
7   Urbanism can assume a variety of forms depending upon the particular function of the urban centre with respect to the total pattern of circulation of the socially defined social product.
8   There need not be a direct relationship between urbanism and economic growth. Urbanism is very much a social product.
9   Urbanism depends upon the geographic concentration of a social surplus. If there is no concentration of this surplus, urbanism does not occur.

Underlying all these propositions is the assumption that urbanism may be regarded as a particular form or patterning of social processes. Therefore, the city is very much a product of its society (Harvey 1988: 196). However, it is a surplus product, because the existence of a city is not a necessity to fulfil the minimum calorific requirements of a population. In Roman Italy, the social surplus was expressed via urbanism. Roman urbanism was a social form, or a way of life distinct from that of the countryside or of the barbarians outside the Roman world. It would appear that the realisation of the social surplus in the form known as urbanism was the dominant mode of social production and reproduction in the Roman Empire. However, it needs to be recognised that the city as a social product was not realised overnight. The Roman city seen at any given date was the result of earlier accumulation and production. Furthermore, the Roman city and urbanism coincided with the need for Roman society to remain stable and reproduce itself. In many ways, the city in Roman Italy was the mode of production of Roman society:

it was the centre of power, the centre of privilege, the centre of culture and the centre of knowledge (Harvey 1988: 203). Therefore, in Roman Italy, the social surplus was concentrated at one point in space, i.e. in the city (Harvey 1988: 226). This argument runs in a different direction to that of Peregrine Horden and Nicholas Purcell (2000: 91), who have stressed that, in the *longue durée*, the city becomes a location integrated into an economic network of flows of resources and goods, but they do not wish 'to show that town life is here somehow of only marginal interest' (see their discussion, 2000: 89–105). However, the desire to create cities as places of concentration in the network saves the city as a social product derived from surpluses produced, particularly in the first century AD, when Pompeii's network of connections in Italy and across the Mediterranean was at its most extensive (see De Sena and Ikäheimo 2003 for evidence). Surpluses and connectivity in Italy during the first century AD were at their apogee, as was the presence of towns across the peninsula. In terms of the *durée* of Roman urbanism, we are looking at a relatively short period in which the phenomenon is fully integrated into the connectivity of empire and, hence, we should not be deceived by the concept of a long *durée* in which the city (ancient and/or medieval) remained in the same format, deriving its existence from an unchanging source of surplus product.

Urbanism needs to be seen as a social product in time and space. It goes without saying that a city is a projection of society upon space. This is an elementary but at the same time crucial concept (Castells 1977: 115). The nature, and seeming uniformity, of Roman urbanism would have allowed anyone arriving for the first time in a city such as Pompeii to find their way to the forum, the centre of power. In this, they would have been aided by their own perception of the city and experiences of other cities (Lefebvre 1991: 162). Moreover, they would have been aided by a series of signs and an ability to comprehend them (Foucault 1984a). For example, the forum would have been found by observing the position of the tallest temple, and following the wider streets in its general direction. There would also have been subtler signs, such as the degree to which street fronts were used for commercial purposes or the number of people in the street. The stranger would also categorise people from their appearance and gestures. In doing so, the stranger would not enquire to learn more about them, but categorise them according to a series of signs (Raban 1974; Harvey 1990: 3–7). For example, the prostitute would have been immediately categorised according to her dress. This is an extreme example: others would have been perceived according to subtler signs. The stranger, in fact, would have re-created the city visited according to their own personal preconceptions of what they saw and had experienced.

This accounts for how the city was viewed, but what was the process that produced the urban form familiar to us from Pompeii? The urban fabric of Pompeii was the result of a process of accumulation. Urban history is the history of accumulation in cities. For example, the original layout of Pompeii was gradually transformed as the requirements and priorities of the inhabitants changed. However, no urban space completely vanishes without trace: 'each new addition inherits and reorganises what has gone before'; each period carries its own preconditions into the next period (Lefebvre 1991: 164). In this process we need to recognise that:

> an existing space may outlive its original purpose and its *raison d'être* which determines its forms, functions and structures; it may thus in a sense become vacant and susceptible to being diverted, reappropriated and put to a use quite different from its initial one.
>
> (Lefebvre 1991: 167)

In other words, people use a space in ways that need not coincide with the intentions of its creator, as we saw in Chapter 10 in relation to the institution of *Iuventus*. This can also be seen to result in the inscription of activities and events in the urban fabric over time. Frequently, in Pompeii, we observe the raised pavements outside houses that have been rebuilt at a higher level (see Plate 11.1). The alteration of the internal arrangement of space in the

Plate 11.1 Raised pavement outside 8.2.37

house has an effect upon external space. In this case, the internal space of the house has been transformed, but the external space of the street struggles to remain the same. The roadway has not been altered, but the pavement has been raised to allow access to the new building. This results in a greater separation between the roadway and the pavement. The street structure is different, but continues to reflect its previous reality. In this example, we see how a human intention to alter the structure of a house has caused the unintended consequence (Giddens 1984: 8) that the roadway has become separated from the pavement so that the street cannot be crossed at this point. Therefore, in the Roman city, as in all social situations, we need to remember that there were intentional actions, but unintentional consequences. Furthermore, these intentional actions took place within the existing spatial fabric of the city, which meant that any action to alter that fabric was conditioned by the ideology of those wishing to alter it. In effect, this ideology was strongly influenced by the urban surroundings into which the human actors had been born (Lefebvre 1991: 210).

When we view the public buildings of Pompeii, we begin to see the city and its inhabitants expressing what it is to be a Pompeian. The public buildings concentrated around the forum, the amphitheatre and the theatres are monuments that enshrine the *mentalité* of the ancient world. These monuments offer each individual inhabitant an image of their position in society (Lefebvre 1991: 220). The monuments of the early colony emphasised the defeat and the destruction of the community that had opposed Sulla. The settlement of Roman veterans demanded a new identity for the city, and to accompany that identity a new set of monuments that reflected the new situation. These monuments reflected the colonists' triumph and the original inhabitants' capitulation. The shift in ideology associated with the first emperor was naturally reflected in the monuments of the forum. The inhabitant of Pompeii viewed with awe the shrines associated with the imperial cult, but they could also see the proximity and relevance to their own lives of the imperial family. Once established, temples simply existed (Lefebvre 1991: 250). There was no need to problematise or consider a change for these spaces in the city: they were sacred and viewed as an enduring part of the city's existence. Indeed, the city's existence may have been bound up with the continued maintenance and re-invention of these sacred spaces. In the forum, there was a close association between the government of the city and these sacred monuments. It should come as no surprise that the position of the emperor was so prominent in the locus of the city's power, the forum. Other public buildings with an emphasis upon ritual, the theatres and the amphitheatre, were also bound up with the emperor's person. For the viewer of the games, their position in society with respect to others was made apparent. Moreover, the exclusion and regulation of those who viewed the games emphasised the inhabitant's position in the city. This is most apparent when we consider the position of women and slaves: in the amphitheatre they were excluded, whilst in the theatres they were confined to the rear. In contrast, the magistrates of the city were located closest to the place of performance. It was here that the festivals were celebrated and, by that celebration, the spaces associated with the amphitheatre and theatres were made sacred. The use of sacred space, in ritual performance, varied from city to city. Ritual could celebrate a city's history or myth, or the myths associated with particular deities who had special meaning for the inhabitants of a particular city. In its festivals, a city visualised or articulated its identity. However, overriding this unique identity of the individual city was its association with a common Roman present. This was made apparent with reference to the festivals associated with the Capitoline triad, Jupiter, Juno and Minerva, and the imperial cult. In Pompeii, the unique identity of the city was bound up with its relationship to Venus and Hercules. Often, however, it would have been impossible for the inhabitant to distinguish objectively which ritual associated them with Rome, and which expressed their uniqueness as a Pompeian. Naturally, the two were intertwined in this city in Campania that had become a Roman colony.

The city as an element distinct from the countryside is a consistent image in Western thought (Williams 1973). The inhabitants of Pompeii may well have considered themselves to be differentiated from those who lived in the countryside outside the city. The city walls, guarded by the *Lares*, defined the bounds of the city. A series of stones outside the gates marked the boundary of the city's *pomerium*. You could either be within or outside the city. The dead were buried outside the city. There was a clear symbolic division here, as well as two clearly defined spaces marked by the physical presence of the city wall. The meaning of this boundary around the city is not easy to understand. The inhabitants of the countryside regularly visited the city; equally, those living in the city may have visited the countryside and towns close by, such as Nuceria. Therefore, the boundary is permeable. The city has a close relationship to its rural hinterland in pre-industrial societies, particularly when the city does not cover a large area or have a large population. However, it would appear that cities were sacred places differentiated from the countryside. Their boundaries were sanctified; the city was a space, which excluded the dead and contained not only a population but also a mythical and historical past. It was a node in the landscape that had a series of accumulated meanings, unlike the countryside, which had few places that had a past meaningful to those travelling through it. Cities had a history, whereas the countryside had none. Myth in the countryside was associated with the taming of nature (for example, the giants, so strongly associated with Vesuvius, were defeated by Hercules, who later brought the land under cultivation: Diod. 4.21; Dio 56.21–3). Features of the landscape, for example volcanoes, also gave the countryside meaning. In contrast, the city had meaning because of the actions of its inhabitants in the past and in the present.

However, those actions included the inhabitants of the city's rural hinterland, because collective action and decision making took place in the city. The rural inhabitants also associated themselves with the city and saw themselves as part of that community. The city played a major part in their lives as the place to which produce was taken, the place at which markets were held, the place at which the major festivals were celebrated. In fact, the city cannot be removed or isolated from its rural hinterland. The people of the countryside fundamentally associated themselves with their local city, and their identity was bound up with it. They were a regular feature of the city's *durée*, at markets, festivals and other events. Their history and identity involved the city at all levels. Equally, we cannot say that the inhabitants of the city were isolated from the countryside, because the rural inhabitants were a prominent feature in the city as regular visitors. The urban inhabitant may have known these people and where they were from. Indeed, in terms of local geography, the countryside was not an alien world, but as familiar as the geography of the city. In effect, we cannot divide the city from the countryside, or the countryside from the city. They are both part of the Roman conceptual landscape.

To a certain extent, it is the way in which this conceptual landscape was used that begins to define the city. There was a structure underlying an individual's actions and use of the city. This tends to be associated with a society's spatio-temporal dialectic (Giddens 1984: 17). An individual's actions were bound up with their notions of time, when it happened, and space, where it happened. For example, a religious festival took place in the city, space, at a certain date, time. Equally, markets were held on a weekly basis in Pompeii (Storchi Marino 2000; Frayn 1993: 40; MacMullen 1970; Fentress 2005). This would have caused many people who may not have used the city otherwise to come to Pompeii on market day. For the elite, the daily cycle was dominated by the meeting of clients at the *salutatio*, followed by business in the forum, followed by bathing and finally dinner. Others may have worked from dawn to dusk with a break at midday (the sixth hour). This daily pattern would have been broken at festivals and other public holidays. However, the daily cycle of timed activities would have structured the day and the use of the city. For example, the baths were at their most desirable at the eighth hour, but only the elite had the *otium* to utilise the baths at that hour, when the majority of the urban population were still working. In contrast, at a festival, the city would have been full of people from the countryside, the urban population and the elite enjoying their free time. People used the city in different ways at festivals, compared with their normal *durée* of everyday life. Moreover, people of unequal status used the city in different ways on a daily basis. In fact, the city structured itself to allow for this: the baths were at their hottest when the elite used them at the eighth hour, but at their coolest at the tenth or later, when the *mercennarius* managed to reach them after a day's work; we might doubt whether the *mercennarius* ever found time to bathe. Therefore, the timing of activities created a distance between the elite and others. There was also a spatial aspect to how people used the city. Each action in the elite's day was separate from the previous action: they left home for the forum, from the forum they went to the baths, and from the baths they went home to dine. In contrast, the urban inhabitants worked close to their place of residence with little cause to move far beyond it.

The elite ranged further across the city and utilised its resources to their optimum advantage. However, for the majority of the population activity was confined to the locality of their place of residence. The *durée* of their lives was limited and closer to home. Seldom would they have needed to stray far to find all their daily needs. Their local identity was bound up with that of their neighbours and concentrated upon the neighbourhood shrine to the *Lares*. The provision of a public fountain in the locality may have reinforced this division of the city into a series of *locales*. These *locales* should not be seen as socially homogeneous: the inhabitants might vary in status and wealth. Members of the elite did not segregate their place of residence from the place of residence of others of lower status. Other members of the *locale* may have been *magistri vicorum* or clients of others. It should be noted that the elite may not have drawn support in the form of clients from a single locality within the city. To gain the widest support, a person would have had clients from a wide range of geographical and social locations. Clients identified with the interests of their patrons; indeed, their lives and use of the city were bound up with the actions of their patron. For example, clients could have been expected to accompany their patron until the ninth hour. However, they would still have identified with their own *locale*, where their own importance as a client of X may have added to their status. The slaves in the city may not have ventured far from the household; indeed, a slave's social action was constrained by the demands of the owner. Slaves were prominent in the household and involved in work in the household, or tasks associated with it. Their knowledge and use of the city were controlled by the needs of their owner and their household. Those slaves employed to work in bakeries, for example, were tied to a similar time schedule to that of the *mercennarius*. Therefore, the slaves' use of the city was limited by the constraints placed upon them by their owner (see examples in Columella, book 11). The use of the city by women and children is problematic given the nature of our male-orientated sources. Women who worked would have followed a structure similar to that of the male *mercennarius*. If employed in the *popinae*, they would have worked during and just before opening and just after closing. For elite females, activity may well have been centred upon the household, once the adult males had left after the *salutatio*. Women could bathe separately from men in Pompeii, in a set of baths that were on a smaller scale than those designed for men. Therefore, in the Roman city, there was a whole series of individuals using the city in different ways, at a variety of times during the day, and in different ways on certain days. This cumulative pattern of use defined the city itself. In other words, the Roman city can be defined by the way the inhabitants and visitors used it.

The spatial organisation of this pattern reflects the use of the city in its temporal framework. The forum was the centre of public activity. The major through-routes leading from the city gates to the forum were the major arteries of activity. Shops tended to be located on the through-routes. This pattern describes the strong link between the city and the countryside. Workshops were distributed throughout the city, but there was a stronger concentration of workshops in *Regio 7*, to the east of the forum. Inns tended to be located close to the city gates, or in the heart of the city to the east of the forum. The purpose-built brothels were also located in this area. In fact, the area to the east of the forum was the integrating core of the city. The network of narrow irregular streets linked the major through-routes together. The area was isolated from the residences of the elite, and in many ways, it may have been seen as morally corrupting. However, for many using the city, this area was the location of the pleasures of city life; moreover, there was a concentration of small-scale craft production in it. Much was located here that the elite found sordid, so that for them, it was important to have a house that was located upon a through-route, or one of the wider streets, such as Via di Mercurio. Their view of the city may have avoided the central area to the east of the forum. It was for the aediles to police this area of moral corruption. The elite distanced themselves from this area of the city; although the rear of some *atrium* houses backed on to this area, the *atrium* house was designed to be viewed from the *fauces*. Thus, it can be concluded that the elite structured their lives around a series of formal activities (the *salutatio*, the forum, the baths and dining). The daily routine of the rest of the population was confined to their *locale*, with forays into other parts of the city for resources and recreation unavailable in their neighbourhood. Similarly, the inhabitant of the countryside came to the city to acquire resources and recreation that they could not provide for themselves.

Economic models, such as the consumer or service city, fail to account for this complexity by reducing all social activity to its economic function. The Roman city had an important social aspect. The city in the first century AD, if not in the previous century, was a surplus product, which formed the means of Roman social reproduction; in effect, it was part of the means of production in Roman Italy. It was the place in which politics, economics, history, myth and *urbanitas* were concentrated. To discuss the Roman Empire without reference to the city is to miss the point (Horden and Purcell 2000: 89–105 argue for the integration of the city into a wider *tableau* of historical conditions). The Roman Empire was made up of cities; hence to define the city is to define Roman society. However, the city should never be viewed as isolated from the countryside or from the institutional network of Roman imperialism. In the end, we must say that the

Roman city consisted of the social actions of its inhabitants and visitors in space and time. These were inscribed upon the fabric of the city, and they accumulated to produce urban formations such as Pompeii upon the eve of its destruction in AD 79.

BIBLIOGRAPHY

AAVV (1911) *Transacations of the Town Planning Conference, London 10–15 October 1910*, London.

AAVV (1995) *Archäologie und Seismologie*, Munich.

Adam, J.-P. (1980) *Dégradation et restauration de l'architecture pompéienne*, Paris.

—— (1986) 'Osservations techniques sur les suites du séisme de 62 à Pompéi', in C. Albore Livadie (ed.) *Tremblements de Terre, Éruptions Volcaniques et Vie des Hommes dans la Campanie Antique*, Naples: 67–85.

Allison, P.M. (1992a) 'The relationship between wall-decoration and room-type in Pompeian houses: a case study of the Casa della Caccia Antica', *Journal of Roman Archaeology* 5: 235–49.

—— (1992b) 'Artefact assemblages: not "the Pompeii Premise"', in E. Herring, R. Whitehouse and J. Wilkins (eds) *Papers of the Fourth Conference of Italian Archaeology 3: New Developments in Italian Archaeology*, London: 49–56.

—— (1992c) 'The distribution of Pompeian house contents and its significance', PhD thesis, University of Sydney.

—— (1997) 'Aretefact distribution and spatial function in Pompeian houses', in B. Rawson and P. Weaver (eds) *The Roman Family in Italy: Status, Sentiment, Space*, Oxford: 321–54.

—— (2004) *Pompeian Households. An Analysis of Material Culture*, Costen Institute of Archaeology Monograph 24: Los Angeles.

—— and F.B. Sear (2002) *Casa della Caccia Antica*, Munich.

Ambrose, J. and Vergun, D. (1980) *Simplified Building Design for Wind and Earthquake Forces*, New York.

Andreau, J. (1973) 'Histoire des séismes et histoire économique: le tremblement de terre de Pompéi (62 ap.J-C.)', *Annales ESC* 28: 369–95.

—— (1974) *Les Affaires de Monsieur Jucundus*, Rome.

—— (1980) 'Pompéi: mais où sont les vétérans de Sylla?', *Revue Etudes Anciennes* 82: 183–99.

—— (1984) 'Il terremoto del 62', in F. Zevi (ed.) *Pompei 79. Raccolta per il decimo centenario dell'eruzione Vesuviana*, Naples.

—— (1999) *Banking and Business in the Roman World*, Cambridge.

Arthur, P. (1986) 'Problems of the urbanisation of Pompeii', *Antiquaries Journal* 66: 29–44.

Ashworth, W. (1965) *The Genesis of Modern Town Planning*, London.

Atkinson, D. (1914) 'A hoard of Samian ware from Pompeii', *Journal of Roman Studies* 4: 27–64.

Ayeni, B. (1979) *Concepts and Techniques in Urban Analysis*, London.

Balsdon, J.P.V.D. (1969) *Life and Leisure in Ancient Rome*, London.

Barrett, J.C. (2004) 'Temporality and the study of prehistory', in R.M. Rosen (ed.) *Time and Temporality in the Ancient World*, Philadelphia: 11–27.

Barthes, R. (1986) 'Semiology and the urban', in M. Gottdiener and A. Ph. Lagopoulos (eds) *The City and the Sign. An Introduction to Urban Semiotics*, New York: 87–98.

Beacham, J.R.C. (1991) *The Roman Theatre and its Audience*, London.

Becker, H.S. (1987) 'Outsiders', in E. Rubinstein and M.S. Wennberg (eds) *Deviance: The Interactionist Perspective*, New York.

Bernstein, F. (1988) 'Pompeian women and the *Programmata*', in R.I. Curtis (ed.) *Studia Pompeiana et Classica in Honor of Wilhelmina F. Jashemski*, New Rochelle, NY: 1–17.

Berry, D.H. (1996) *Cicero Pro P. Sulla, Edited with Introduction and Commentary*, Cambridge.

Berry, J. (1997a) 'The conditions of domestic life in Pompeii in AD 79: a case study of Houses 11 and 12, Insula 9, Region I', *Papers of the British School at Rome* 65: 103–25.

—— (1997b) 'Household artefacts: Towards a reinterpretation of Roman domestic space', in R. Laurence and A. Wallace-Hadrill (eds) (1997): 183–95.

——(1998) *Unpeeling Pompeii*, Rome.

Biundo, R. (1996) 'I rogatores nei programmata elettorali pompeiani', *Cahiers Glotz* 7: 179–88.

——(2003) 'La propaganda elettoral a Pompei: la funzione e il valore dei *progammata* nell'organizzazione della campagna', *Athenaeum* 91: 53–116.

Bloomfield, J. (2003) 'The "Tabernae" of imperial Rome: Design, function and designation', unpublished MA dissertation, University of Reading.

Boardman, P. (1978) *The Worlds of Patrick Geddes*, London.

Bonghi Jovino, M. (1984) *Ricerche à Pompei: l'insula 5 della Regio VI dalle origini al 79 d.C.*, Rome.

Bradley, M. (2002) 'It all comes out in the wash: Looking harder at the Roman *Fullonica*', *Journal of Roman Archaeology* 15: 20–44.

Buckland, W.W. (1921) *A Text-book of Roman Law from Augustus to Justinian*, Cambridge.

Bulmer, M. (1986) *Neighbours. The Work of Philip Abrams*, Cambridge.

Callendar, M.H. (1965) *Roman Amphorae*, Oxford.

Camodeca, G. (1977) 'L'ordinamento in *Regiones* e i *vici* di Puteoli', *Puteoli* 1: 62–98.

—— (1999) *Tabulae Pompeianae Sulpicorum (TPSulp.). Edizione critica dell'archivio puteolano dei Sulpicii*, Rome.

Carandini, A. (1977) *L'instrumentum domesticum di Ercolano e Pompei nella prima età imperiale*, Rome.

——(1988) *Schiavi in Italia. Gli strumenti pensanti dei Romani fra tarda Repubblica e medio Impero*, Rome.

Carlstein, T. (1982) *Time Resources, Society and Ecology. On the Capacity for Human Interaction in Space and Time. Volume 1: Preindustrial*, London.

Carocci, F., de Albentis, E., Gargiuto, M. and Pesando, F. (1990) *Le Insulae 3 e 4 della Regio VI di Pompei*, Rome.

Carroll, M. and Godden, D. (2000) 'The Sanctuary of Apollo at Pompeii: Reconsidering chronologies and excavation history', *American Journal of Archaeology* 104: 743–54.

Castells, M. (1977) *The Urban Question: A Marxist Approach*, London.

Castiglione, V., Del Franco, M. and Vitale, R. (1989) 'L'insula 8 della Regio 1: un campione d'indagine socio-economica', *Rivista di Studi Pompeiane* 3: 185–221.

Castiglione Morelli, N. (1983) 'Le lucerne della casa di Giulio Polibio à Pompei', *Bollettino dell'Associazione Internazionale Amici di Pompei* 1: 213–58.

Castrén, P. (1975) *Ordo Populusque Pompeianus. Polity and Society in Roman Pompeii*, Rome.

Cerulli Irelli, G. (1977) 'Officina di lucerne fittili à Pompei', in *L'instrumentum domesticum di Ercolani e Pompei nella prima età imperiale*, Rome: 53–72.

Champion, T.C. (1989) *Centre and Periphery. Comparative Studies in Archaeology*, London.

Cherry, G.E. (1988) *Cities and Plans. The Shaping of Britain in the Nineteenth and Twentieth Centuries*, London.

Chiaramonte Treré, C. (1986) *Nuovi contributi sulle fortificazioni Pompeiane*, Milan.

Chiavia, C. 2002. *Manifesti elettorali nella colonia romana di Pompei*, Turin.

Clarke, J.R. (1991) *The Houses of Roman Italy 100 BC–AD 250: Ritual, Space and Decoration*, Berkeley.

——(1998) *Looking at Love Making: Constructions of Sexuality in Roman Art 100 BC–AD 250*, Berkeley.

—— (2003) *Art in the Lives of Ordinary Romans: Visual Representations and Non-Elite Viewers in Italy, 100 BC–AD 315*, Berkeley.

Coarelli, F. (1980) *Roma. Guide archeologiche Laterza*, Bari.

——(1987) *I santuari del Lazio in età repubblicana*, Rome.

—— (1989) 'Il Santuario della Fortuna Primigenia. Struttura architettonica e funzioni cultuali', in B. Coari (ed.) *Urbanistica ed Architettura dell'Antica Praeneste*, Palestrina: 115–35.

——(2001) 'Il Foro Triangulare: decorazione e funzione', in P.G. Guzzo (ed.) *Pompei: Scienza e Società*, Milan, 97–107.

Cohen, B. (1980) *Deviant Street Networks: Prostitution in New York City*, Toronto.

Cohen, D. (1991) 'The Augustan law on adultery: the social and cultural context', in D.I. Kertzer and R.P. Saller (eds) *The Family in Italy from Antiquity to the Present*, New Haven: 109–26.

Cohen, S. (1985) *Visions of Social Control*, Cambridge.

Coleman, K.M. (1990) 'Fatal charades: Roman executions staged as mythological enactments', *Journal of Roman Studies* 80: 44–73.

Connolly, P. (1979) *Pompeii*, London.

Conticello, B. (1990) *Rediscovering Pompeii*, exhibition catalogue, Rome.

Cooley, A.E. (2003) *Pompeii*, London.

——and Cooley, M.G.L. (2004) *Pompeii: A Sourcebook*, London.

Corbeill, A. (1996) *Controlling Laughter: Political Humour in the Late Roman Republic*, Princeton.

Corbin, A. (1990) *Women for Hire. Prostitution and Sexuality in France after 1850*, London.

Coulton, J.J. (1987) 'Roman aqueducts in Asia Minor', in S. Macready and F.H. Thompson (eds) *Roman Architecture in the Greek World*, London.

Crawford, M.H. (1969) *Roman Republican Coin Hoards*, London.

——(1970) 'Money and exchange in the Roman world', *Journal of Roman Studies* 60: 40–8.

——(1996) *Roman Statutes*, London.

Crook, J.A. (1967) *Law and Life of Rome*, London.

Curtis, R.I. (1979) 'The garum shop of Pompeii (1.12.8)', *Cronache Pompeiane* 5: 5–23.

——(1983) 'In defense of garum', *Classical Journal* 78: 232–48.

——(1984a) 'A personalised floor mosaic from Pompeii', *American Journal of Archaeology* 88: 557–66.

——(1984b) 'The salted fish industry of Pompeii', *Archaeology* 37, 58 and 74.

——(1985) 'Product identification and advertising on Roman commercial amphorae', *Ancient Society* 16: 209–28.

——(1991) *Garum and Salsamenta. Production and Commerce in Maleria Medica*, Leiden.

Dalby, A.F. (1972) *Small Buildings in Earthquake Areas*, Watford.

D'Alessio, M.T. (2001) *Materiali votivi dal Foro Triangulare di Pompei*, Rome.

D'Ambrosio, A. and Borriello, M. (1990) *Le terrecotte figurate di Pompei*, Rome.

D'Ambrosio, A. and De Caro, S. (1983) 'La necropoli di Porta Nocera', in L. Vlad Borelli, F. Parise Badoni, O. Ferrari, A. D'Ambrosio and S. De Caro, *Un impegno per Pompei*, Milan: 23–42.

D'Arms, J.H. (1970) *Romans on the Bay of Naples. A Social and Cultural Study of the Villas and their Owners from 150 BC to AD 400*, Cambridge, Mass.

——(1981) *Commerce and Social Standing in Ancient Rome*, Cambridge.

——(1988) 'Pompeii and Rome in the Augustan Age and beyond: the eminence of the *Gens Holconia*', in R.I. Curtis (ed.) *Studia Pompeiana et Classica in Honor of Wilhelmina F. Jashemski*, New Rochelle, NY, 1: 51–74.

—— and Kopff, E.C. (1980) *The Seaborne Commerce of Ancient Rome. Studies in Archaeology and History*, published as *Memoirs of the American Academy at Rome* 36.

De Caro, S. (1974) 'Le lucerne dell'officina LVC', *Rendiconti dell'Academia di Archeologia Lettere e Belli Arti di Napoli* 49: 107–34.

——(1985) 'Nuove indagini sulle fortificazioni di Pompei', *Annali dell'Instituto Universitario Orientale di Napoli* 7: 75–114.

——(1986) *Saggi nell'area del tempio di Apollo à Pompei*, Naples.

De Felice, J. (2001) *Roman Hospitality: The Professional Women of Pompeii*, Pennsylvania.

De Franciscis, A. (1976) 'Sepolcro di M. Obellius Firmus', *Cronache Pompeiana* 2: 246–8.

Degrassi, A. (1935) 'Sui fasti di *Magisti Vici* rinvenuti in Via Marmorata', *Bullettino della Commissione Archeologia Communale di Roma* 43: 173–8.

——(1947) *Inscriptiones Italiae* 13.1, Rome.

De Haan, N. (2001) '*Si auae copia patiatur:* Pompeian private baths and the use of water', in A.O. Koloski-Ostrow (ed.) *Water Use and Hydraulics in the Roman City*, Dubuque, Iowa: 41–50

Della Corte, M. (1913) 'Il *pomerium* di Pompei', *RendLincei* 22: 261–2.

——(1924) *Iuventus*, Arpinum.

——(1928) 'Pompei-Borgo Marinaio', *Notizie degli Scavi* 369–72.

——(1939) 'Pompeii: Le inscrizioni della Grande Palestra ad occidente dell'Anfiteatro', *Notizie degli Scavi* 239–327.

——(1965) *Case ed abitanti di Pompei*, 3rd edition, Naples.

De Ruggiero, E. (1948–58) *Dizionaria Epigrafico di Antichita Romane*, Rome.

De Ruyt, C. (1983) *Macellum. Marché alimentaire des romains*, Louvain.

De Sena, E.C. and Ikäheimo, J.P. (2003) 'The supply of amphora-borne commodities and domestic pottery in Pompeii 150 BC–AD 79: preliminary evidence from the House of the Vestals', *European Journal of Archaeology* 6: 301–21.

Descœudres, J.P. (1993) 'Did some Pompeians return to their city after the eruption of Mt Vesuvius in AD 79? Observations in the House of the Coloured Capitals', in L. Franchi dell'Orto (ed.) *Ercolano 1738–1988, 250 anni di ricerca archeologica*, Rome: 165–78.

—— and Sear, F. (1987) 'The Australian expedition to Pompeii', *Rivista di Studi Pompeieane* 1: 11–36.

Deutsche, R. (1991) 'Boys Town', *Environment and Planning D: Society and Space* 9: 5–30.

De Waele, J.A.K.E. (2001) *Il tempio dorico del Foro triangolare di Pompei*, Rome.

Dixon, S. (1992) *The Roman Family*, Baltimore.

Dobbins, J.J. (1992) 'The altar in the sanctuary of the Genius of Augustus in the forum at Pompeii', *Mitteilungen des Deutschen Archaeologischen Instituts, Romische Abteilung* 99: 251–63.

——(1994) 'Problems of chronology, decoration, and urban design in the forum at Pompeii', *American Journal of Archaeology* 98: 629–94.

——(1996) 'The imperial cult building in the forum at Pompeii', in A. Small (ed.) *Subject and Ruler: The Cult of the Ruling Power in Classical Antiquity* (*Journal of Roman Archaeology Supplement* 17): 99–114.

Döhl, H. and Zanker, P. (1984) 'La scultura', in F. Zevi (ed.) *Pompei 79. Racolta per il decimo centenario dell'eruzione Vesuviana*, Naples, pp. 177–210.

Dowdall, H.C. and Adshead, S.D. (1910) 'The Town Planning Act 1909', *Town Planning Review* 1: 39–50.

Dunbabin, K. (1989) '*Baiarum grata voluptas:* pleasures and dangers of the baths', *Papers of the British School at Rome* 44: 6–46.

——(2003) *The Roman Banquet: Images of Conviviality*, Cambridge.

Duncan-Jones, R.P. (1982) *The Economy of the Roman Empire: Quantitative Studies*, Cambridge.

——(1990) *Structure and Scale in the Roman Economy*, Cambridge.

Dwyer, E. (1991) 'The Pompeian atrium house in theory and in practice', in E.K. Gazda (ed.) *Roman Art in the Private Sphere*, Ann Arbor.

Dyson, S.L. (1993) 'From new to new age archaeology: archaeological theory and classical archaeology – a 1990s perspective', *American Journal of Archaeology* 97: 195–206.

Ehrhardt, W. (1988) *Casa dell'Orso (VII 2, 44–46)*, Munich.

Ellis, S.J.R. (2004) 'The distribution of bars at Pompeii: archaeological, spatial and viewshed analyses', *Journal of Roman Archaeology* 17: 371–84.

Elsner, J. (1995) *Art and the Roman Viewer*, Cambridge.

Engels, D. (1990) *Roman Corinth. An Alternative Model for the Classical City*, Chicago.

Eschebach, H. (1973) 'Untersuchungen in den Stabianer Thermen zu Pompeji', *Mitteilungen des Deutschen Archaeologischen Instituts Römische* 80: 235–42.

—— (1979) 'Probleme der Wasserversorgung Pompejis', *Cronache Pompeiane* 5: 24–60.

——(1982) 'Die Casa di Ganimede in Pompeji VII 13, 4', *Mitteilungen des Deustschen Archaeologischen Instituts Römische* 89: 229–436.

—— and Schäfer, T. (1983) 'Die Öeffentlichen Laufbrunnen Pompejis Katalog und Beschreibung', *Bulletino di Associazione Internazionale Amici di Pompei* 1: 11–40.

Etienne, R. (1992) *Pompeii: The Day a City Died*, London.

Fagan, G.G. (1999) *Bathing in Public in the Roman World*, Ann Arbor.

Fentress, E. (2005) 'On the block: *catastae, chalcidica,* and *cryptae* in early imperial Italy', *Journal of Roman Archaeology* 18: 220–34.

Fienga, F. (1932/3) 'Esplorazione del pago marittino Pompeiana', in *Atti dell'III Congresso Nazionale di Studi Romani* 11: 172–6.

Finley, M.I. (1973) *The Ancient Economy*, London.

Fiorelli, G. (1875) *Descrizione di Pompei*, Naples.

Fishwick, D. (1995) 'The inscription of Mamia again: the cult of the *Genius Augusti* and the temple of the imperial cult on the *forum* of Pompeii', *Epigraphica* 57: 17–43.

Flambard, J.M. (1977) 'Clodius, les collèges, la plèbe et les esclaves', *Mélanges d'Archeologie et d'Histoire de l'Ecole Française de Rome* 89: 115–56.

——(1981) '*Collegia compitalicia*: phénomène associatif, cadres territoriaux et cadres civiques dans le monde Romain à l'époque républicaine', *Ktema* 6: 143–66.

Flemming, R. (1999) '*Quae corpore quaestum facit:* the sexual economy of female prostitution in the Roman Empire', *Journal of Roman Studies* 89: 38–61.

Flohr, M. (2003) '*Fullones* and Roman society: a reconsideration', *Journal of Roman Archaeology* 16: 447–50

Foucault, M. (1977) *Discipline and Punish. The Birth of the Prison*, London.

——(1984a) 'Space, knowledge and power', in P. Rabinow (ed.) *The Foucault Reader*, London, pp. 239–56.

——(1984b) *The Care of the Self. History of Sexuality*, vol. 3, London.

Franklin, J.L. (1978) 'Notes on Pompeian prosopography: *Programmatum Scriptores*', *Cronache Pompeiane* 4: 54–74.

—— (1986) 'Games and a *Lupanar*: prosopography of a neighborhood in ancient Pompeii', *Classical Journal* 81: 319–28.

—— (1987) 'Pantomimists at Pompeii: Actius Anicetus and his troupe', *American Journal of Philology* 108: 95–107.

——(1990) *Pompeii: The 'Casa del Marinaio' and its History*, Rome.

——(2001) *Pompeis Difficile Est. Studies in the Political Life of Imperial Pompeii*, Ann Arbor.

Frayn, J.M. (1993) *Markets and Fairs in Roman Italy*, Oxford.

Frederiksen, M. (1980/1) 'Puteoli e il commercio del grano in epoca romana', *Puteoli* 4–5: 5–27.

——(1984) *Campania*, Oxford.

Frier, B.W. (1977) 'The rental market in early imperial Rome', *Journal of Roman Studies* 67: 27–37.

——(1978) 'Cicero's management of his urban properties', *Classical Journal* 74: 1–6.

——(1980) *Landlords and Tenants in Imperial Rome*, Princeton.
Fröhlich, T. (1991) *Lararien- und Fassadenbilder in den Vesuvstädten: Untersuchungen zur 'Volkstümlichen' Pompejanischen Malerei*, Mainz am Rhein.
Fulford, M. and Wallace-Hadrill, A. (1999) 'Towards a history of pre-Roman Pompeii: excavations beneath the House of Amarantus', *Papers of the British School at Rome* 67: 37–144.
Gardner, J.F. (1986) *Women in Roman Law and Society*, London.
Garnsey, P. (1970) *Social Status and Legal Privilege in the Roman Empire*, Oxford.
—— (1976) 'Urban property investment', in M.I. Finley (ed.) *Studies in Roman Property*, Cambridge: 123–36.
——(1988) *Famine and the Food Supply in the Graeco-Roman World*, Cambridge.
Geddes, P. (1906) *City Development: A Report to the Carnegie Dunfermline Trust*, Edinburgh.
Gibbs, S.L. (1976) *Greek and Roman Sundials*, Berkeley.
Giddens, A. (1981) *A Contemporary Critique of Historical Materialism*, London.
——(1984) *The Constitution of Society*, Oxford.
Gigante, M. (1979) *Civiltà delle forme letterarie nell'antica Pompei*, Naples.
Giordano, C. (1974) 'Iscrizioni grafitte e dipinte nella Casa di C. Iulio Polibio', *Rendiconti dell'Accademia di Archeologia, Lettere e Belle Arti* 39: 21–8.
Gleason, M.W. (1995) *Making Men: Sophists and Self-Representation in Ancient Rome*, Princeton.
Goodie, E. (1984) *Deviant Behaviour*, Englewood Cliffs.
Gosden, C. (2004) 'Shaping life in the late prehistoric and Romano-British periods', in R.M. Rosen (ed.) *Time and Temporality in the Ancient World*, Philadelphia: 29–44.
Gradel, I. (1992) 'Mamia's dedication: emperor and genius. The imperial cult in Italy and the Genius Coloniae in Pompeii', *ARID* 20: 43–58.
——(2003) *Emperor Worship and Roman Religion*, Oxford.
Grahame, M. (2000) *Reading Space: Social Interaction and Identity in the Houses of Roman Pompeii*, BAR International Series 886, Oxford.
Gralfs, B. (1988) *Metallverarbeitende Produktionsstätten in Pompeji*, BAR International Series 433, Oxford.
Grassner, V. (1986) 'Die Kaufläden in Pompeii', unpublished dissertation, University of Vienna.
Greene, K. (1986) *The Archaeology of the Roman Economy*, London.
——(1992) *Roman Pottery*, London.
Guidoboni, E. (1989) *I terremoti prima del mille in Italia e nell'area mediterranea*, Bologna.
Hardy, D. (1991) *From Garden Cities to New Towns. Campaigning for Town and Country Planning 1899–1946*, London.
Harlow, M. and Laurence, R. (2002) *Growing Up and Growing Old in Ancient Rome*, Routledge.
Harmand, L. (1957) *Le Patronat sur les collectivités publiques*, Louvain.
Harris, W.V. (1980) 'Roman terracotta lamps: the organisation of an industry', *Journal of Roman Studies* 70: 126–45.
Harrison, M. (1986) 'The ordering of the urban environment: time, work and the occurrence of crowds 1790–1835', *Past and Present* 110: 134–68.
Harvey, D. (1988) *Social Justice and the City*, Oxford.

——(1990) *The Condition of Postmodernity*, Oxford.

Harvey, P.B. (1973) 'Socer Valgus, Valgii and C. Quinctius Valgus', in E.N. Borza and R.W. Carrubba (eds) *Classics and the Classical Tradition. Essays presented to Robert E. Dengler*, Pennsylvania: 79–94.

Haverfield, F. (1910) 'Town planning in the Roman world', in *Transactions of the Town Planning Conference, London, 10–15 October 1910*, London, RIBA.

——(1913) *Ancient Town Planning*, Oxford.

Herbert, D.T. and Thomas, C.J. (1982) *Urban Geography: A First Approach*, London.

Hermansen, G. (1978) 'The population of imperial Rome: the *regionaries*', *Historia* 27: 129–68.

——(1981) *Ostia: Aspects of City Life*, Edmonton.

Hillier, B. and Hanson, J. (1984) *The Social Logic of Space*, Cambridge.

Hopkins, K. (1978) 'Economic growth and towns in classical antiquity', in P. Abrams and E.A. Wrigley (eds) *Towns in Societies*, Cambridge, pp. 35–77.

—— (1983) *Death and Renewal. Sociological Studies in Roman History*, vol. 2, Cambridge.

Horden, P. and Purcell, N. (2000) *The Corrupting Sea: A Study of Mediterranean History*, Oxford.

Ioppolo, G. (1992) *Le Terme del Sarno a Pompei*, Rome.

Jaczynowska, M. (1970) *Les organizations des iuvenes et l'aristocratie municipale*, in *Recherches sur les structures socials dans l'antiquité classique*, Paris: 265–74.

Jansen, G.C.M. (1991) 'Water systems and sanitation in the houses of Herculaneum', *Mededelingen van het Nederlands Institut te Rome* 50: 145–66.

——(2001) 'Water pipe systems in the houses of Pompeii: distribution and use', in A.O. Koloski-Ostrow (ed.) *Water Use and Hydraulics in the Roman City*, Dubuque, Iowa: 41–50.

Jashemski, W. (1964) 'A Pompeian copa', *Classical Journal* 59: 337–49.

——(1979) *The Gardens of Pompeii*, New York.

Jones, R. and Robinson, D. (2004) 'The making of an elite house: the House of the Vestals at Pompeii', *Journal of Roman Archaeology* 17: 107–30.

Jongman, W. (1988) *The Economy and Society of Pompeii*, Amsterdam.

—— (2000) 'Wool and the textile industry of Roman Italy: a working hypothesis', in Lo Cascio (2000): 187–97.

Kampen, N. (1981) *Image and Status: Roman Working Women in Ostia*, Berlin.

Kleberg, T. (1957) *Hôtels, restaurants et cabarets dans l'antique romaine: études historiques et philologiques*, Uppsala.

Klejn, L.S. (1993) 'To separate a centaur: on the relationship of archaeology and history in Soviet tradition', *Antiquity* 67: 339–48.

Koloski-Ostrow, A.O. (1997) 'Violent stages in two Pompeian houses: imperial taste, aristocratic response and messages of male control', in A.O. Koloski-Ostrow and C.L. Lyons (eds) *Naked Truths. Women, Sexuality and Gender in Classical Art and Archaeology*, London: 243–66.

Laidlaw, A. (1985) *The First Style in Pompeii: Painting and Architecture*, Rome.

Landes, D.S. (1987) 'Ordering the urban environment: time, work and the occurrence of crowds 1790–1835', *Past and Present* 116: 192–8.

La Torre, G.F. (1988) 'Gli impianti commerciali ed artigianali nel tessuto urbano di Pompei' in L. Franchi dell'Orto (ed.) *Pompei l'informatica al servizio di una città antica*, Rome, pp. 75–102.

Laurence, R. (1991) 'The urban *vicus*: the spatial organisation of power in the Roman city', in E. Herring, R. Whitehouse and J. Wilkins (eds) *The Archaeology of Power*, vol. 1, London: 145–52.

——(1994a) *Roman Pompeii: Space and Society*, 1st edn, London.

——(1994b) 'Rumour and communication in Roman politics', *Greece and Rome* 61: 62–74.

——(1997) 'Space and text', in R. Laurence and A. Wallace-Hadrill (eds) (1997), pp. 7–14.

——(1999) *The Roads of Roman Italy: Mobility and Cultural Change*, London.

——(2004) 'The uneasy dialogue between ancient history and archaeology', in E. Sauer (ed.) *Archaeology and Ancient History*, London: 99–113.

——and A. Wallace-Hadrill (eds) (1997) *Domestic Space in the Roman World: Pompeii and beyond* (*Journal of Roman Archaeology* Suppl. 22).

Lefebvre, H. (1991) *The Production of Space*, Oxford.

Le Goff, P. (1960) 'Au moyen âge: temps de l'église et temps au marchand', *Annales ESC* 15: 417–33.

Leppmann, W. (1968) *Pompeii in Fact and Fiction*, London.

Le Roux, P. (1983) 'L'armée Romaine au quotidian: deux graffiti legionaires de Pompei et Rome', *Epigraphica* 45: 65–77.

Ling, R. (1983) 'The Insula of the Menander at Pompeii: an interim report', *Antiquaries' Journal* 63: 34–57.

——(1990) 'A stranger in town: finding the way in an ancient city', *Greece and Rome* 14: 157–70.

——(1991) 'The architecture of Pompeii', *Journal of Roman Archaeology* 4: 248–55.

——(1997) *The Insula of the Menander, Volume I: The Structures*, Oxford.

——(2005) *Pompeii: History, Life and Afterlife*, Stroud.

——and Ling, L. (2005) *The Insula of the Menander, Volume II: The Decorations*, Oxford.

Lo Cascio, E. (1996) 'Pompei dalla città sannitica alla colonia sillana: le vicende istitutionali', in M. Cébeillac-Gervasonid (ed.), *Les elites municipals de l'Italie péninsulaire des Gracques à Néron*, Naples-Rome: 111–23.

——(ed.) (2000) *Mercati permanenti e mercati periodici nel mondo romano*, Bari.

Løs, A. (1995) 'La condition sociale des affranchis privées au 1ᵉʳ siècle après J.-C.', *Annales HSS* 90: 1011–44.

Lott, J.B. (2004) *Neighbourhoods of Augustan Rome*, Cambridge.

MacDonald, W.L. (1986) *The Architecture of the Roman Empire II: An Urban Appraisal*, New Haven.

MacMullen, R. (1970) 'Market-days in the Roman Empire', *Phoenix* 24: 333–41.

Maiuri, A. (1942) *L'ultima fase edilizia di Pompei*, Rome.

——(1973) *Alla ricerca di Pompei preromana*, Naples.

Manacorda, D. (1977) 'Anfore spagnole à Pompei', *L'instrumentum domesticum di Ercolano e Pompei*, Rome: 121–34.

Mancini, G. (1935) 'Fasti consolari e censorii ed elenco di *Vicomagistri* rinvenuti in Via Marmorea', *Bullettino della Commissione Archeologia Communale di Roma* 43: 35–79

Massey, D. (1991) 'Flexible sexism', *Environment and Planning D: Society and Space* 9: 31–57.

Matthews, J. (1989) *The Roman Empire of Ammianus*, London.

Mau, A. (1899) *Pompeii: Its Life and Art*, Washington.

Mayeske, B.J.B. (1972) 'Bakeries, bakers and bread at Pompeii: a study in social and economic history', Ph.D. thesis, Maryland.

McGinn, T.A.J. (1998) *Prostitution, Sexuality and the Law in Ancient Rome*, Oxford.

—— (2002) 'Pompeian brothels and social history', *Journal of Roman Archaeology Supplement* 47: 7–46.

——(2004) *The Economy of Prostitution in the Roman World*, Ann Arbor.

Meiggs, R. (1973) *Roman Ostia*, Oxford.

Meller, H. (1990) *Patrick Geddes: Social Evolutionist and City Planner*, London.

Michel, D. (1990) *Casa dei Cei (I 6, 15)*, Munich.

Miller, M. (1992) *Raymond Unwin: Garden Cities and Town Planning*, Leicester.

Moeller, W.O. (1970) 'The riot of AD 59 at Pompeii', *Historia* 19: 84–95.

——(1975) 'The date and dedication of the building of Eumachia', *Cronache Pompeiana* 1: 232–6.

——(1976) *The Wool Trade of Ancient Pompeii*, Leiden.

Mols, S.T.A.M. and Moorman, E.M. (1993–4) '*Ex parvo crevit*. Proposta per una lettura iconografia della Tomba di Vestorius Priscus fuori Porta Vesuvio a Pompei', *Rivista di Studi Pompeiane* 6: 15–52.

Moreland, J. (2001) *Archaeology and Text*, Duckworth.

Morley, N. (1996) *Metropolis and Hinterland. The City of Rome and the Italian Economy 200 BC–AD 200*, Cambridge.

—— (1997) 'Cities in context: urban systems in Roman Italy', in H. Parkins (ed.) *Roman Urbanism: Beyond the Consumer City*, London: 42–58.

——(2000) 'Markets and marketing and the Roman elite', in Lo Cascio (2000): 212–21.

Morris, A.S. (1987) 'Mendoza. Land use in the Adobe city', in C.S. Yadav (ed.) *The Morphology of Towns*, New Delhi.

Mouritsen, H. (1988) *Elections, Magistrates and Municipal Elite. Studies in Pompeian Epigraphy*, Rome.

—— (1990) 'A note on Pompeian epigraphy and social structure', *Classica et Mediaevalia* 61: 131–49.

——(1996) 'Order and disorder in late Pompeian politics', in M. Cébeillac-Gervasonid (ed.), *Les Elites municipales de l'Italie péninsulaire des Gracques à Nérone*, Clermont Ferrand: 139–44.

—— (1999) 'Electoral campaigning in Pompeii: a reconsideration', *Athenaeum* 87: 515–23.

—— (2005) 'Freedmen and decurions: epitaphs and social history in imperial Italy', *Journal of Roman Studies* 95: 38–63.

——and Gradel, I. (1991) 'Nero in Pompeian politics: *Edicta Munerum* and imperial flaminates in late Pompeii', *Zeitschrift für Papyrologie und Epigraphik* 87: 145–55.

Mumford, L. (1961) *The City in History*, Harmondsworth.

Mustilli, D. (1950) 'Botteghe di scultori, marmorarii, bronzieri e caelatores in Pompei', in A. Maiuri (ed.) *Pompeiana*, Naples: 206–29.

Mygind, H. (1917) 'Die Wasserversorgung Pompejis', *Janus* 21: 294–351.

——(1921) 'Hygienische Verhältnisse im alten Pompeji', *Janus* 25: 251–383.

Nappo, S.C. (1988) 'Regio I Insula 20', *Rivista di Studi Pompeiane* 2: 186–92.

——(1991) 'Fregio dipinto dal praedium di Giulia Felice con rappresentazione del foro di Pompei', *Rivista di Studi Pompeiani* 3 (1989): 79–96.

——(1996) 'L'impianto idrico a Pompei nel 79 d.C.: nuovi dati', in N. de Haan and G.C.M. Jansen (eds) *Cura Aquarum in Campania* (Babesch suppl. 4), Leiden: 37–45.

—— (1997) 'The urban transformation of domestic space in Hellenistic Pompeii', in Laurence and Wallace-Hadrill (eds) (1997): 91–120.

Nielsen, I. (1990) *Thermae et Balnea. The Architecture and Cultural History of Roman Public Baths*, Aarhus.

Nippel, W. (1984) 'Policing Rome', *Journal of Roman Studies* 74: 20–30.

Nishida, Y. (1991) 'Measuring structures in Pompeii', *Opuscula Pompeiana* 1: 91–102.

Nishida, Y. and Hori, Y. (1992) 'The investigations of *Regio* VII *Insula* 12', *Opuscula Pompeiana* 2: 48–72.

Ostrow, A.K. (1990) *The Sarno Bath Complex*, Rome.

Owens, E.J. (1989) 'Roman town planning', in I.M. Barton (ed.) *Roman Public Buildings*, Exeter, pp. 7–30.

—— (1991) *The City in the Greek and Roman World*, London.

Packer, J.E. (1971) *The Insulae of Imperial Ostia*, published as Memoirs of the American Academy at Rome 31.

—— (1978) 'Inns at Pompeii: a short survey', *Cronache Pompeiane* 4: 5–53.

Painter, K.S. (2001) *The Insula of the Menander at Pompeii, Volume IV: The Silver Treasure*, Oxford.

Panella, C. (1974/5) 'Per uno studio delle anfore di Pompei. Le forme 8 e 10 della tipologia di R. Schoene', *Studi Miscellanei* 22: 149–62.

—— (1981) 'La distribuzione e i mercati', in A. Giardina and A. Schiavone (eds) *Società Romana e Produzione Schiavistica*, vol. 2, Bari: 55–80.

—— and Fano, M. (1974/5) 'Le anfore con anse bifide conservate a Pompei, contributo ad uno loro classificazione', in G. Vallet (ed.) *Méthodes classiques et méthodes formelles dans l'étude des amphores*, Rome, pp. 133–77.

—— and Tchernia, A. (2002) 'Agricultural products transported in Amphorae: oil and wine', in W. Scheidel and S. von Reden (eds) *The Ancient Economy*, Edinburgh: 173–89.

Parker, H.N. (1997) 'The teratogenic grid', in M.B. Skinner and J.P. Hallett (eds) *Roman Sexualities*, Princeton: 47–65.

Parkins, H. (1997) *Roman Urbanism: Beyond the Consumer City*, London

—— and Smith, C. (1998) *Trade, Traders and the Ancient City*, London.

Paterson, J. (1998) 'Trade and traders in the Roman world: scale, structure and organisation', in Parkins and Smith (1998): 149–67.

Peacock, D.P.S. (1977) 'Pompeian Red Ware', in D.P.S. Peacock (ed.) *Pottery and Early Commerce: Characterisation and Trade in Roman and Later Ceramics*, London: 147–62.

—— (1980) 'The Roman millstone trade: a petrological sketch', *World Archaeology* 12: 43–53.

—— (1982) *Pottery in the Roman World: An Ethnoarchaeological Approach*, London.

—— (1986) 'The production of millstones near Orvieto, Umbria, Italy', *Antiquaries Journal* 66: 45–51.

—— (1989) 'The mills of Pompeii', *Antiquity* 63: 205–14.

—— and Williams, D.F. (1986) *Amphorae and the Roman Economy*, London.

Pelling, M. (1978) *Cholera, Fever and English Medicine 1825–1865*, Oxford.

Peters, W.J.J. (1993) *La casa di Marcus Lucretius Fronto à Pompei e le sue pitture*, Amsterdam.

Pirson, F. (1997) 'Rented accommodation at Pompeii: the evidence of the *Insula Arriana Polliana* VI 6', in R. Laurence and A. Wallace-Hadrill (eds) (1997): 165–82.

Poccetti, P. (1979) *Nuovi documenti italici: a complemento del Manuale di E. Vetter*, Pisa.

Porteous, J.D. (1977) *Environment and Behavior: Planning and Everyday Urban Life*, Reading, Mass.

Pucci, G. (1977) 'Le terre sigillate Italiche, Galliche e Orientali', in *L'instrumentum domesticum di Ercolano e Pompei nella prima età imperiale*, Rome: 9–22.

——(1981) 'La ceramica Italica (terra sigillata)', in A. Giardina and A. Schiavone (eds) *Società Romana e Produzione Schiavistica*, vol. 2, Bari: 99–122.

Quilici, L. (1980) 'L'impianto urbanistico della città bassa di Palestrina', *Romische Mitteilungen* 87: 171–214.

——(1989) 'La struttura della città inferiore dei Praeneste', in B. Coari (ed.) *Urbanistica ed Architettura dell'Antica Praeneste*, Palestrina: 49–67.

Raban, J. (1974) *Soft City*, London.

Raper, R.A. (1977) 'The analysis of the urban structure of Pompeii: a sociological study of land use', in D. Clarke (ed.) *Spatial Archaeology*, London, pp. 189–221.

Rawson, E. (1985) 'Theatrical life in Republican Rome and Italy', *Papers of the British School at Rome* 81: 97–113.

——(1987) '*Discrimina Ordinum*: the Lex Julia Theatralis', *Papers of the British School at Rome* 55: 83–114.

Richardson, L. (1974) 'The archaic Doric temple of Pompeii', *La Parola del Passato* 29: 281–90.

——(1978) 'Concordia and Concordia Augusta: Rome and Pompeii', *La Parola del Passato* 33: 260–72.

——(1982) 'The city-plan of Pompeii', in *La regione sotterrata dal Vesuvio: atti de convegno internazionale 11–15 Novembre 1979*, Naples: 341–51.

——(1988) *Pompeii. An Architectural History*, Baltimore.

Rickman, G. (1980) *The Corn Supply of Rome*, Oxford.

Riggsby, A.M. (1997) 'Private and public in Roman culture: the case of the *Cubiculum*', *Journal of Roman Archaeology* 10: 36–56.

——(2003) 'Pliny in space (and time)', *Arethusa* 36: 167–86 and 255–62.

Robinson, O. (1991) *Ancient Rome. City Planning and Administration*, London.

Rodriguez-Almeida, E. (1980) *Forma Urbis Marmorea: aggiornamento generale*, Rome.

Rossi, A. (1982) *Architecture and the City*, Cambridge, Mass.

Rostovtzeff, M. (1900) 'Pinnirapus Iuvenum', *Romische Mittheilungen* 15: 223–8.

——(1957) *Social and Economic History of the Roman Empire*, Oxford.

Rousselle, A. (1992) 'Body politics in ancient Rome', in P. Schmitt Pantel (ed.) *A History of Women in the West I: From Ancient Goddesses to Christian Saints*, London: 296–336.

Rubington, E. and Wennberg, M.S. (1987) *Deviance: The Interactionist Perspective*, New York.

Ruddell, S.M. (1964) 'The inn, restaurant and tavern business in ancient Pompeii', M.A. thesis, University of Maryland.

Rykwert, J. (1976) *The Idea of a Town. The Anthropology of Urban Form in Rome, Italy and the Ancient World*, London.

Sabbatini Tumolesi, P. (1980) *Gladiatorum Paria: annunci di spettacoli gladiatorii a Pompei*, Rome.

Sakai, S. (1991) 'Some considerations of the urbanism in the so-called "Neustädt in Pompeii"', *Opuscula Pompeiana* 1: 35–57.

Salas, E. (1966) 'L'Evolution de la notion au temps et les horlogers à l'époque coloniale au Chili', *Annales ESC* 21: 141–58.

Saller, R.P. (1987) 'Men's age at marriage and its consequences in the Roman family', *Classical Philology* 82: 21–34.

——(1991) Review of Engels 1990, *Classical Philology* 86: 351–7.

——(1994) *Patriarchy, Property and Death in the Roman Family*, Cambridge.

——(2003) 'Framing the debate over growth in the ancient economy', in W. Scheidel and S. von Reden (eds) *The Ancient Economy*, Edinburgh: 251–69.

—— and Shaw, B.D. (1984) 'Roman tombstones and Roman family relations in the principate', *Journal of Roman Studies* 74: 124–57.

Saunders, P. (1986) *Social Theory and the Urban Question*, London.

Savunen, L. (1995) 'Women and elections in Pompeii', in R. Hawley and B. Levick (eds) *Women in Antiquity: New Assessments*, London: 194–206.

——(1997) *Women in the Texture of Pompeii*, Helsinki.

Scheid, J. (1992) 'The religious roles of women', in P. Schmitt Pantel (ed.) *A History of Women I: From Ancient Goddesses to Christian Saints*, London, 377–408.

Scheidel, W. and von Reden, S. (eds) (2002) *The Ancient Economy*, Edinburgh.

Searle, G.R. (1971) *The Quest for National Efficiency*, Oxford.

——(1976) *Eugenics and Politics in Britain 1900–1914*, Leiden.

Seifert, D.J., O'Brien, B. and Balicki, J. (2000) 'Mary Ann Hall's first-class house: the archaeology of a capital brothel', in R.A. Schmidt and B.L. Voss (eds) *Archaeologies of Sexuality*, London: 117–28.

Seiler, F. (1992) *Casa degli Amorini Dorati (VI 16, 7.38)*, Munich.

Setala, L. (1997) *Women in the Urban Texture of Pompeii*, Helsinki.

Shaw, B.D. (1987) 'The age of Roman girls at marriage: some reconsiderations', *Journal of Roman Studies* 77: 30–46.

——(1991) 'The cultural meaning of death: age and gender in the Roman family', in D.I. Kertzer and R.P. Saller (eds) *The Family in Italy from Antiquity to the Present*, New Haven: 66–90.

Sjoberg, G. (1960) *The Preindustrial City*, Glencoe, Ill.

Slane, K.W. (1989) 'Corinthian ceramic imports: the changing pattern of provincial trade in the first and second centuries AD', in S. Walker and A. Cameron (eds) *The Greek Renaissance in the Roman Empire*, *BICS* Supplement 55, London: 219–25.

Small, A. (1996) 'The shrine of the imperial family in the macellum at Pompeii', in A. Small (ed.) *Subject and Ruler: The Cult of the Ruling Power in Classical Antiquity (Journal of Roman Archaeology Supplement* 17): 115–35.

Smith, M.P. (1992) 'Postmodernism, urban ethnography, and the new social space of ethnic identity', *Theory and Society* 24(4): 493–531.

Snow, J. (1965) *Snow on Cholera. Being a Reprint of Two Papers by John Snow*, New York.

Sogliano, A. (1901) 'Il Borgo Marinaio presso il Sarno', *Notizie degli Scavi*: 423–40.

Soja, E.W. (1989) *Postmodern Geographies. The Reassertion of Space in Critical Social Theory*, London.

Solmsen, F. (1979) *Isis among the Greeks and Romans*, London.

Spinazzola, V. (1953) *Pompei alla luce degli scavi nuovi di Via dell'Abbondanza (anni 1910–1923)*, Rome.

Storchi Marino, A. (2000) 'Reti interregionali integrate e circuiti di mercato periodico negli *indices nundinarii* del Lazio e della Campania', in Lo Cascio (2000): 93–130.

Strocka, V.M. (1984) *Casa del principe di Napoli (VI 15.7–8)*, Munich.

——(1991) *Casa del labirinto (VI 11, 8–10)*, Munich.

Tchernia, A. (1986) *Le Vin de l'Italie romaine*, Rome.

Thompson, E.P. (1967) 'Time, work-discipline and industrial capitalism', *Past and Present* 38: 56–97.

Todd, F.A. (1939) 'Three Pompeian wall-inscriptions and Petronius', *Classical Review* 53: 5–9.

Treggiari, S.M. (1980) 'Urban labour in Rome: *mercennarii* and *tabernarii*', in P. Garnsey (ed.) *Non-Slave Labour in the Greco-Roman World*, Cambridge: 48–64.

Trevor Hodge, A. (2002) *Roman Aqueducts and Water Supply*, 2nd edn, London.

Tsujimura, S. (1991) 'Ruts in Pompeii. The traffic system in the Roman city', *Opuscula Pompeiana* 2: 58–86.

Unwin, R. (1909) *Town Planning in Practice*, New York.

Van Andringa, W. (2000) 'Autels de carrefour, organization vicinale et rapports de voisinage à Pompéi', *Rivista di Studi Pompeiane* 11: 47–86.

Vanderbroeck, P.J. (1987) *Popular Leadership and Collective Behaviour in the Late Roman Republic*, Amsterdam.

Varone, A. (2002) *Erotica Pompeiana*, Rome.

Verney, P. (1979) *The Earthquake Handbook*, London.

Vetter, E. (1953) *Handbuch der italischen Dialekte*, vol. 1, Heidelberg.

Veyne, P. (1990) *Bread and Circuses*, Harmondsworth.

Vlad Borelli, L., Parise Badoni, F., Ferrari, O., D'Ambrosio, A. and De Caro, S. (1983) *Un impegno per Pompei*, Milan.

Wallace-Hadrill, A. (1988) 'The social structure of the Roman house', *Papers of the British School at Rome* 56: 43–97.

—— (1990) 'The social spread of Roman luxury: sampling Pompeii', *Papers of the British School at Rome* 58: 145–92.

——(1991) 'Houses and households: sampling Pompeii and Herculaneum', in B. Rawson (ed.) *Marriage, Divorce and Children in Ancient Rome*, Oxford: 191–227.

——(1994) *Houses and Society in Pompeii and Herculaneum*, Princeton.

——(1995) 'The urban texture of Pompeii', in T. Cornell and K. Lomas (eds) *Urban Society in Roman Italy*, London: 39–62.

—— (1996) 'Engendering the Roman house', in D.E.E. Kleiner and S.B. Matheson (eds) *I Claudia, Women in Ancient Rome*, New Haven: 104–15.

—— (1997) 'Rethinking the Roman atrium house', in R. Laurence and A. Wallace-Hadrill (eds) (1997): 219–40.

Wallat, K. (1995) 'Der Zustand des Forums von Pompeji an Vorabend des Vesuvausbruchs 79 n. Chr.', in AAVV (1995): 75–92.

——(1997) *Die Ostseite des Forums von Pompeji*, Frankfurt.

Walvin, J. (1978) *Leisure and Society, 1830–1950*, London.

Ward, R.B. (1992) 'Women in the Roman Baths', *Harvard Theological Review* 85: 125–47.

Ward-Perkins, J.B. (1974) *Cities of Ancient Greece and Italy: Planning in Classical Antiquity*, New York.

Watts, C. (1987) 'A pattern language for houses at Pompeii, Herculaneum and Ostia', Ph.D. thesis, University of Texas at Austin.

Weber, M. (1958) *The City*, New York.

Welch, K. (1994) 'The Roman arena in late-republican Italy: a new interpretation', *Journal of Roman Archaeology* 7: 59–79.

Whittaker, C.R. (1990) 'The consumer city revisited: the *vicus* and the city', *Journal of Roman Archaeology* 3: 110–18.

Williams, C. (1999) *Roman Homosexuality: Ideologies of Masculinity in Classical Antiquity*, Oxford.

Williams, R. (1973) *The Countryside and the City*, Oxford.

Williams-Thorpe, O. (1988) 'Provenancing and archaeology of Roman millstones from the Mediterranean area', *Journal of Archaeological Science* 15: 253–305.

Wilson, A. (2002) 'Urban production in the Roman world: the view from North Africa', *Papers of the British School at Rome* 57: 231–73.

——(2003) 'The Archaeology of the Roman *Fullonica*', *Journal of Roman Archaeology* 16: 442–6.

Wilson, E. (1991) *The Sphinx in the City*, London.

Wiseman, T.P. (1977) 'Cicero *pro Sulla* 60–61', *Liverpool Classical Monthly* 2: 21–2.

Wolff, J. (1992) 'The real city, discursive city, the disappearing city: postmodernism and urban sociology', *Theory and Society* 24(4): 553–60.

Wyke, M. (1997) *Projecting the Past: Ancient Rome, Cinema, and History*, London.

Zanker, P. (1988a) *Pompeji: Stadtbilder als Spiegel von Gesellschaft und Herrschafts-form*, Mainz.

——(1988b) *The Power of Images in the Age of Augustus*, Ann Arbor.

——(1998) *Pompeii: Public and Private Life*, Cambridge, Mass.

Zevi, F. (1982) 'Urbanistica di Pompei', in *La regione sotterrata dal Vesuvio: atti de convegno internazionale 11–15 Novembre 1979*, Naples: 353–63.

——(1994) 'Sul Tempio di Iside a Pompei', *Parola del Passato* 274: 37–56.

—— (1996) 'Pompeii della città sannitica alla colonia sillana: per un'interpretazione dei dati archeologici', *Les elites municipals de l'Italie péninsulaire des Grecques à Néron*, Naples-Rome: 125–38.

INDEX

Printed in Great Britain
by Amazon.co.uk, Ltd.,
Marston Gate.